Resisting Militarism

Series Editors: Victoria M. Basham and Sarah Bulmer

The Critical Military Studies series welcomes original thinking on the ways in which military power works within different societies and geopolitical arenas.

Militaries are central to the production and dissemination of force globally, but the enduring legacies of military intervention are increasingly apparent at the societal and personal/bodily levels as well, demonstrating that violence and war-making function on multiple scales. At the same time, the notion that violence is an appropriate response to wider social and political problems transcends militaries: from private security, to seemingly 'non-military' settings such as fitness training and schooling, the legitimisation and normalisation of authoritarianism and military power occurs in various sites. This series seeks original, high-quality manuscripts and edited volumes that engage with such questions of how militaries, militarism and militarisation assemble and disassemble worlds touched and shaped by violence in these multiple ways. It will showcase innovative and interdisciplinary work that engages critically with the operation and effects of military power and provokes original questions for researchers and students alike.

Titles in the *Advances in Critical Military Studies* series include:

Published:

Resisting Militarism: Direct Action and the Politics of Subversion
Chris Rossdale

Forthcoming:

The Military-Peace Complex: Gender and Materiality in Afghanistan
Hannah Partis-Jennings

Inhabiting No-Man's-Land: Army Wives, Gender and Militarisation
Alexandra Hyde

Disordered Violence: Gendered Neo-Orientalism and Terrorism
Caron Gentry

Militarisation, Aesthetics and Embodiment in International Politics
Catherine Baker

Resisting Militarism

Direct Action and the Politics of Subversion

CHRIS ROSSDALE

EDINBURGH
University Press

Edinburgh University Press is one of the leading university presses in the UK. We publish academic books and journals in our selected subject areas across the humanities and social sciences, combining cutting-edge scholarship with high editorial and production values to produce academic works of lasting importance. For more information visit our website: edinburghuniversitypress.com

© Chris Rossdale, 2019, 2021

First published in hardback by Edinburgh University Press 2019

Edinburgh University Press Ltd
The Tun – Holyrood Road, 12(2f) Jackson's Entry, Edinburgh EH8 8PJ

Typeset in 10.5/13 ITC Giovanni Std by
Servis Filmsetting Ltd, Stockport, Cheshire

A CIP record for this book is available from the British Library

ISBN 978 1 4744 4303 6 (hardback)
ISBN 978 1 4744 4304 3 (paperback)
ISBN 978 1 4744 4305 0 (webready PDF)
ISBN 978 1 4744 4306 7 (epub)

The right of Chris Rossdale to be identified as the author of this work has been asserted in accordance with the Copyright, Designs and Patents Act 1988, and the Copyright and Related Rights Regulations 2003 (SI No. 2498).

CONTENTS

Acknowledgements vii
List of Abbreviations x

Introduction 1
   Militarism and Anti-Militarism 3
   Researching British Anti-Militarism 7
   Structure of the Book 12
1. Anti-Militarist Direct Action 16
   A Brief History of British Anti-Militarist Direct Action 22
   (Anti-)Representation 27
   Prefiguration 33
   (Anti-)Strategy 38
   Empowerment 40
2. Conceptualising Militarism 45
   Militarism and Institutions 46
   Banal Militarism 53
   White Poppies, Blue Hoodies 60
3. Feminist and Queer Anti-Militarism 65
   Feminist Anti-Militarism? 68
   Three Cases 71
4. Agents of Security 82
   Critical Security Studies and the Politics of Agency 85
   Doing Security 90
   Negotiating Agency 95
5. Resisting Security 108

Deconstructing Security	109
Unsecurability	114
Politics of In/Security	123
Spectacular Resistance	134
6. Contestations	139
Peace Camps	143
Vulnerability	147
Humour	151
Desiring Militarism	164
7. Diversity	173
Diversity of Tactics	175
Violence and Nonviolence	184
The (White) Limits to Diversity	196
8. Dis/Obedience	206
Disobedient Subjects	210
Obedient Subjects	216
Strategies of Dis/Obedience	227
Making Mischief	233
9. Regimes	237
The Arms Trade Treaty	239
Repressive Regimes	242
Liberal Militarism	248
Racialisation	252
Recovering Radicalism	257
Conclusion	261
List of Interviews	271
References	272
Index	307

ACKNOWLEDGEMENTS

This project has been enriched at every turn by the communities of scholarship it has been my extraordinary good fortune to encounter over the past nine years. Much of this time was spent at the Department of Politics and International Studies at the University of Warwick, where I found myself part of an exciting research environment, first as a PhD student and later as a member of staff. Shorter stints at Royal Holloway and City University London injected fresh energy, and more recently the LSE has been an ideal base from which to finish the project. I have presented material from the book at the Universities of Cardiff, Exeter, Goldsmiths, Manchester and Warwick, as well as at International Studies Association, British International Studies Association, European International Studies Association, Political Studies Association and Anarchist Studies Network events, and benefited hugely from the insightful feedback and questions from colleagues in these spaces.

Writing a book is a mostly solitary and sometimes lonely experience. Nevertheless, I have been blessed with the friendship and support of some outstanding colleagues, who through exchanges on panels and in pubs and over e-mail have contributed more to the project than I can say. Particular thanks are due to Linda Åhäll, Liam Barrington-Bush, Chris Browning, Olimpia Burchiellaro, Alex Christoyannopoulos, Lara Coleman, Jesse Crane-Seeber, Stuart Croft, Jonathan Dean, James Eastwood, Madeline Fagan, Uri Gordon, Paul Higate, Tom Houseman, Kim Hutchings, Matt McDonald, Kevin McSorley, Akanksha Mehta, Hidefumi Nishiyama,

Ciaran O'Connor, Louiza Odysseos, Maria do Mar Pereira, Sharri Plonski, Nicola Pratt, Alex Prichard, Doerthe Rosenow, Meera Sabaratnam, Anna Stavrianakis, Katrine Steenland, Maurice Stierl, Nick Taylor, Lisa Tilley, Nick Vaughan-Williams, Stellan Vinthagen, David Wearing, Julia Welland and Musab Younis. The tribulations of academic life were softened by the companionship and camaraderie of Mikey Bloomfield, Chris Emery, Kathryn Fisher, Myriam Fotou, Yuna Han, Joe Hoover, Marta Iñiguez de Heredia, Sophie Loup, Diego de Merich, Tristen Naylor, Amin Samman, Elke Schwarz, Nick Srnicek and Michel van Ingen.

I especially want to thank Paul Kirby, Nivi Manchanda and Katharine Millar, who, as well as being patient sounding boards and wonderful friends, read the manuscript in its entirety and provided invaluable feedback. Aggie Hirst has read more drafts over the years than I can count, and has been a constant source of inspiration. And the book simply would not exist without the mentorship of James Brassett, whose generosity and encouragement have made so much possible.

The book began life as my PhD thesis, which was funded by the ESRC; I am deeply grateful for the opportunities that funding provided. I am also indebted to Victoria Basham and Sarah Bulmer for including the book in their exciting new series, and to the editorial team at Edinburgh University Press for their guidance.

I would like to thank Darren Cullen and the Space Hijackers for allowing me to reprint their artwork. I am also grateful for permission to reproduce an extract from *Last Post* by Carol Ann Duffy. Published by The BBC, 2009. Copyright © Carol Ann Duffy. Reproduced by permission of the author c/o Rogers, Coleridge & White Ltd, 20 Powis Mews, London W11 1JN. Some material in the section headed '11 September 2007. East London. The Tank Auction' in Chapter 5 is adapted from Chris Rossdale (2016). 'Activism, Resistance and Security.' In *Ethical Security Studies: A New Research Agenda*, edited by Jonna Nyman and Anthony Burke, 201–15. Abingdon; New York: Routledge, and is reproduced with permission.

My sincerest thanks go to the many activists who have contributed to this project, especially those interviewees who generously volunteered their time and their stories. Furthermore, I am indebted to those alongside whom I have taken part in anti-militarist actions and campaigns over the years, many of whom I am proud to call close friends. Their hard work, dedication and subversive imaginations are at the heart of this book, and their encouragement and solidarity has been as invaluable personally as it has intellectually.

Finally, my family were constant sources of joy and comfort during this long process. David, Karen, Paul, Hayley and Pamela have understood my frequent disappearances from human contact and always made me feel loved. Kat Hobbs, my partner and best friend, has been my most valued interlocutor, while also helping to remind me that sometimes there are more important things to do than sit and write a book.

LIST OF ABBREVIATIONS

AMN	Anti-Militarist Network
ATT	Arms Trade Treaty
CAAT	Campaign Against Arms Trade
CIRCA	Clandestine Insurgent Rebel Clown Army
CND	Campaign for Nuclear Disarmament
CSS	Critical Security Studies
DAC	Direct Action Committee Against Nuclear War
DSEI	Defence and Security Equipment International
DSO	Defence & Security Organisation
EF!	Earth First!
GBC	Green and Black Cross
NCF	No Conscription Fellowship
NGO	Non-Governmental Organisation
NPIW	No Pride in War
PPU	Peace Pledge Union
SNS	Sparkles Not Shrapnel
STAF	Stop the Arms Fair
VfP	Veterans for Peace
WRI	War Resisters' International

Introduction

It is January 2017. A coalition of Gulf forces led by Saudi Arabia continues its bombardment of Yemen, visiting daily horrors amidst thin claims of fighting terrorism. The intervention has been marked by continual attacks against civilians, and an accompanying blockade has precipitated what one UN staffer has referred to as a 'humanitarian catastrophe' (O'Brien 2015, 2016). In the twenty-one months since the US- and UK-backed forces began their airstrikes, thousands of Yemenis have been killed and millions have been forced to flee their homes. One of the biggest attacks came last October, when an airstrike on a funeral in Sana'a killed more than 140 people, injuring over 550. For many years the Gulf states have bought British, and in this conflict have made extensive use of jets and missiles made in the UK. Sensing an opportunity, and despite evidence of coalition war crimes, the British government has licensed over £5 billion in fresh arms sales to coalition members since the conflict escalated in March 2015 (Amnesty International 2017).[1] Back in the UK, activists are campaigning for a halt in arms sales to Saudi Arabia. Amongst other initiatives, Campaign Against Arms Trade (CAAT) are taking the government to court, hoping to get these arms sales ruled unlawful. Unfortunately, progress on the case is glacial. It is in this context that Sam Walton, a Quaker from London, and the Reverend Daniel 'Woody' Woodhouse, a Methodist minister from Leeds, attempt a more direct approach.

On a cold Monday morning, under cover of darkness, the two men cut through a perimeter fence and sneak undetected into

Wharton Aerodrome. This is the gigantic airfield and testing facility owned by BAE Systems, and it is where Eurofighter Typhoon jets are assembled and tested prior to delivery to the Royal Saudi Air Force. Sam and Woody are armed with crowbars, a bolt cutter and a sledgehammer. Woody is wearing vestments and carrying a bible. They also have a detailed map of the facility and list of every plane currently on the site. Those destined for Saudi Arabia are clearly marked – these are their targets. They hurry across the runway to the hangar where the planes are stored, chancing upon an unlocked door that lets them inside. One more door, locked, separates them from the Eurofighters, which are tantalisingly visible through the security glass. They set to work using their crowbars to force open the door, knowing that they are just seconds away from their goal.

However, this is as far as they get. With the door almost open, Sam and Woody are discovered by an unsuspecting security guard carrying out a routine patrol. Making no attempt to overpower him or escape, the two men calmly explain that they have travelled here in order to cause as much damage as possible to the Typhoons. They show the guard their list of planes, a document they are really not supposed to have. This is all above the guard's pay-grade, and the police are called; Sam and Woody allow themselves to be arrested. In twelve hours' time they will be released from Blackpool Police Station with the story of their action already national news. Both refuse to accept a police caution and insist on being taken to trial. In nine months they will be found not guilty of criminal damage, having successfully argued that their actions were proportional to the wrongs they wished to prevent.

Their actions beg questions. What did they hope to achieve by smashing planes? How did they organise such an action, and keep it a secret? What are the networks and social relations that made this possible? Why did the two confess so readily to their crime, and insist on going to court? In what ways did their religions shape their action? And – having been apprehended before they could reach the planes – did Sam and Woody fail? This book tries to make sense of this action, and many others like it. The book is an ethnography of anti-militarist politics. It moves from public demonstrations and open meetings to clandestine actions and courtrooms, in order to provide an in-depth account of the tactics, strategies and philosophies at the heart of anti-militarist campaigning in the UK. The stories contained within allow us to think through questions of vital importance for anyone interested in the politics of militarism and resistance. To the above we can add: does anti-militarism have to be nonviolent? What kinds of alternatives to militarism do anti-militarists envisage? To what extent are anti-militarists able to contend with militarism's entanglement in patriarchal and racialised systems of power? In what ways do anti-militarists resist the politics of militarism? In what ways do they reproduce it?

Through these questions, the book works to enliven our understanding of both militarism and resistance. This undertaking is animated by a recognition that power and resistance can be productively read in tension with one another. Systems of power are revealed by examining attempts to uproot them, insofar as practices of resistance expose fault-lines, tensions, and ever-deeper lines of penetration (Bleiker 2000: 26; Foucault 1982). And practices of resistance can be critically engaged with insofar as they are always to some extent produced and implicated within the very fields of power they seek to contest. My contention is that we understand more about both militarism and resistance when we examine them together.

Militarism and Anti-Militarism

Militarism, which can be broadly defined as 'the social and international relations of the preparation for, and conduct of, organised political violence', is an ambitious concept (Stavrianakis and Selby 2012: 3). While it is sometimes used to refer to a particular kind of political environment, one that is saturated by military power, it is more usefully understood as a way of making sense of the social and political processes through which political violence is made possible. Militarism provokes an account of how particular wars, coercive state practices and other forms of violence are embedded within, legitimised through, and function to reshape a wide range of social relations. It challenges us to think about the complex networks of political institutions, value systems, social practices, rationalities and forms of subjectivity which tend towards the normalisation and reproduction of political violence. It shows us how violence and the instruments of violence are glorified, legitimised, or rendered unremarkable and banal on an everyday level, and traces the historical and contemporary processes through which violence is woven into society. Militarism thus links macro-level topics of war, conflict and state violence to more intimate relations of power, authority and domination.

There is no single type of militarism. The social relations which underpin political violence are context specific, their form determined by particular configurations of culture and political economy, by legacies and enduring experiences of colonialism and imperialism, by particular hierarchies of race, class, ethnicity, gender, sexuality and (dis)ability, and by various formations of nationalism and national identity. Militarism also shifts and adapts in response to new forms of technology, new objects of violence, and new practices of resistance. It is not a static entity, but a complex of social, political and economic processes which have no firm unity other than our capacity to conceptualise them as tending towards particular forms of (violent) practices. As such, it is an ambiguous referent; the task of identifying a particular practice, idea, or subject as militarised is not straightforward. Despite these complexities, the concept of militarism is a powerful one for thinking critically about the politics of violence. At its best, it situates particular violent acts within a social context, recognises the co-constitution of war and society, and draws in an account of racism, patriarchy, capitalism and imperialism (without being reducible to any of these). It therefore invites nuanced accounts of the processes through which violence is made possible while offering opportunities to link political struggles and critical traditions together.

This broad understanding of militarism is useful but deliberately vague, abstracted from the contexts through which more specific accounts (and critiques) are possible. My approach in this book is to build from this account by engaging with anti-militarist practices through a series of conceptual frames, in order to engage with or speak to different dimensions of militarism. I explore militarism and anti-militarism through the politics of gender and sexuality, security, (non)violence, disobedience, liberal militarism and race, demonstrating how each framing allows us to recognise and think critically about the relationship between militarism and resistance. The task is not to produce a broad conceptualisation or statement about the nature of militarism, but to engage with particular features, elements, contradictions, and to look at some of the ways these might be contested. The context through which this analysis will take place is that of contemporary Britain, and much of what I say about militarism is focused through that lens. However, the arguments and insights that emerge are not necessarily restricted to that national context; they clearly resonate with other sites of Western and liberal militarism.

Anti-militarism refers to politics organised in opposition to militarism. There is a long, rich and diverse history of politics directed in this manner and, as with militarism, the particular nature of anti-militarism depends on context. In this book I use the concept to identify a particular movement active in the UK, though cautiously and with three important reservations. The first is an issue of definition; while some who appear in the book use the label of anti-militarism readily, others use it less, and others not at all. Other signifiers – notably 'peace movement', 'anti-war movement' and 'anti-arms trade movement' – circulate widely. The second issue concerns cohesion. There is no clear way to determine the boundaries of this movement and its terms of inclusion and exclusion, and while the study takes place in a context where there are multiple connections binding together various individuals, groups and organisations, there are also plenty of sites and subjects who fall away (either from my analysis or by processes of exclusion at work within the movement). The third issue is the dangerous sense of completion or innocence that can accompany the identification of a movement as a space of pure opposition, obscuring how anti-militarist politics are themselves implicated in the reproduction of militarism. All three of these reservations are explored in the book, as integral to understanding the politics of the movement. With them in mind, I nonetheless refer to and engage with something approximating a movement, an intentional community operating in opposition to certain features of British militarism. It is the wager of this book that this is an interesting and productive space from which to approach the politics of militarism and resistance.

My particular focus lies on those elements of anti-militarism which engage in direct action – that is, in forms of political intervention which bypass more formal processes of political representation and instead seek to act 'directly' on situations, through tactics including occupations, blockades and property damage. Direct action tactics are widespread within the movement, though the particular form they take and rationalities at play vary significantly. Throughout the book I argue that the performances, negotiations, and debates which surround direct action practices are a fruitful site through which to read the politics of both militarism and resistance. The concept of prefiguration is central here. Prefiguration is the idea that the means used in political struggle should embody the ends that are sought – indeed, that the means will tend to become the ends. It is a way of contending with the tendency of radical political movements to end up replicating what they are fighting, and of insisting that the creative work of generating new forms of politics should be integral to the practice of resistance. It therefore functions both as an analytic (and so a critique of those who believe that militaristic means can produce nonviolent ends), and as a way of articulating a politics which takes this analytic seriously.

The book reads anti-militarist action as prefigurative. I argue that activists seek to avoid replicating militarised social relations, that they work to cultivate alternative forms of contestation, subjectivity and relationality, and that a prefigurative lens provides the tools to think critically about the limits of these processes. This approach is rooted in the understanding that anti-militarists do not operate externally to militarism; they are subjects of it, participants in it, they reinscribe it. Such entanglements clearly set the stage for critiques of anti-militarist practice, but they also provide opportunities; it is precisely through our implications within systems of power that rewritings are possible. The conceptual framings of militarism through which the book moves are used to explore the limits and disruptive potentials of anti-militarism. Each chapter identifies particular tensions and lines of contestation, between militarism and anti-militarism and/or internally to anti-militarism, and uses these to think through the ways that anti-militarist politics resist, subvert, and even reproduce militarism. The book explores a series of debates and tensions amongst anti-militarists, including those surrounding contrasting approaches to illegality, the role of pacifism and nonviolence, and those concerning the gendered and racialised politics of the movement, situating these as attempts to determine the particular nature of militarism, the imperatives of resistance, and the relationship between the two.

The central arguments of this book turn on the ambiguous nature of direct action. On the one hand, I read direct action as an incredibly valuable form of resistance. It disrupts normal rules of political participation, expands the capacity for so-called ordinary people to make meaningful interventions, and breaks down distinctions between the local and the global. In side-stepping depoliticising injunctions to appeal to the proper authorities, it demands that we carry out the endless task of resisting militarism in a far more tangible fashion. And, in calling attention to the prefigurative dimensions of political action, it is generative of subjects and movements that subvert militarism in many different ways. On the other hand, direct action is also deeply problematic. It is too swiftly a space for heroes, more accessible for those who enjoy certain forms of social privilege, easily fetishised over other less immediate forms of action, and in other ways frequently shaped and conducted by those very social relations which constitute militarism. It is at the tensions between these readings that direct action becomes a powerful lens through which to read the intersecting and co-constitutive politics of militarism and resistance.

Researching British Anti-Militarism

I have conducted the research for the project while being an active member of the movement in question, in a manner that has allowed me to gain a more intimate and empathetic understanding of the politics of British anti-militarism than other research methods would allow. The ethnographic approach that I use moves beyond those which treat ethnography as an empiricist data-collection method, an engaging writing style, or a 'close to the ground' epistemology that claims some privileged encounter with truth (Vrasti 2008). My intention is not to capture the truth or totality of those anti-militarist practices with which I engage, nor to formulate an assessment of movement capabilities or trajectories. Instead, I mobilise a series of avowedly and explicitly political interpretations which situate anti-militarist practices within debates about the nature of militarism and the possibilities for resistance. There is an explicit attempt to blur the lines of theoretical and empirical content, to allow each to structure and condition the other. What results is a series of interrogations which are never purely empirical or purely theoretical, and which remain sensitive both to the ways in which social practices are always already deeply theoretical interventions, and to the embedded and contextualised nature of theory (Zalewski 1996).

Ethnographies tell stories. It is often the custom to leave interventions, theoretical digressions and clarifications for footnotes, endnotes, or separate publications, and so to leave the text as a relatively clean narrative. I take a different approach; the stories I tell are frequently interrupted and juxtaposed with interpretations, problematisations and theoretical connections. While perhaps at times inelegant, this is precisely an attempt to play between the lines of theory and practice, narrative and deconstruction, to recognise and make visible their mutual constitution. More in keeping with ethnographic convention, my focus lies not on the macro-level politics of the movement, but on gestures, moments and experiments, the micropolitics of subverting and reproducing militarism. There is also no grand theory or single principle of interpretation; theory is deployed tactically to enliven particular analyses. Nevertheless, there are clear principles which guide my accounts, both with respect to the consistent focus on the relationship between militarism and resistance, and to the general commitment to a critical, post-foundational theoretical ethos which draws variously on poststructural, feminist, queer, postcolonial and anarchist political thought.

The interpretations are also guided by clear normative commitments. I am writing as an anti-militarist, with a desire to understand the relationships between militarism and resistance such that militarism can be better resisted. While the book speaks to academic literatures on both militarism and resistance, it also looks to engage anti-militarist politics more directly. In so doing, my aim is not to suggest strategic directions for action. Instead, I follow Jeffrey Juris, who suggests that 'by providing critically engaged and the-

oretically informed analyses generated through collective practice
... ethnography can provide tools for activist (self-)reflection and
decision making while remaining pertinent for broader academic
audiences' (2008: 22). On similar grounds, attempting to move
beyond the conventions of 'vanguardist revolutionary intellectual
practice', David Graeber argues that

> [e]thnography is about teasing out the hidden symbolic, moral, or pragmatic logics that underlie certain types of social action; how people's habits and actions make sense in ways that they are not themselves completely aware of. One obvious role for a radical intellectual is precisely that: looking first at those who are creating viable alternatives on the ground, and then trying to figure out what the larger implications of what they are (already) doing might be. (Graeber 2007: 305–6)

Graeber and Juris have both written in ways which attempt to do just this (Graeber 2009; Juris 2008), and this book takes influence and inspiration from their approach. My intention has been to try in different ways to make sense of what anti-militarists are doing, and to read anti-militarist practices within the field of power relations in which they are situated and which they are always working to (un)make. This involves both working with and casting critical reflection on the dominant conceptual frameworks employed within the movement (Coleman 2015). Some of these interpretations and critiques may have resonance, might help to rethink and reframe what the movement is doing. Others may not. My expectation is that different anti-militarists will have very different reactions; my hope is to stimulate discussions on these terms within and around the movement.

My own positionality is very present in the book. I take an active role in the movement I am discussing. I paint banners, facilitate meetings, wait for arrestees in police stations and support them in court. I take part in secret and illegal actions, am trusted with privileged information, and at one point during the research period was arrested and prosecuted for my role in anti-militarist direct action. Some of my 'research subjects' are also my closest friends.[2] This level of intimacy between researcher and subject shifts what kinds of claims can be made. All pretensions to objectivity are gone, but in their place lie particular resources. Roxanne Doty argues that the self is *always* present in research, always applying value systems and frameworks of interpretation which reveal (and yet conceal) the intimacy of our investments. Far better to make this presence visible and itself part of the research process than to pretend otherwise (2010: 1048). Doing so, and doing so reflexively, can help to break down the idea of the detached, sovereign author. It can also allow us to draw on faculties excluded from other forms of analysis (Brigg and Bleiker 2010: 794). My emotional investments in and responses to anti-militarist action clearly shape the analysis, and at times they may limit it, but they also provide opportunities to explore the affective qualities of anti-militarist action in a manner which allows for certain kinds of insight about the politics of both militarism and resistance.[3]

This kind of autoethnographic approach clearly carries dangers of indulgence, of an auto-essentialism that takes our experiences as an encounter with truth (Inayatullah 2011: 8). I take my lead from Morgan Brigg and Roland Bleiker, and their suggestion that 'methodological uses of the self should be judged by their ability to open up new perspectives on political dilemmas' (2010: 781). My intention is not to position myself as a site of pure knowledge, but to work with the understanding that our own entanglements in relations of power (as it relates to both militarism and resistance) is always already the condition of knowledge and a space from which to interrogate the world (Inayatullah 2011; Lorde 2007). This positionality and approach does not absolve me from the violence of (mis)representation that is the condition of all attempts to tell the stories of others, but it does perhaps allow for a more straightforward form of reflexivity (Dauphinee 2010). Throughout the book I outline debates or tensions within anti-militarism, frequently in a manner which makes clear my own sympathies; I have sought to do so in a manner which give enough of a sense of what is going on to invite other ways of reading the movement.

The book draws on research conducted from 2009 to 2017. During that time I participated in well over a hundred anti-militarist events including demonstrations, blockades, workshops, meetings, trials, peace camps and pickets. Much of the discussion throughout the book draws on first-hand accounts; these are supplemented with other examples from UK-based anti-militarism, alongside a series of interviews conducted with activists over the course of the study.

There are a large number of collectives and organisations in the UK which are, in some fashion, anti-militarist. I engage, even if briefly, with around thirty of these. My focus turns most often towards anti-militarist action directed against the arms trade and to groups who use some form of direct action, albeit with plenty of digressions. While the book touches on the activities of many anti-militarist groups, there is a smaller number which receive specific attention and more detailed analysis. These include:

- Campaign Against the Arms Trade (CAAT): A London-based organisation, established in 1974 by a coalition of anti-militarist groups, which campaigns for the abolition of the international arms trade. Alongside more traditional campaigning activities such as parliamentary lobbying and awareness-raising, CAAT has a long history of facilitating direct action. I have been closely involved with CAAT since 2010, including as a member of its Steering Committee.
- Stop the Arms Fair (STAF): A coalition which includes direct action groups, individuals, and some non-governmental organisations (NGOs), STAF was established in 2011 to coordinate resistance to Defence and Security Equipment International (DSEI), the large arms fair which takes place biennially in London. I have been involved with STAF since its formation, and have helped to organise action against four DSEI events.
- Smash EDO: A Brighton group, active between 2004 and 2014, which carried out a diverse, direct action-focused campaign against the EDO MBM factory in their hometown. Their tactics included weekly noise demonstrations, blockades, rooftop occupations and mass demonstrations. While never directly involved in the campaign, I attended a number of demonstrations and events.
- Plowshares (or Ploughshares): A (broadly) Christian pacifist movement which is well known for actions in which small groups of activists physically dismantle weapons or military equipment, often with hammers and fake or real blood.

- The Space Hijackers: A London-based Situationist-inspired group of 'anarchitects', active between 1999 and 2014, who carried out a series of hilarious stunts in public spaces. Although they focused predominantly on the privatisation of public space, they also carried out high-profile anti-militarist actions.

Structure of the Book

The book is structured as a series of frames through which we can read the politics of both militarism and anti-militarism. My aim is not to assemble a grand conception of militarism, or a general claim about the nature of anti-militarism, but rather to stage a series of encounters between militarism and resistance, so as to better understand their antagonistic but mutually constitutive relationship. The first two chapters establish the groundwork for the rest of the book. Chapter 1 outlines the understanding of direct action that guides the analysis. After looking briefly at how direct action tactics became popularised within British anti-militarism, I introduce four concepts through which we can interrogate the politics of direct action. These concepts – (anti-)representation, prefiguration, (anti-)strategy and empowerment – and the debates that surround them help to situate direct action not only as a particular practice or tactic, but as generative of particular kinds of subjects, movements and approaches to social transformation. In Chapter 2 I engage in broad terms with how militarism has been conceptualised, both by anti-militarist movements and by social theorists. The chapter looks first at how anti-militarists recognise militarism as an institutional formation, a (localised) network encompassing militaries, branches of government, the arms industry, public institutions and more. In the second part I draw on academic accounts to show how militarism can be understood as a complex of value systems, rationalities, social practices and subjectivities which tend towards the production and legitimisation of political violence.

The next seven chapters explore militarism and anti-militarism through a series of contexts. Chapter 3 looks at how feminist and queer anti-militarists have understood the relationships between militarism, gender and sexuality. Those relationships have been theorised in some detail by academics working at these intersections, and have occasionally taken centre-stage in British anti-militarist politics, most notably at the time of the Greenham Common Women's Peace Camp in the early 1980s. However, they are not often highlighted in contemporary British anti-militarism. The chapter considers the politics of this limited attention, before turning to a series of cases where anti-militarists *have* focused on the militarised politics of gender and sexuality. Here, we can see activists challenging central dynamics of militarism while also calling attention to the reproduction of militarised gender orders within anti-militarism.

Chapters 4 and 5 focus on how anti-militarists engage with the politics of security. In Chapter 4 I argue that anti-militarist direct action can be understood as a form of anti-hegemonic security agency, where statist/militarist approaches to the politics of security are displaced by activists putting alternative forms of security into practice. Chapter 5 suggests that, beyond viewing activists as alternative agents of security, we might read them as *resisting* security, both by evading state security practices and by subverting the political and conceptual terrain of security/insecurity.

In Chapter 6 I examine peace camps, die-ins, and the use of humour by activists to demonstrate how, in their modes of resistance, anti-militarists challenge militarised forms of contestation by prefiguring alternatives. The chapter also reflects on how anti-militarism is shaped not just by opposition to militarism, but by desire for it.

Chapter 7 looks more closely at the internal movement dynamics of British anti-militarism. I focus on the contested organising principle known as 'diversity of tactics', and on the role of nonviolence within the movement, suggesting that here we see attempts to develop movement practices which do not reproduce militarism. I make the potentially controversial argument that anti-militarism should not necessarily insist on nonviolence. In the last part of the chapter I discuss the role of whiteness in British anti-militarism. I show how solidarity politics, direct action tactics and the particular conceptions of militarism operating within the movement depend on some form of white privilege, and reproduce racialised forms of exclusion.

In Chapter 8 I look at how anti-militarists attempt to become 'disobedient' in the conduct of direct action, with a particular focus on how they constitute themselves as (il)legal subjects. I consider the ways in which anti-militarist disobedience is always intertwined with some form of obedience, and outline how different negotiations of the disobedience/obedience relationship have important political implications.

Chapter 9 turns to look at how anti-arms trade activists develop critiques of the international arms trade. I argue that the overwhelming focus on the sale of arms to 'repressive regimes' risks reproducing liberal militarism and racialised discourses of the international, showing how apparently radical anti-militarism can become folded within and circumscribed by militarist discourse. The chapter ends by outlining the need for a more explicit focus on liberal and racialised forms of militarism within the movement.

In the Conclusion I return to the politics of prefiguration and political coalition. There are certain dangers involved in practices of resistance which set themselves in opposition to coherent and stable enemies, and which seek to build hegemonic coalitions. Such practices often struggle to contend with the ways resistance is shaped and produced by those very power relations it seeks to oppose. I outline some of these challenges, before suggesting how an understanding of anti-militarism as a prefigurative ethic of resistance which seeks to reveal, limit, or disrupt violence, and which recognises that its task is never complete, may offer some pathways through.

Notes

1. Data on UK arms export licences is provided in an easily accessible format on CAAT's website, available at https://www.caat.org.uk/resources/export-licences.
2. On the ethics of conducting ethnography when research subjects are also friends, see Ellis (2007).
3. In situating my own emotional and affective responses as central, I am also working with Juris's understanding of 'militant ethnography', wherein the lived experience of participating in protest action becomes an important component of understanding movements. Juris argues that 'anyone who has participated in mass direct actions or demonstrations can attest [that] such events produce powerful emotions, involving alternating sensations of anticipation, tension, anxiety, fear, terror, solidarity, celebration, and joy. These affective dynamics

are not incidental; they are central to sustained processes of movement building and activist networking. In this sense, I use my body as a research tool, particularly during moments of intense passion and excitement, to generate what Deidre Sklar (1994) calls "kinesthetic empathy"' (Juris 2008: 20-1).

CHAPTER 1

Anti-Militarist Direct Action

29 January 1996. Preston, Lancashire. Seeds of Hope
It's 2 a.m., freezing, and Andrea Needham, Lotta Kronlid and Joanna Wilson are using bolt cutters to break through the fence and sneak into Wharton Aerodrome. It is twenty-one years to the day before Sam and Woody will attempt the same. The three women pause to tie Japanese peace cranes to the fence and then move quickly into the base and towards the main hangar, the location familiar after months of patient reconnaissance. They prise the door open with their crowbars, the sound of smashing glass deafening in the winter silence. No security guards this time. They head inside.

The hangar is packed with planes that are capable of causing considerable destruction, but the trio are here for very particular targets: Hawk jets, specifically any of the twenty-four Hawks that British Aerospace (now BAE Systems) have agreed to sell to the Indonesian government. Hawks are ostensibly training aircraft, but they have been deployed in operations as part of Indonesia's genocidal occupation of East Timor. Thanks to meticulous planning, the women know the serial numbers of these twenty-four planes. By chance, one of them – serial number ZH 955 – is nearby when they enter the hangar.

Each woman has a hammer, and their actions are carefully choreographed. Lotta takes hers to the bomb targeting and release controls in the cockpit. Jo starts on the nose. Andrea makes one token blow and then moves further into the hangar to see if there are more Indonesian Hawks, before returning to ZH 955. They are calm and deliberate, paying particular attention to the symbolic dimensions of their action. A banner is attached to the plane which reads 'women disarming for life and justice'. Copies of a video and booklet explaining the action are left in the pilot's seat. Andrea leaves a photograph of her baby niece on the wing of the plane.

With the jet disarmed – the damage will later be estimated at £1.7 million – the three eat some food, sing together, and use a phone they find to call friends and journalists. They then wait calmly to be arrested. They will spend the next six months in jail, alongside their friend, Angie Zelter, who helped to plan the action. In July they will face trial for committing criminal damage, the charges carrying a potential ten-year prison sentence. They will argue that their actions were justified, a necessary response to Indonesia's genocide and the British government's complicity. Against the wishes of the judge, the jury will find them not guilty of all charges. The verdict is unprecedented, and the action will become a landmark moment in contemporary British anti-militarism. The action is given the name Seeds of Hope (Needham 2016; Nepstad 2008: 184–8; Zelter 2004).

7 September 2015. Newham, London. Stop Arming Israel
It's lunchtime on a warm late-summer day when I arrive at the small patch of grass next to the main road that leads into ExCeL, London's colossal exhibition centre that will soon play host to the DSEI arms fair. Today is the first day of a week of action, during which hundreds of anti-militarist activists will attempt to disrupt the set-up of the fair. Each day in this week of action will be centred around a particular theme, including faith, environmentalism and education. Today's action is focused on Palestine.

A large group of activists are gathered on the grass, surrounded by Palestinian flags and a multitude of anti-arms trade banners. Palestinian hip-hop fills the air and two gazebos stand on the verge of the road. These gazebos mirror the large pavilion that will showcase Israel's arms companies during the arms fair: one, the 'Pavilion of Israeli National Shame', details the violence with which Israel's weapons industry is deeply intertwined; the other, the 'Pavilion of Palestinian National Remembrance', makes space for those voices and lives excluded from and effaced by the everyday business of the arms industry.

The week of action has been months in the planning and the mood is upbeat but uncertain. Maintaining people's energy while gathered at the side of the road, in a part of London unfrequented by passers-by, is a difficult task, and while people are pleased to be here, there is an aimless quality to the proceedings. That changes abruptly when several activists spot a flat-bed lorry carrying a SELEX Armoured Surveillance Vehicle driving up the road towards ExCeL. Half-formed plans spring into action as they run into the road, stand in the way of the lorry, and unfurl a banner reading 'Stop Arming Israel'. The vehicle comes to a halt, at which point more of us run into the road, several jump onto the lorry's back, and a man wearing a Tony Blair mask chains himself to its rear. Within two minutes there are eighty people in the road, chanting and shouting and dancing and singing. The atmosphere has electrified.

For a short period, attention focuses on the four people standing on the back of the lorry. One is waving a Palestinian flag, two more hold a banner, while the last reads out testimony from Palestinians recounting the brutal realities of life under occupation. The mood, while still highly charged, has become more sombre, the unnerving reminder of the action's purpose sending a collective chill through the crowd. After some time this sober pause gives way to something more carnivalesque. The music returns, people report that exhibition traffic is backed up and that deliveries are being turned away from the site, and our numbers swell. In front of the lorry about fifty people take part in a dabke dance, circling in delight while asserting Palestinian culture at a site normally reserved for the commodification of its destruction. The police are trying unsuccessfully to shift us. They walk amongst the crowd suggesting that people move, insisting that people move, and issuing countless fifteen-minute ultimatums. The crowd, predominantly composed of seasoned activists, ignore the police, and the police fail to make good on their periodic threats. The dabke is particularly baffling to the police, and their attempt to issue threats of arrest are drowned out by its music.

After three hours in the road the police's attitude and approach become notably more uncompromising. Somewhere, someone has clearly decided that enough is enough. They form into lines and begin to push us off the road. In five days' time, on the 'big day of action', such a tactic will be met with fierce resistance by activists. Today, we disperse quickly. It is only the first day of the week, and people are unwilling to seriously risk arrest (and, more significantly, being bailed away from the site) at this early stage. The crowd moves back to the grass, where people from different organisations, including War on Want and the Boycott Israel Network, give talks about their campaigns. A worker from inside ExCeL comes out, offers us a tray of sandwiches left over from an event in the building, and amiably tells us about the chaos the action has caused within.

So ends the first day of the week of action. Over the coming five days the road will be blocked repeatedly, causing major disruption to the set-up of the arms fair. Around ten people will be arrested; in six months, they too will be acquitted, this time because the judge himself agrees that those arrested had sought to prevent greater crimes from taking place inside the arms fair (Stone 2016a).

*

These two stories are paradigmatic examples of anti-militarist direct action, as well as themselves being important moments in contemporary British anti-militarism. The former, drawing on tactics developed by the Plowshares movement, is regularly cited by activists as a source of inspiration. The latter was the outcome of several years of tactical and organisational development through which mass direct action has become commonplace and the DSEI arms fair has become the flagship target of anti-arms trade activists. The basic tactic demonstrated in both examples – direct action against institutions connected with militarism – is one which unites the sometimes disparate movements, groups and actions explored in this book. Whilst it is by no means the only tactic used by British anti-militarists, it plays a major role in the constitution of the contemporary movement. Whether it be hundreds of people shutting down an arms factory, or a handful of activists in canoes preventing a battleship from reaching an arms fair, it is very often moments of direct action that centre the collective imagination.

Throughout this book, I argue that what is often most important about direct action is less the action itself than the relationships, debates and ideas that give rise to and are expressed through such action. Direct action therefore stands not only as an important political practice in its own right, but as a lens through which to read the political and social dynamics of anti-militarism. Later chapters develop this understanding through encounters with the politics of gender and sexuality, security, subjectivity, violence, disobedience, legalism and more. This chapter lays the groundwork for those discussions. I begin by outlining some basic definitions of direct action, before providing a brief account of the development of direct action tactics within British anti-militarism. The main part of the chapter introduces four concepts which are integral to the politics of direct action: (anti-)representation, prefiguration, (anti-)strategy and empowerment. I argue that these concepts and the contestations concerning their particular meanings and respective importance allow us to understand direct action in a manner which goes beyond its status as a particular practice or tactic in order to highlight the role it plays in the construction of particular kinds of subjects and movements, and particular understandings of social transformation.

Direct action is primarily signified by a refusal to appeal to a 'higher power' to achieve one's aims, and by replacing such appeals with interventions which seek to impact directly upon a situation. Or, in the words of one interviewee, 'direct action is when we do it for ourselves' (Interview N). In David Wieck's terms, direct action *'realizes the end desired'*:

> To take a homely example. If a butcher weighs one's meat with his or her thumb on the scale, one may complain about it and tell him he is a bandit who robs the poor, and if he persists and one does nothing else, this is mere talk; one may call the Department of Weights and Measures, and this is indirect action; or one may, talk failing, insist on weighing one's own meat, bring along a scale to check the butcher's weight, take one's business somewhere else, help open a co-operative store, etc., and these are all direct actions. (Wieck 1996: 375; original emphasis)

Polly Pallister-Wilkins demonstrates how this sentiment works in the context of radical politics when discussing direct action against the Israeli West Bank wall. She examines the group Anarchists Against the Wall, who have worked with Palestinians to physically pull down or dismantle sections of the barrier. As opposed to other activist groups in Israel such as Peace Now, Anarchists Against the Wall are defined through 'a refutation of the assumption that as a collective of people hoping to change something they will take their claim to the state' (2009: 398). There are three reasons why they act 'directly' instead of appealing to 'legitimate' authorities: the first is a refusal to render power to dominant institutions, in this case the Israeli state; the second is the understanding that, even if they did make an official appeal, the state simply would not listen; the third is the 'almost impossible task of identifying all those interest groups who have converged to benefit from the separation Wall and thus cast a large and almost impenetrable network of domination' (2009: 402). For these reasons, the group do not appeal to the state to rectify the situation and instead intervene directly, attempting to halt or hinder construction themselves.

Another notable account of this ethos can be found in the anarchist Emma Goldman's critique of the women's suffrage campaign, which she argued merely served to bring women into line with the violence and limitations of existing political structures, and did little to disrupt core patriarchal attitudes; '[n]ow, woman is confronted with the necessity of emancipating herself from emancipation, if she really desires to be free. This may sound paradoxical, but is, nevertheless, only too true' (1969: 215). She writes that

> [t]he right to vote, or equal civil rights, may be good demands, but true emancipation begins neither at the polls nor in courts. It begins in woman's soul. History tells us that every oppressed class gained true liberation from its masters through its own efforts. It is necessary that woman will learn that lesson, that she realize that her freedom will reach as far as her power to achieve her freedom reaches. (Goldman 1969: 224)

Goldman's argument is that the freedom to partake in, or achieved through, established political frameworks is a limited and potentially counterproductive victory. Against these conventional conceptions of emancipation, Goldman insisted that anarchists 'believe with Stirner that man has as much liberty as he is willing to take.

Anarchism therefore stands for direct action, the open defiance of, and resistance to, all laws and restrictions, economic, social, and moral' (1969: 65). Instead of relying upon (and thereby reinforcing) dominant power relations, Goldman argues for a praxis which encourages people to directly break down, transform and recreate the conditions of their lives.

In these basic accounts of direct action we can identify three distinct but interrelated motivations for the use of direct action. The first is that direct action is a strategically more effective tactic than indirect action. The second, that direct action is more politically transformational than indirect action. And third, that direct action is more personally transformational than indirect action. As I outline below, all of these motivations are present in British anti-militarism, albeit often in ambiguous or contested form.

A Brief History of British Anti-Militarist Direct Action

The role of direct action within British anti-militarism has expanded considerably over the past hundred years. There is a long history of organised British anti-militarism, going back at least as far as the foundation of the Peace Societies in 1816. As Nigel Young demonstrates, this history is one both of 'discontinuities and divisions' and of peaks and troughs in activity (1987a: 9–10). It is also a history which incorporates a number of overlapping political traditions, the most influential of these being anarchist, feminist, religious pacifist, secular pacifist, liberal internationalist, and Marxist-socialist (1987a: 12–14). While a full account of this history is beyond my scope here, the development of direct action can best be traced by looking at a series of periods during which anti-militarist activity intensified.[1]

The first two of these peaks occurred during the two world wars, at which time anti-militarists were predominantly focused on organising opposition to conscription. While conscription was introduced at an earlier point in other European nations, the British government only took such a step in 1915–16. Opposition to conscription was organised by the No Conscription Fellowship (NCF), bringing together pacifists, socialists, anarchists and libertarians in a campaign that became more radical as the war drew on (Young 1987b: 28–37). Thousands of young men registered as conscientious objectors, with others refusing to even register. Of those who did register, many refused to undertake alternative forms of service: '[a]s the war continued, non-co-operation amongst all types of objectors intensified, including refusal to work, sit-down strikes and hunger strikes' (Young 1987b: 31). This domestic upheaval was accompanied by 'desertion, mutiny, inertia and disorganisation' on the front, causing considerable frustration for the government (Young 1987b: 35). High levels of conscientious objection were also seen during the Second World War, with the government's figure of 67,000 counting only those who *officially* registered. The majority of these objectors were church members, with a sizeable proportion of anarchists. Many pacifists focused on providing advice and support to conscientious objectors, despite the government suppression of literature and organisations who engaged in 'conspiracy' to encourage draft refusal. Both the influential peace movement newspaper *Peace News* and the NCF were at various points suppressed.[2]

While activists from a number of different social and political traditions were involved in opposition to conscription, the influence of the Quakers in these movements was of utmost importance. Quakers have been primary actors in British peace movements since the 1650s, and remain a significant presence (Vipont 1960: 250–87). There are two longstanding features of Quakerism that have shaped their influence on anti-militarism. The first of these is a desire to effect a distance between the self and warfare, to '[s]earch out whatever in your own way of life may contain the seeds of war' (Yearly Meeting of the Religious Society of Friends (Quakers) in Britain 2009: 1, 31). Such a sentiment sets the terms for a moral and political justification for conscientious objection. The second feature is an ongoing search for the means of preventing war. This has meant that Quakers have played an integral role in the development of anti-militarist tactics, including civil disobedience, non-violence and direct action, as well as mediation, conflict resolution and peace education (Young 1987a: 16–17).

The conscientious objection movement played a vital role in institutionalising civil disobedience and non-compliance within British anti-militarism. The development of direct action tactics came slightly later, as part of the first wave of the anti-nuclear movement. A key figure here was Hugh Brock, who, as editor of *Peace News* during the 1940s, sought to draw Gandhi's nonviolent methods into the movement. He was secretary of a small organising group called Operation Gandhi, which in 1952 began to organise sit-downs and demonstrations at the War Office and at the Atomic Energy Research Establishment in Aldermaston. He and others connected with *Peace News* also built close links with both anti-colonial movements in Africa and the Civil Rights movement in the US, learning from their tactics as well as alerting people to their struggles (Randle 1987: 132–3). The role of direct action in British anti-militarism intensified in 1957 with the formation of the Direct Action Committee Against Nuclear War (DAC), which was 'influenced by ideas inherited from the Independent Labour Party, Guild Socialism, anarchism, and the libertarian left in general' (Randle 1987: 147). Alongside organising large marches, the DAC carried out actions with a more straightforwardly obstructive intention. In December 1958 activists broke into the Thor intermediate-range rocket base in Norfolk and stopped work from taking place inside (Randle 1987: 134–5). This action was highly unusual and had a significant effect on the movement; writing in *Peace News* shortly afterwards, Gene Sharp said that the DAC 'has hit upon the method for undermining policies which threaten humanity: *withdraw* support and peacefully *act* against such policies' (1959; original emphasis).[3]

The DAC wound up its operations in 1961; in its place emerged the Committee of 100, so named for the hundred public signatories who accompanied its birth. The Committee formed largely out of a sense frustration with the aversion of the Campaign for Nuclear Disarmament (CND) to civil disobedience and illegal action.[4] It organised a series of mass acts of civil disobedience which were at the time considered unprecedented.[5] These included staging a three-hour sit-in at the Ministry of Defence in February 1961 that involved 5,000 participants (with no arrests) and another in April involving 2,500 people (with 1,000 arrests). A mass action planned for September was threatened when the police pre-emptively arrested around fifty of the organisers, including Bertrand Russell. These arrests gained worldwide attention, and the demonstration drew between 12,000 and 17,000 people. In December of the same year the Committee sought to shift the focus of their attention to military bases rather than city centres, and attempted to organise simultaneous demonstrations across seven locations. Their aim was to draw 50,000 people; it is indicative of how quickly the goalposts shifted in 1961 that the eventual turnout of 7,000 people (with 840 arrested) was considered a failure (Randle 1987: 136–41). The Committee's energy waned in 1962, largely as a result of burn-out from the previous year's activities, and organisers focused on smaller actions at bases similar to those carried out by the DAC.[6]

The DAC and Committee of 100 had a far-reaching impact on the conduct of British anti-militarism and on radical politics more broadly. As the Committee disbanded, many of its members moved into the anarchist, feminist, anti-fascist and anti-racist movements, taking their experience of direct action and civil disobedience with them. As Michael Randle argues, the two groups' key effect

> was to establish a tradition of NVDA [non-violent direct action] within the political culture. It is difficult now to realise just how controversial such action was in the late 1950s: if it is far less so today that is because its use has become so much more widespread, and because the intellectual case for the discriminate use of non-violent direct action in a democratic society has largely been won. (Randle 1987: 157–8)

The groups are also notable for their promotion of action above ideology; whilst members of the Committee comprised anarchists, pacifists, liberals, socialists and more, it 'was an ideological no man's land': 'This was a time for action, not argument: for movement, not *a* movement: for propaganda by deed, not word . . . You were identified not by your uniform but by your behaviour, not by what you might say but by what you would do' (Walter 2011: 91).

A second major wave of anti-militarist direct action took place in the early 1980s, again organised largely around opposition to nuclear weapons. This period is most notable for the Women's Peace Camp that was established in 1981 at RAF Greenham Common, in protest against the stationing of cruise missiles at the site. Over the course of three years the camp repeatedly drew tens of thousands of people in a series of mass protests at the camp, as well as smaller blockades and many instances of activists cutting through the fences and entering the base (Roseneil 1995; Laware 2004). Events at the camp were widely reported, generating now-iconic images and videos of women encircling the base, chaining themselves to the perimeter fence, and dancing on the missile silos (Young 1990). This media attention led to a number of other camps forming at bases elsewhere in the UK and in Europe (Cortright 2008: 146–9).

Greenham's legacy in the formation of the contemporary movement and its tactics has been substantial. In a very material sense, this is because it introduced and prepared thousands of people – many of them still active in anti-militarist politics – for direct action (Roseneil 1995: 172). It also prioritised an account of the gendered and patriarchal dimensions of militarism, linking feminist and anti-militarist politics to a hitherto unseen degree, while also placing a greater emphasis on the prefigurative dynamics of direct action than had previously been the case (Roseneil 1995: 71–96). Perhaps most significantly, the substantial media attention Greenham received, alongside the large numbers of people who took part in the demonstrations, played a major role in normalising mass, obstructive and illegal direct action within anti-militarist politics. This normalisation ran alongside a presentation of military bases as surprisingly vulnerable to direct action; whilst they may have been able to defend against a Soviet airstrike, they were unable to prevent anti-militarist women from repeatedly entering the base and causing chaos.[7]

The development of direct action politics moved through another important phase in the 1990s. Until that point, direct action had largely been a particular tactic used by movements; it was at this point that it became a defining feature, such that one would refer to the 'direct action movement' (rather than 'anti-racist movement' or 'environmental movement'). This shift was closely tied to the emergence of the Earth First! (EF!) network in the UK. EF! has little organisational structure and no formal political positions, instead operating largely as a banner under which different groups take action autonomously. Over the course of the 1990s thousands of EF! protest actions took place; these involved occupations of forests and woods as part of the anti-roads movement, sabotage of GM crop trials, property damage against multinational corporations, and occupations and blockades of military and nuclear bases. EF! annual gatherings and the monthly newsletter linked these disparate actions together, and local EF! groups also built campaigns with other organisations not so focused on direct action (Wall 1999; Doherty et al. 2003: 670–4). This substantial normalisation of direct action tactics, and emphasis on decentralised and small-scale actions, was integral to the alter-globalisation and climate movements which emerged in the UK in the early 2000s. It also sets the context for today's anti-militarist direct action politics.

The role of direct action within the contemporary movement is complex. In some ways, it is simply one amongst a wide variety of tactics in common use, part of a repertoire that includes parliamentary lobbying, awareness raising, picketing, marches, union organising, web-based activism, and so forth. For many, perhaps most, activists within the movement, carrying out direct action constitutes a relatively small proportion of their anti-militarist activity. However, direct action is also pedestalised, recognised both as a highly effective means of resisting militarism and as an important method for galvanising the movement. The scale of direct action also varies, from regular blockades of military bases and arms factories to the kinds of large set-piece actions seen against the DSEI arms fair in recent years. Direct action is therefore both normal and exceptional. Its meaning and role is not singular, nor the same for different anti-militarists. Later chapters outline some tensions with regard to how it is practised and negotiated; first, I look in more detail at the conceptual terrain within which direct action is situated.

(Anti-)Representation

We can understand the particular role played by direct action in the political constitution of movements through the status and negotiation of four concepts. The first of these concerns direct action as a critique or rejection of political representation. Insofar as we can understand direct action as a 'principle of action without intermediaries' (Gordon 2018: 529), it is largely through a critical relationship with those potential intermediaries that direct action takes its character. This builds on the understanding that representative forms of politics tend to entrench hierarchies, fail to deliver radical outcomes, and co-opt or weaken social movements (Carter 1970, 1992, 2005; de Cleyre 2005: 273-86). As such, in bypassing the normal processes of representation and intervening 'directly', direct action reaches towards more radical forms of social change. However, there is some dispute amongst anti-militarists about the extent to which direct action is to be regarded as part of a wider process of political transformation, or as simply one amongst a series of useful tactics.

One important contemporary exposition of the radical critique of political representation comes from Richard Day's reading of the logic of and struggle against hegemony in radical thought. In *Gramsci Is Dead*, Day notes the centrality of conceptions and analyses of hegemony for radical political praxis. By the logic of hegemony, he means

> a process through which various factions struggle over meaning, identity and political power. To use the words of Antonio Gramsci, a key thinker in this lineage, a social group which seeks hegemony strives to 'dominate antagonistic groups, which it tends to "liquidate," or to subjugate perhaps even by armed force', at the same time as it attempts to 'lead' kindred and allied groups (Gramsci 1971: 57). Hegemony is a simultaneously coercive and consensual struggle for *dominance*. (Day 2005: 6-7; original emphasis)

Day argues that the response to hegemony, in Marxist and liberal theory and in most radical social movements, has traditionally been to seek a *counter*-hegemony, to 'shift the historical balance back, as much as possible, in favour of the oppressed' (2005: 8). He criticises that counter-hegemonic instinct by insisting that '[t]o argue in this way . . . is to remain within the logic of neoliberalism; it is to accept what I call the *hegemony of hegemony*', by which he means 'the assumption that effective social change can only be achieved simultaneously and *en masse*, across an entire national or supranational space' (2005: 8; original emphasis). For Day, counter-hegemonic projects do little to displace the onto-political totalisations which underpin extant hegemonies, and which are likely to rely on and sustain relations of domination.

Day argues that radical politics should not seek to produce a counter-hegemony, but should work to displace the very logic of hegemony itself. The mobilisation of a counter-hegemony, an alternative regime which promises emancipation, is only ever a partial challenge, which does not fundamentally subvert the legitimisation of and impulse towards authority, domination and mastery of its counterpart. A radical politics which wishes to avoid reproducing central axes of domination should instead operate against or beyond the logic of hegemony. Day suggests that action on these terms can be seen in those social movements that demonstrate what he calls an *'affinity for affinity*, that is, for non-universalizing, non-hierarchical, non-coercive relationships based and [sic] mutual aid and shared ethical commitments' (2005: 9; original emphasis). He argues that those groups that display an affinity for affinity might help to displace, rather than reproduce, the hegemony of hegemony.

Tied to his twin reading of hegemony and affinity, Day develops the concepts of the 'politics of demand' and 'politics of the act'. The politics of demand is understood as a 'mode of social action [which] assumes the existence of a dominant nation attached to a monopolistic state, which must be persuaded to give the gifts of *recognition* and *integration* to subordinate identities and communities' (2005: 14–15; original emphasis); that is, as a form of social action which proceeds through petition and representation, and which thereby fetishises relations of hierarchy and domination. As Day argues,

> every demand, in anticipating a response, *perpetuates* those structures, which exist precisely in anticipation of demands. This leads to a positive feedback loop, in which the ever-increasing depth and breadth of apparatuses of discipline and control create ever new sites of antagonism, which produce new demands, thereby increasing the quantity and intensity of discipline and control . . . Clearly, the fundamental fantasy of the politics of demand is that the currently hegemonic formation will recognize the validity of the claim presented to it and respond in a way that produces an event of emancipation. Most of the time, however, it does not; instead

Day contrasts this politics of demand with a politics of the act, an alternative form which

> relies upon, and results from, getting over the hope that the state and corporate forms, as structures of domination, exploitation and division, are somehow capable of producing effects of emancipation. By avoiding making demands in the first place, it offers a way out of the cycle through which requests for 'freedom' or 'rights' are used to justify an intensification of the societies of discipline and control. (Day 2005: 15)

A politics of the act is based on the recognition that 'what we think can only be done via the state and corporate forms . . . can in fact be done, and done more effectively, without passing through these mediating institutions' (Day 2005: 18). Day gives examples of the 'newest social movements', including anarchist groups, indigenous movements, postcolonial movements, queer identity groups and others, which are rejecting a reliance upon the politics of demand in favour of a politics of the act. His work serves to displace the assumption that the only possible means of political intervention are those which conform to the logics of hegemony, and suggests that an affinity-based approach might hold more interesting possibilities.

Many of the examples in this book can be read as anti-hegemonic practices of resistance, as manifestations of a politics of the act which seek to directly limit or transform conditions, spaces or policies connected with militarism. In this sense, they operate beyond the terms of political representation. However, to emphasise those features is not to deny that activists do also appeal to (or seek to influence) representative political structures, including the state. Even when not explicitly articulated, direct action practices are legible largely insofar as they can be seen to issue particular demands. Yotam Marom highlights this point in conversation with Naomi Klein, while responding to her concern that its absence of demands meant that the Occupy Movement became defined by what it was not:

> We don't have demands in the way that other people want to hear them. But of course we have demands, of course we want things. When we reclaim a foreclosed home for a foreclosed-on family, or organize students to do flash mobs at the banks keeping them in debt, or environmental activists to do die-ins at banks that invest in coal, these are ways of speaking our demands in a new language of resistance. (Klein and Marom 2012)[8]

What is at stake is perhaps less that something is demanded, rather the particular politics of legitimacy, duty and intelligibility that are reproduced by the performance of any particular demand. In this sense, the politics of demand and the politics of the act should not be understood as secure and separate categories, as ways of distinguishing between fundamentally different types of actor and action, or as distinct properties of an intervention. Instead, we can see these categories as frames of interpretation which might help to unpick different trends and tendencies within a set of practices. In Chapters 4 and 5 I demonstrate how attention to the anti-representative and anti-hegemonic qualities of direct action practices allows us to see how anti-militarists resist statist and militarised security politics, while in Chapter 9 I draw on Day's account to show how anti-militarist practices rooted in the politics of demand can function to reproduce hegemonic forms of militarism.

Common to all approaches to anti-militarist direct action is a do-it-yourself sensibility which centres the role that can be played by 'ordinary' people. This attitude is elegantly summarised in Andrea Needham's reflections on the Seeds of Hope action:

> One of the beautiful things about Ploughshares actions is that anyone can do them. You don't need to be a technical genius or an engineer, you don't need to be physically strong, you don't need any expensive equipment or special skills. All you need is a hammer and a functioning arm. We each had both of these things. We started hammering. (Needham 2016: 91–2)

However, within that outlook lies a long-running tension about the political nature of direct action. While for most people the purchase of the tactic lies in its apparent exteriority from the political system, the extent to which this is simply one amongst many possible tactics, or is in itself politically transformational, varies. For some, direct action is the 'preferred way of doing things', a means of creating a more localised and democratic approach to politics (Doherty et al. 2003: 670). Beyond its immediate tactical purchase, it has significant value as a prefigurative intervention. Others argue that there is a troubling tendency to over-valorise direct action or to engage in a kind of purism, rather than picking the most appropriate tactics for any one campaign. Several of my interviewees cautioned against a 'knee-jerk' approach to activism which opts for the most spectacularly direct approach irrespective of strategic thinking; as one put it, 'direct action is part of your toolbox; it's not *the* toolbox' (Interview P).

These contrasts are by no means new. Craig Calhoun argues that the motivations for direct action in nineteenth-century radical movements were divided between those, such as the Luddites, for whom direct action was a matter of necessity by virtue of exclusion from the 'legitimate' political sphere, and those, including many Owenites and anarchists, for whom the refusal to participate in conventional politics had a more romantic, aesthetic, or ethical component (1993: 406–7). In his reflections on the Committee of 100, Randle identifies a distinction between those, such as Bertrand Russell, for whom direct action was simply 'a way of drawing media and public attention to the nuclear issue', and those for whom it was part of a wider programme of radical change 'that would affect almost every aspect of social and political life' (1987: 148). Whilst few today see direct action as inherently revolutionary, the extent to which it is conceptualised as generative of a radical politics, or more straightforwardly as a useful tactic, varies significantly. As I discuss more substantially in Chapter 7 (and as was the case in mid-nineteenth- and twentieth-century movements), such variation often remains hidden because movements are determined more by the action they seek to take than the motivations behind it. These differences are further elaborated in Chapter 8 when considering contrasting attitudes towards political disobedience within the movement.

One further tension related to direct action's (anti-)representational character concerns the role of symbolism. One of the principle reasons why people engage in direct action is the 'directness' of the action – the fact that one is, immediately, impacting on a situation. When planning actions, many activists will insist that trying to gain media attention should not be a primary goal (especially if this interferes with other aims); the chief effect should be on the particular situation or target. However, this focus on directness clearly does not mean that the politics of direct action are not also determined by how action is represented, or that direct action is not constituted by the representations that surround it. The most celebrated direct actions, even (or perhaps especially) when lauded for their 'directness', are overdetermined by their representation within the movement. In Chapters 4 and 5 I argue that it is insofar as it provokes imaginaries beyond the confines of representative politics that direct action is powerful; this is its own form of representation. Activists are attentive to these representations and the symbolism that shapes them. In the vignette that opened this chapter I highlighted how the Seeds of Hope women used carefully considered symbols in their actions; this symbolism was further exemplified when, on the twenty-first anniversary of the Seeds of Hope action, Sam and Woody carried out Seeds of Hope 2, at the same site and while using the exact same hammer as the original action.[9] The point, then, is not to establish a dichotomy between directness and representation, but to be attentive to how the particular conduct and presentation of direct action politics reshapes certain expectations and practices of political action.

Prefiguration

A second concept that operates in close proximity to direct action is prefiguration. The principle of prefiguration rests on the idea that the means used to achieve political change should correspond to the ends that are desired, so that 'there is no distinction between how we fight and what we fight for' (Maeckelbergh 2009: 66). It represents a 'broadening of the idea of direct action' (Gordon 2007: 35), insofar as it insists that the do-it-yourself ethos of transformation applies within movements as much as to the world around them. Over the past twenty years prefiguration has become an axiomatic feature for many direct action movements worldwide.[10]

The prefigurative ethos is underpinned by a series of arguments about the nature of political transformation. The most important of these emerged from early anarchist critiques of Marxism. Anarchists like Mikhail Bakunin insisted that a revolutionary process organised in an authoritarian manner would lead not to an equal society, but to a fresh tyranny, a 'highly despotic government of the masses by a new and very small aristocracy' (Bakunin 1990: 178–9). They argued that revolutionary organisations and processes must embody the society they wish to create. Reflecting on her experiences in post-1917 Russia, Goldman insisted that

> [n]o revolution can ever succeed as a factor of liberation unless the MEANS used to further it be identical in spirit and tendency with the PURPOSES to be achieved . . . Today is the parent of tomorrow. The present casts its shadow far into the future. That is the law of life, individual and social. Revolution that divests itself of ethical values thereby lays the foundation of injustice, deceit, and oppression for the future society. The *means* used to *prepare* the future become its *cornerstone*. (Goldman 1996: 402–3; original emphasis)

Arguments like these are rooted in a generative temporality which recognises that the future is produced in the present, as opposed to vanguardist accounts which hold the social relations of the future as a matter for later (Gordon 2018). By this logic, all political action is to be regarded as in some sense prefigurative, with 'prefigurative' actors being those who recognise and seek to work within the contours of that understanding.

The early twentieth-century anarchist writer Gustav Landauer developed an account of prefiguration which stresses the importance of exploring new forms of social relation as part of the revolutionary process. Landauer differed from many of his contemporaries in his refusal to conceptualise the state as a corporeal institution which could be destroyed. Instead, he advanced a relational ontology which placed very different demands on what it means to resist. In his most well-known passage, he argues that

> [a] table can be overturned and a window can be smashed. However, those who believe that the state is also a thing or a fetish that can be overturned or smashed are sophists and believers in the Word. The state

is a social relationship; a certain way of people relating to one another. It can be destroyed by creating new social relationships; i.e., by people relating to one another differently.

> The absolute monarch said: I am the state. We, who we [sic] have imprisoned ourselves in the absolute state, must realize the truth: *we* are the state! And we will be the state as long as we are nothing different; as long as we have not yet created the institutions necessary for a true community and a true society of human beings. (Landauer 2010: 214; original emphasis)

Simply attacking abstracted notions of the state ignores the relational and participatory dynamics which make systems of violence and domination possible. Following from this view of power and the state which, as Day notes, was influenced by Nietzsche's method and critique of modernity (2005: 34), Landauer insisted that forms of protest which adhered to the logics and relations of that which was opposed would only ever serve to entrench the state form.

Landauer instead advocated the creation of 'functioning enclaves of libertarianism' as a 'prefigurative framework for emancipation' (Horrox 2010: 195). If participation in dominant systems and relations is unacceptable, and mere opposition a reification, then constructing alternative social relations as a means to weakening relations of domination is necessary. Landauer envisaged these project(s) of creation on both micro and macro scales, ranging from setting up soup kitchens and guerrilla gardening to larger social movements; indeed, Landauer's ideas were influential in the early kibbutz movement (Horrox 2010: 198). He displays contempt for resistances not preoccupied with the task of creating society anew, feeling that the fetishisation of many of his contemporaries was a reactive position. Criticising anarchists who engaged in assassinations, he argued that

> what drives them is vanity – a craving for recognition. What they are trying to say is: 'We are also doing politics. We are not idle. We are a force to be reckoned with!' These anarchists are not anarchic enough for me. (Horrox 2010: 84)

To argue that Landauer was a fierce advocate of creativity is not to say that he rejected contestation, negation and destruction;

discussing his admiration for Nietzsche, he applauds how 'there was activity in Nietzsche's spiritual quest, there was permanent destruction and creation, collapsing and rebuilding' (Horrox 2010: 64). It is more accurate to say that Landauer was sceptical of *confrontation*, of resistance which defined itself only in opposition to (and so on the terms of) another force. Landauer certainly wanted to do away with the state, with totalising and hegemonic visions of politics, with violence, but he refused to let this overwhelm and define his desire to create something new.

In focusing attention on the generative and creative dimensions of radical politics, prefiguration should not be narrowly conceptualised as the rational configuration of means to align with predetermined ends, nor the straightforward embodiment of idealised utopias. Instead, it is a process of experimentation, through which speculative mobilisations of possibility might be explored and broken down within the context of resistance. It is not so much the attempt to live utopias as it is the necessary (and necessarily problematic) work to imagine ways of being and relating otherwise. Efforts to enact a politics which move beyond existing forms of domination must continuously run against, make visible, and contest those relations of domination which will emerge in the process, which are woven throughout the social form. In this sense they are a potent learning space, where 'the tension between aspiration and experience is continuously worked out' (Gordon 2018: 530). Prefigurative politics might then be understood as a process through which we come to know ourselves, and to become otherwise.

At the heart of this ethos is a recognition that practices of resistance cannot be thought outside of the power systems they seek to contest. In Nathan Jun's terms, '[t]o resist power as though it were somehow *elsewhere* or *outside* is merely to react against power'. Radical history reminds us that 'such reactive resistance is either quickly defeated by extant power structures or else ends up replicating those power structures at the micropolitical level' (2011: 243). As I outline in Chapter 3, accounts like this have been crucial for feminist anti-militarists, who have called attention to how militarised gender orders are reproduced within anti-militarist spaces. One consequence of these understandings for activists has been an increased focus on *process*, on attempts to organise in ways which reflect movements' ideals (such as equality, autonomy, non-domination). In Uri Gordon's terms,

> [t]he effort to create and develop horizontal functioning in any collective action setting, and to maintain a constant awareness of interpersonal dynamics and the way in which they might reflect social patterns of exclusion, are accorded just as much importance as planning and carrying out campaigns, projects and actions. Considerations of efficiency or unity are seldom alleged to justify a weakening of this emphasis. (Gordon 2007: 35)

The practical and political implications of this commitment are substantial, insofar as the organisation of movements thus becomes a political rather than merely strategic question (Howard and Pratt-Boyden 2013; Maeckelbergh 2009, 2011; Sancho 2014). Despite these substantial commitments, it has become commonplace for contemporary social movements to adopt a prefigurative ethos through which they attempt to 'create the institutions of a new society in the shell of the old' (Graeber 2011).

It is a central argument of this book that anti-militarist politics should be recognised as prefigurative. This stems first from the understanding that all political action is in some sense prefigurative, generating and reproducing particular social relations and subjectivities, albeit perhaps in ways that are contrary to the intentions of those involved. Prefiguration here operates as a lens of analysis that helps to reveal the politics and contradictions of social movements. The second reason for focusing on prefiguration is that it animates a rich series of anti-militarist practices as engagements with and against the terms of militarism. Much of contemporary anti-militarism operates in an organising context where the fundamental ideas of prefiguration – particularly with respect to the idea that there should be a confluence between means and ends – have become political common sense. Third, reading anti-militarism as prefigurative allows us to recognise the ways militarism operates and is contested as a series of social relations. While much of the practical focus of anti-militarist activism rests with particular institutions, it would be problematic to reduce militarism to these and thereby miss the system of values, ideologies, subjectivities and everyday social practices within which they are embedded. It is here that Landauer's invocation is so important; as with the state, militarism is not a thing that can be smashed, but a series of social relations that must be disassembled by relating otherwise. Throughout the book (but most explicitly in Chapters 6 and 7) I demonstrate how much of anti-militarist politics goes beyond challenging institutions and critiquing militarised social relations, and works to prefigure alternatives. Those prefigurations are not straightforwardly transformative, and often do more to reveal the depths of our imbrication within militarised relations of power than to challenge them, but they are nonetheless crucial practices through which to read the politics of anti-militarism.

(Anti-)Strategy

Direct action has an ambiguous relationship with political strategy. This might seem counter-intuitive; activists favour direct action tactics largely because they are highly effective at disrupting the normal conduct of militarism, at putting pressure on weak points in networks, and at forcing institutions into a crisis of legitimacy. It is often unexpected, unpredictable, and difficult to prevent. In one activist's terms, 'it's like the chess piece on the board that moves of its own accord' (Interview O). It has something of a double effect, weaving together symbolism and tangibility, contributing towards wider campaigns while also having direct effects on particular situations. These features mean that direct action is frequently viewed as a good strategic option.

However, there are important reasons to also see direct action as *non*-strategic, and even *anti*-strategic. Direct action politics tend to be organised in a relatively autonomous manner, with targets and tactics determined by those who will be taking part and their supporters. While there are occasionally mass direct action campaigns, such as Faslane 365 in 2006–7 and against DSEI in more recent years, the specific actions taken as part of these campaigns are largely organised by small autonomous groups. This does not mean that groups like Plowshares and CAAT do not encourage, support and train people to take direct action, or call attention to some strategic opportunities. But they rarely govern this with any level of coordination; there is always something of an incidental quality. Indeed, the broadly decentralised and non-hierarchical nature of the movement means that even very concerted attempts at strategic organisation are always somewhat fragile. This, understandably, leads to certain frustrations. Actions will take place that not everyone agrees with. Actions will not happen when they would have been highly effective, or do happen when they are not particularly useful. Few involved in anti-militarist direct action politics (or indeed any direct action politics) would claim that the full strategic possibilities of direct action are realised.

There are certain virtues in this prioritisation of autonomy over the general strategic imperative. As a tendency, it emerges from a suspicion of vanguardist instrumentalism, and the ways in which the disciplining of effective action in line with 'The Cause' has authoritarian and even militarising dimensions (Foucault 2002: 453). In this sense it is closely tied to the prefigurative qualities of direct action, signifying a refusal to allow short-term or narrow calculations of effectiveness, or fixed long-term programmes, to overdetermine the directions of movements such that their more quotidian political dynamics are overlooked (Franks 2003). Whilst this may lead to less effectively targeted political action in an immediate sense, it is insofar as it centres prefigurative politics that an anti-strategic ethos may be more effective in the long run. An anti-strategic ethos also holds open spaces for creativity, deriving from feminist and anarchist traditions which refuse to set out in advance what the subjects of revolution must *be*:

> there cannot be social change without the construction of new kinds of desiring subjects as molecular, nomadic, and multiple. One must start by leaving open spaces of experimentation, of search, of transition: becoming-nomads.
> This is no call for easy pluralism, either – but rather a passionate plea for the recognition of the need to respect the multiplicity and to find forms of action that reflect the complexity – without drowning in it. (Braidotti 1994: 171)

In these terms, the anti-strategic dimensions of direct action (can) operate as a space of political exploration. Nonetheless, as Rosi

Braidotti's nod to the risk of 'drowning in' complexity indicates, the total absence of strategic thought is potentially as problematic as its dominance.

To highlight a certain anti-strategic ethos is not to suggest that anti-militarists do not engage in discussions about strategies or long-term plans; rather, it is to claim that activists have a critical relationship with strategy (Rossdale and Stierl 2016), or a more expansive account of strategy than traditional vanguardist approaches (Maeckelbergh 2011). The question then becomes how to juggle that anti-strategic ethos with the desire to mount effective challenges to militarism – or as one interviewee put it, 'how we build these smaller, tactical decisions now into the broader long-term challenge we want to see':

> I don't think the aim should ever be how can we basically make people do what we want. That's the classic approach to strategy and I think it's a bad one. Like, the aim as I see it is more, like, how can we get critical people to do what they want to do, and how can we try and thread those things together into a coherent plan. (Interview L)

There are, of course, no straightforward answers here. There exists a certain faith that maintaining these conflicting imperatives – autonomy and coherence – holds open the space to develop movements and strategies which do not impose more restrictive approaches to strategy. Nonetheless, these imperatives cannot but generate tensions. While they appear at various points in the book, they are engaged most explicitly in Chapter 7, where I examine how anti-militarists negotiate the limits of acceptable tactics without establishing general strategic terms.

Empowerment

The final concept to draw out here concerns the specifically empowering qualities that activists frequently identify in direct action. The understanding of direct action as politically transformational is closely tied to its status as personally transformational, as a practice that generates an experience of agency or potency that is often lacking in more traditional forms of politics. This was a common theme for my interviewees. During a group interview one, referring to her experience of blockading a road into a military base, noted that the action gave her a new-found 'sense of worth', a belief that she had the capacity to intervene politically in a manner previously unavailable, while another referred to the empowering dimensions of conducting her own defence in court (Interview D). In an introductory talk about their campaign, the group Target Brimar explained that they had chosen a campaign based on direct action precisely because they felt it to be a more empowering route than petitioning the state. Another interviewee summed up his politics by explaining that

> we're not going to get what we want by politely asking the ruling classes for it, ever, and you could argue that you're not going to get it by direct action either because only .01 per cent of the population will ever actually take that step. But if we're not going to win either way, I know which brick wall I'd rather be banging my head against, because it'll give me more self-respect to not be asking for it. (Interview F)

That sense of empowerment can extend beyond those involved in any one action or campaign, reshaping understandings of what kinds of action are possible. Activists often share stories about actions that have inspired them and shaped their political imagination. Direct action can also create 'a ripple or a spark that is discernible to people who you're in solidarity with', as one activist told me:

> for example, when I was in Gaza and friends went and smashed up EDO MBM technologies in Brighton,[11] I told people in Gaza that that's what happened, and they were really pleased, you know? They were suddenly like, oh wow, somebody did this risky thing that we hadn't heard people do before ... we saw the demonstrations – they didn't amount to anything, whereas this was like, yeah, this was a company that got smashed to stop them. (Interview O)

An optimistic account of this sense of empowerment situates it as transformational, as helping to cultivate subjects who intervene in ways that subvert representational and hegemonic political forms.

This experience is central to the accounts developed in Chapters 4 and 5. Nevertheless, there are also certain pitfalls here, which might be thought in relation to direct action's tangibility.

It is precisely in the experience of tangibility that activists locate the empowering and effective dimensions of direct action – the material destruction of a weapons system or blockade of a base, which other forms of campaigning would almost certainly fail to effect. However, and notwithstanding the effectiveness of such action, that affective relationship with direct action can be seductive. As with Landauer's critique of anarchists who engaged in assassinations, the desire for immediate and concrete successes risks displacing more intangible processes of social change. Two different quotes from interviewees reveal contrasting attitudes here:

> I don't think it's valueless for people to, you know, raise consciousness around things that are important in the world. I just think it's hard to track and so I'll never make it my core thing . . . Like, have it as the side aim that you try and structure into all the things you do about, like, running trainings for things and making sure you give out flyers to people walking past and that sort of thing. But it will never be the aim in itself because it's always going to be a thing where you're, like, 'Did we do it?' 'Who knows!' Until the point where a whole town turns out to burn down a factory, and then you'll probably be like 'Look, I've raised a bit of awareness'. (Interview L)

> a lot of those campaigns . . . we wanted to shut this down, we wanted to persuade them to do this, we did like this and then they did it. But actually . . . we're trying to change the mind-set and attitudes of a whole society, a whole culture, a whole world in a sense, and some things aren't measurable; if next year ten thousand more people wear white poppies than this year and therefore forty thousand more people see a white poppy than this year, who can measure at this stage what effect that's had? But actually, if we only do things we can measure, we'll only win small victories. (Interview M)

The first quote here privileges forms of action which have a concrete and measurable outcome, recognising that these can be vital for maintaining energy within a campaign. However, as the second quote points out, these positions can also limit political imagination, potentially in a manner which struggles to contend with the subjectifying and ideological dynamics of militarism that are discussed in the next chapter. At several points in the book, but most explicitly in Chapters 6 and 8, I demonstrate how it is potentially precisely in those situations where direct action *feels* good, effective, tangible, that we might need to think most critically about the kinds of politics we may inadvertently be reproducing.

*

Not every anti-militarist practice with which this book engages can be categorised as direct action; nonetheless the tactic does collect and guide the study. This is not because direct action is necessarily superior to other tactics, but because the practice of direct action, and the sentiments and negotiations which accompany it, are productive spaces from which to read the politics of the movement. The critique of political representation, the attention to prefiguration, the caution around political strategy and the desire for some form of political empowerment draw activists into intimate engagements (and dilemmas) with both the conduct of resistance and the nature of militarism. Through them we can understand the role played by direct action in the cultivation of particular kinds of subjects and movements, and particular understandings of social transformation. The accounts here therefore ground the analyses which follow. The next chapter begins to put these practices of resistance into more explicit conversation with the systems of power they seek to contest.

Notes

1. For histories of anti-militarist and peace movements, see Carter (1992); Cortright (2008); Grünewald and van den Dungen (1995).
2. During the two world wars, British public opinion was not on the side of the objectors. However, this does not mean that British society during this period was unproblematically pro-war. As Anne Summers demonstrates, prior to 1914, British attitudes towards both the regular army and its imperial adventures were sceptical. In the exhausted, horrified aftermath of the First World War, the rapid whipping of the British population into a military spirit was viewed as something of a fraud (1976). At the time of the Peace Ballot in 1934–5, large portions of the population appeared to hold highly positive – if not

outwardly pacifist – attitudes towards disarmament and demobilisation (Ceadel 1980).
3. It was while she was secretary of the DAC that April Carter wrote her classic pamphlet on direct action (1970).
4. For a CND insider's perspective on this dispute, see Hudson (2005: 66–75).
5. Nicolas Walter wrote that our 'means seem unfamiliar, in spite of the long illegal tradition of the Levellers, Radicals, Chartists, Suffragettes, and hunger marchers, in spite of the long non-violent tradition of Winstanley, Fox, Godwin, Thoreau, and Tolstoy, and in spite of the work of Gandhi who united these two traditions' (Walter 2011: 80).
6. For further discussion, see Bradshaw et al. (1981); Carter (1992: 45–57); Driver (1964); Taylor (1988: 115–272).
7. That vulnerability was also being revealed in North America, where the Plowshares movement was getting started and itself demonstrating that advanced weapons systems are often poorly equipped to defend against peace activists with hammers.
8. For a more substantive account of the resistance to issuing demands in the Occupy Movement, see Rossdale and Stierl (2016).
9. The Plowshares movement pay particularly close attention to the symbolic dimensions of their direct action (Tobey 2017).
10. See Howard and Pratt-Boyden (2013); Maeckelbergh (2011); Mason (2014); Sancho (2014); Yates (2015).
11. The EDO Decommissioners' action is discussed in more detail in Chapter 4.

CHAPTER 2

Conceptualising Militarism

At the most basic level, militarism can be understood as the social and international relations of the preparation for and conduct of organised political violence (Stavrianakis and Selby 2012: 3). There is no singular type of militarism; its form is context specific, determined by the particular configurations of power at operation in any particular environment. My task in this book is not to begin from or build towards a precise account of militarism, but to retell the story of militarism and resistance from a series of perspectives. It is nonetheless useful to introduce some more substantive accounts of what militarism is, from which later chapters can then depart.

The first half of the chapter looks at how activists' most straightforward relationship with militarism concerns militarism as it is embodied within and produced through a series of institutions. It is through resistance to these institutions that anti-militarist politics gains much of its coherence. I focus on anti-arms trade activists, showing how they target organisations ranging from arms companies and government departments to museums and churches. After introducing a number of campaigns against institutions, I show how activists situate these institutions within a conception of militarism that is specifically *local* and *networked*; an ontologisation which renders militarism accessible (and vulnerable) to democratic and grassroots-based political action.

While these institutions are vitally important, they do not exhaust the terms of militarism. To think about militarism (and therefore resistance) more carefully, we need an account which recognises the concept as a way of engaging forms of social and political organisation that run throughout society. A far more nuanced account (and critique) of resistance becomes available when we understand militarism in these terms. The second half of the chapter therefore introduces an account of everyday or 'banal' militarism, drawing more heavily on academic accounts to show how militarism is constituted through a series of values, subjectivities and social practices. I close the chapter by introducing two anti-militarist organisations that explicitly campaign against militarism on these terms.

Militarism and Institutions

This book is broadly concerned with what we might call the micropolitics of militarism. In taking an ethnographic approach, I am interested in drawing out how anti-militarists resist, subvert, or reproduce militarised value systems, modes of contestation, and forms of subjectivity. This approach can be highly effective at recognising the subtleties through which everyday social relations are implicated in and shaped by militarism. However, it also runs the risk of overlooking (or undervaluing) the institutional contexts which give militarism its specificity and considerable social power. As Bryan Mabee argues, we have to see militarism as both 'a disposition that justifies particular security or military practices' *and* 'a particular constellation of social forces surrounding the military and the institutionalization of military power' (2016: 243). This institutionalisation relates both to the political-economic context within which particular militarised societies are situated, and to the operation of certain networks of institutions through which military power is conducted and legitimised. Such institutions include the military, government ministries (principally defence, foreign affairs, trade, and development), the arms industry, border agencies, police forces, and private military and security companies.[1]

For activists too, it is the institutions, and their attendant practices and policies, which draw most attention. As one puts it, militarism 'takes into account the whole group of interests that is served by and has an interest in perpetuating militarised conflict and militarised economic policy' (Interview O). And while this book examines activist practices in the micropolitical terms noted above, the context of those practices is generally one where activists are concerned with particular institutions. Much of the empirical material that follows focuses on direct action against the British arms industry. A strong, state-supported arms industry has been fundamental to British militarism since the industrial revolution, and remains integral to Britain's status as a leading power. Where Britain may have lacked a comparative advantage with respect to competitors in terms of industry, commerce, or population size, it has remained at the forefront of weapons technology, translating this into both military power and a powerful manufacturing base (Edgerton 1991; Satia 2018). This has meant that the arms industry (and arms dealers) have long been the principle foes of British anti-militarists. In the contemporary movement we see action directed against a series of interconnected institutions related to the arms industry, including arms companies, government departments, large arms fairs, as well as less obvious organisations including universities, churches and museums.

The primary targets for anti-arms trade activists tend to be arms companies themselves. Over the past fifteen years there have been high-profile campaigns in the UK against companies including Heckler & Koch, Finmeccanica (now Leonardo), Lockheed Martin, Elbit Systems, Raytheon, EDO MBM, Brimar Systems, and Chemring. Dwarfing all of these are campaigns against the UK's largest arms company, BAE Systems (formerly British Aerospace), for whom many activists hold a particular and deep-seated hatred. It was a BAE Systems Hawk that the Seeds of Hope women smashed, a BAE Typhoon that Sam and Woody nearly reached, and many more actions against BAE sites, property, meetings, and trade deals appear in this book. CAAT have run a number of major campaigns against BAE Systems, including several high-profile legal challenges, with such persistence that BAE hired private investigators to spy on the organisation. Campaigns against arms companies tend to weave together attempts to harm the company's legitimacy (with the public, government, investors, or potential employees) alongside action to directly impede production.

Government departments are also a major institutional target for anti-arms trade activists, challenged for their role in promoting and licensing arms sales and giving diplomatic and legal cover to the arms industry. A revolving door between government ministers, senior civil servants and arms industry executives signals the intimacy of the relationships between government and industry here (Perlo-Freeman 2010: 260–3). Since 2008, attention has focused on the Defence & Security Organisation (DSO), which was housed in the UK Trade & Investment department between 2008 and 2016, and has been located in the Department for International Trade from 2016. Civil servants within DSO are tasked with promoting British arms exports (including arranging for high-profile individuals, such as the Royal Family, to help secure sales), and with helping to organise arms fairs within the UK. CAAT have placed a great deal of attention on DSO, viewing it as the government department with the largest role in supporting the British arms industry, and have organised many protests, media stunts and occupations at the DSO offices in Westminster. They do so on the back of a successful campaign. DSO's predecessor, the Defence Export Services Organisation, was based in the Ministry of Defence, and in 2007 CAAT campaigned successfully for its closure (Evans 2007). One activist involved in the campaign noted that this was 'the first time in probably about ten years that the government had made a significant decision that the arms industry didn't agree with' (Interview M).

If government departments and arms companies receive much of the everyday focus of anti-arms trade activists, it is large arms fairs that draw more spectacular attention. The most significant is Defence and Security Equipment International (DSEI – pronounced 'dicey' by activists), a biennial event that has taken place at ExCeL in East London since 2001. DSEI is the world's largest 'fully integrated' defence exhibition, featuring land-, sea- and air-based military technology. Over a thousand exhibitors display products ranging from crowd control equipment and small arms to combat aircraft, drones and tanks, with over 30,000 military and trade delegates in attendance. Activists view DSEI as a major event in the business of the international arms trade, and as one which cements Britain's leading role in the industry. Opposition to DSEI is therefore a major component of the anti-arms trade calendar. Since 2009, the scale of this opposition has increased steadily with each iteration, with the 2017 protests involving thousands of activists and over a hundred arrests. The key organising force in this steady intensification has been the STAF coalition, with heavy support from CAAT. Both opposition to DSEI and the politics of the STAF coalition will be discussed extensively in later chapters. Alongside DSEI there are two other UK-based arms fairs which regularly draw protest: the Farnborough International Air Show, and Security and Policing.

Activists also take action against institutions which do not at first glance appear to be related to the arms trade or to militarism, often in an attempt to call attention to relationships that such institutions might prefer to conceal. Universities have been an important campaign target, with many British institutions having some mix of arms trade investments and research, teaching or recruitment relationships with arms companies (Stavrianakis 2006; Street and Beale 2007). Other targets have included banks with arms trade investments, churches who host arms trade events and, as I discuss further below, exhibitions run by Clarion Events, the company which owns DSEI. Since 2011 there has also been a substantial focus on public institutions with arms trade connections, and in particular on museums that have hosted arms trade events. This began during DSEI 2011, when several hundred activists demonstrated outside the National Gallery as it hosted a gala dinner on behalf of Finmeccanica for arms dealers and government ministers. Since then, there have been similar protests against the National History Museum, London Transport Museum and Science Museum.

As they focus on institutional targets, anti-militarists also conceptualise militarism as a network. In this network militarism is both a localised political form and present in surprising places. These narratives are critical for the forms of resistance mobilised; if the place of militarism is abstracted, or restricted to the corridors of Westminster and Whitehall, then ordinary people cannot make an intervention without seeking to occupy or convince the occupiers of those places. Direct action politics is predicated precisely on subverting such expectations of political representation, and so alternative conceptions are needed.

The Manchester-based Target Brimar provide a good example of how militarism is framed in this manner. At an anti-militarist gathering in the city in 2011 activists from the group explained how understanding militarism as a network was central to their campaign. They outlined how they chose the relatively small company Brimar (which made screens and viewing equipment for Apache helicopters, used in Afghanistan, Iraq and Gaza) in part because there was a chance that they may actually succeed – either by closing the factory down or pushing it to cease military production (which was only one part of its overall business). Doing so would break the 'military–industrial complex' at a point they saw as weak but important – at that time only two factories produced the screens, and Apache helicopters cannot fly without them. This possibility, they explained, was more appealing than taking action against well-guarded military bases like Faslane.

Target Brimar's literature placed significant focus on 'the network', and Brimar's place within it, one pamphlet emphasising that 'Brimar is a small cog in the war machine. A cog located in Greater Manchester' (Target Brimar undated). Similar logics could also be seen underpinning the Smash EDO campaign that relentlessly campaigned against the EDO MBM facility in Brighton between 2004 and 2014. In their publicity, they used a tagline which read: 'Every bomb that is dropped and every bullet that is fired has to be made somewhere and wherever that is, it can be resisted.'[2] Narratives like this implicitly refuse understandings of politics that focus on the centralised and bureaucratised realm, in favour of those which render militarism both accessible and vulnerable. This is not to suggest these narratives are therefore unproblematic or straightforwardly subversive. As Martin Coward argues, the network trope is itself implicated in a series of war-enabling ontological frameworks (2009, 2017). However, it does play an important role in providing the impetus for direct action politics.

The focus on 'the local' dimension is particularly important in this framing. In a segment recorded for BBC's *The One Show* in early 2011, one of the founders of the Shut Down Heckler & Koch campaign took a reporter on a tour of Nottingham to show him the various arms companies operating 'locally' in the suburbs (CAAT 2011b). Similarly, at the CAAT National Gathering in November 2010, a workshop entitled 'What to do about the arms company on your doorstep?' discussed how local people can conduct research into and take action against local arms companies. Activists have developed tools to help with this. Disarm DSEI, a London-based group who organise resistance to DSEI (now as part of the STAF coalition), created a Google Maps-based application that allowed users to search for DSEI exhibitors near them.[3] CAAT built on this idea and developed their own map, including UK-based companies that attend DSEI alongside the Farnborough Air Show, Security and Policing and some overseas arms fairs. Users can search the map by postcode, target market or company name:

> Sometimes the death and destruction that the trade wreaks seems too far away to be relevant to our daily lives. In fact, conflict, repression and destruction around the world are fuelled by weapons, equipment and components made all across the UK.
> Our map aims to help you find out about the arms trade and security industry on your doorstep – and take action. (CAAT 2015a)

It is not uncommon for groups within CAAT's activist network to get in touch with the main office, seeking support in developing a campaign after having used the map to find a local company.

These moves do not signify a romanticisation or fetishisation of the local of the sort critiqued by Michael Hardt and Antonio Negri, amongst others (2003: 43–6; Mohan and Stokke 2000). Rather, they represent a recognition that the local/global dichotomy is problematic, and that narratives which expel 'the local' from understandings of militarism and war serve to defer popular participation. This is why Target Brimar, at the Manchester gathering, referred to militarism as a simultaneously 'local and global' phenomenon, with each predicated on and constituted by the other. They noted that this understanding was inspired by Smash EDO (as was much of their campaign), who made such claims about their Brighton-based focus. Similar ideas were expressed by the Raytheon 9 who, after responding to the 2006 Israel–Lebanon war by entering Raytheon's Derry factory and carrying out major property damage, highlighted the shared context between the ongoing war in Lebanon and Derry's own historical experiences of violence (McCann undated: 7). Several members of the Raytheon 9 subsequently visited Qana in Lebanon, to acknowledge these connections and build new ones (McCann 2007), reflecting Chin and Mittelman's call for a resistance that is 'localised, regionalised and globalised at the same time'

(1997: 35), and Mohan and Stokke's desire for a '"scaling up" of multiple localisms' (2000: 262).

A primary function of the localism frame is to break down the experience of alienation from global politics felt by many people. As one interviewee with many years of experience in local campaigning explained, it 'makes it easier for people to make a connection between what [a factory/business] is doing and how that's affecting somebody in another part of the world' (Interview H). The localisation narrative is in this sense one which builds on the twin senses of possibility and responsibility mobilised by the network trope: the war may be distant, and perhaps too complex for the question of intervening to be thinkable, but the local frame cuts through this and demands some form of reckoning. This sense of reckoning is further advanced by extending the network to incorporate unconventional sites of militarism.

One unconventional site which has become a common target for activists over the past few years is the Baby Show, an exhibition which attracts large numbers of young families, chosen because the owner of the event, Clarion Events, also owns DSEI. Various protests have taken place to draw attention to the links. The Space Hijackers held an action in 2008 during which they invited visitors to visit other Clarion events: '[d]ressed in our smartest attire, we paced the entrance to Earl's Court chatting to glowing mothers and cheerful fathers about the fact that Clarion cater for both extremes of the human experience, both life, and death' (Space Hijackers undated). Dressed as elves, activists have also targeted Clarion's 'Spirit of Christmas' exhibition, mobilising similar ironic narratives (Viesnik 2009). When activists learned that the National Gallery had entered into a sponsorship relationship with the Italian arms manufacturer Finmeccanica, a campaign to Disarm the Gallery started. Activists also dressed as dinosaurs and targeted the Natural History Museum when it hosted a reception for arms dealers during the 2012 Farnborough Air Show, and as scientists when the Science Museum did the same in 2014 and 2016. Such narratives create opportunities to demonstrate the diffusion of militarism throughout society in a manner which disrupts the illusion of 'non-political' spaces. They also allow activists to exploit tensions which might not be found within conventional militarist spaces; it is on such terms that the major narrative of the Disarm the Gallery campaign was the incongruity between the destruction of war and the Gallery's supposed status as a site of creativity and beauty. This particular campaign was successful and, in October 2012, the National Gallery ended its relationship with Finmeccanica.

Recognising local, dispersed and unusual places as nodal points in wider networks of militarism and the arms trade is an important rewriting. It holds open spaces to resist which remain hidden when one begins from centralised and hegemonic accounts of politics, encouraging the anti-representative qualities of direct action tactics and inviting popular participation. Writing about military bases, Cynthia Enloe argues that the consent of local people is a crucial part of what allows militarism to function. However, this relationship, and the vulnerability it reveals in the military apparatus, is necessarily obscured (1989: 67). The arms industry similarly relies on the consent, both active and passive, of ordinary people in unremarkable places. Revealing those dynamics is an important component of resistance.

Banal Militarism

The institutions outlined above are unquestionably central to the functioning of contemporary militarism. However, a more substantive account of both militarism and resistance becomes available when we recognise how those institutional dimensions are underpinned by a deeper penetration of certain ideas and practices into the social fabric. Academic debates about the nature of militarism have stressed the need to view militarism in terms of the general diffusion, circulation and operation of militarised ideas, values, practices, subjects, rationalities and moralities. As Joanna Bourke writes, 'military practices, technologies and symbols have invaded our everyday lives. We rarely even notice it . . . Militarist incursions into our ways of thinking, talking and enjoying ourselves are barely acknowledged' (2014: 3). The conventional (and always questionable) notion of a clear separation between military and civilian, war and peace, is less tenable than ever. Instead, we confront a social world in which the production of organised political violence is a remarkably quotidian process, and in which few if any social domains can claim innocence. Recognising militarism in this manner invites us to consider how the practices of fighting wars, selling weapons, or arming police and border agents are normalised and legitimised through processes which also fold authority, hierarchy and violence into social life. It also demands some contention with how we as subjects are situated and implicated within militarism. Kevin McSorley and Joseph Burridge use the concept of 'banal militarism' to account for these processes, adapting Michael Billig's account of 'banal nationalism'. As they explain, for Billig, 'nationalism is an underlying framework for thought and action, explicitly articulated only rarely, but nonetheless reproduced and inculcated in everyday life at a continuous, subtle and often fundamentally embodied and affective level through mundane cultural interactions' (2013: 73). Such banal or mundane nationalisms are often much harder to shed than more vocal forms of patriotism. McSorley and Burridge view militarism through a similar lens:

> In deploying the concept of banal militarism, we are attempting to draw attention to the various everyday practices, techniques and metaphors – in education, training, fashion, diet and so on – through which war occupies bodies and militarist principles and ideals are inculcated in civilian life. The practices, in other words, through which bodies may be transformed, engendered and incorporated into military 'service', with this more broadly conceived, in a post-conscription age, in terms of wide military support. (McSorley and Burridge 2013: 73)

On similar terms Maryam Khalid argues that the 'language, ideas, and relationships associated with militarism operate in the seemingly mundane, apolitical, everyday' (2015: 637). Such an analytic draws us away from identifying particular ideas and practices as straightforwardly militarised (or not militarised) to recognising how any and all social relations are vulnerable to conscription, often in ways which may not be immediately apparent.

This account of militarism has considerable implications for resistance. While the institutional focus remains essential, substantive political transformation involves contending with the processes through which militarism operates at the level of everyday social relations. This is vital both because those institutions and their practices draw support and legitimacy from these more dispersed aspects, and because the production of violence that militarism captures and signifies is not restricted to such institutions. Viewing militarism in this way is both a burden and an opportunity; as Bourke argues, we are no longer passive actors 'in thrall to a set of amorphous, militaristic ideologies or corrupting institutions. We are involved in the production of violence: it constitutes who we are and might be and, as such, can be resisted' (2014: 3–4). As the arguments throughout this book demonstrate, much of anti-militarist resistance involves contending with, opposing, and at times even reproducing everyday or banal militarism. In the following discussion I introduce in broad terms how we might recognise this banal militarism, suggesting that it can be usefully understood by considering it as simultaneously and co-constitutively a system of values and collection of practices. This sets the terms for the more specific treatments of later chapters.[4]

Many writers have understood militarism as a system of values, ideas, moral codes and rationalities which legitimise, normalise and even glorify warfare. One influential account comes from Alfred Vagts, who writes that

> militarism is more and sometimes less, than the love of war. It covers every system of thinking and valuing in every complex of feelings which rank military institutions and ways above the ways of civilian life, carrying military mentality and modes of acting and decision into the civilian sphere. (Vagts 1959: 17)

This definition powerfully makes space for the ideational nature of militarism, while raising the challenging task of accounting for 'every system of thinking and valuing in every complex of feelings' that underpin a militaristic imaginary. While I will go on to suggest that we should be cautious with respect to sweeping accounts of militarist values and rationalities, there are a number of important attempts to provide a general summary.

Classical understandings of militarism tended to focus on a few specific ideological components, principally concerning the veneration of the military establishment and military action (Berghahn 1984). Certainly, the love of war and armed forces is an unmistakably militaristic sentiment. However, more contemporary approaches look to a wider set of ideas and values. Enloe provides the following list of militaristic core beliefs:

(a) that armed force is the ultimate resolver of tensions;
(b) that human nature is prone to conflict;
(c) that having enemies is a natural condition;
(d) that hierarchical relations produce effective action;
(e) that a state without a military is naïve, scarcely modern and barely legitimate;
(f) that in times of crisis those who are feminine need armed protection;
(g) that in times of crisis any man who refuses to engage in armed violent action is jeopardizing his own status as a manly man. (Enloe 2004: 219)[5]

In contrast with Enloe's focus on particular worldviews, Paul Dixon highlights certain concepts when suggesting a list of 'military' values, these being 'patriotism, unity, hierarchy, discipline, obedience, authoritarianism, pessimism and cynicism', which are opposed to 'equality, diversity, dissent, participation, autonomy' (2012: 112–13).

While Enloe's and Dixon's lists are potentially a little straightforward, they also demonstrate the importance of linking those values, attitudes, moral codes and rationalities which are more obviously connected to the conduct of organised political violence (such as the desirability and utility of violence) with a wider set of ideas about the nature of power and subjectivity. Another such account comes from Wolfi Landstreicher, who argues that

> militarism is not just war as such. It is a social hierarchy of order givers and order takers. It is obedience, domination and submission. It is the capacity to perceive other human beings as abstractions, mere numbers, death counts. It is, at the same time, the domination of strategic considerations and efficiency for its own sake over life and the willingness to sacrifice oneself for a 'Great Cause' that one has been taught to believe in. (Landstreicher 2009: 85)

Landstreicher's account is important partly because it invites consideration of the ways in which left-wing and even anti-militarist organisations can adopt militarised strategic rationalities. Together, Enloe, Dixon and Landstreicher outline a series of values which underpin a militarist imaginary, serve to legitimise militarist institutions, and normalise banal militarism. However, it is not necessarily the case that these comprise the entire scope of militarism, nor that their role within with militarism is so generalisable.

The values and rationalities which constitute militarism are intimately related to the political-ideological underpinnings of other social hierarchies, notably those of gender, race and nation, as well as to the particular political-economic environment. Militarism cannot fully be understood outside of these systems; its particular politics are always determined by (while working to reshape and reproduce) its specific social context. In the next chapter I look in some detail at how feminists and queer theorists have demonstrated the centrality of ideas about gender and sexuality to the conduct and legitimisation of war. Militarism is also constituted by racialised imaginaries concerning the benign or benevolent nature of imperialism, the forms of violence which inhere in particular subjects, and the kinds of bodies which are to be considered expendable,[6] as well as (racialised and gendered) configurations of nationalism and national identity (Nagel 1998; Prividera and Howard III 2006), not to mention social imaginaries and hierarchies of class (Basham 2016b), (dis)ability (Puar 2017) and more.

Historical sociologists have demonstrated how the nature and ideological specificity of militarism is shaped by the particular political-economic context. They have developed the concept of 'liberal militarism' to classify advanced capitalist nations which favour capital-intensive war (and war preparation), high levels of military production, a state–capital relationship that is formally separate but closely related, and 'simultaneous containment of social conflict at home and policing of empire abroad' (Stavrianakis 2016a: 845; see also Edgerton 1991; Mabee 2016). This particular form of militarism, exemplified by the UK, also has certain ideological dimensions. Most significantly, a universalist ideology, a pacific self-image combined with a belief in the legitimacy of humanitarian and civilising missions, and a near-existential level of concern with threats posed to the liberal order, filtered through particular images of security and insecurity (Basham 2018).

These ideational dimensions of militarism cannot be thought outside of the array of social practices that sustain them (and which they in turn work to reproduce). These practices serve to cultivate communities and political subjects for whom militarised values and policies attain the status of common-sense interactions with the world. They also have a more visceral dimension, 'in terms of a broad militarization of sensation, affect, and bodies' (McSorley and Burridge 2013: 73). More and less visible, voluntary, institutionalised, unusual and controversial, we can identify a wide range of contemporary British social practices as integral to the nature of contemporary militarism.

The most visible sites of militarised practices are those relating to the role of the military in public life, largely clustered around the social imperative to 'support the troops'. While these practices are not necessarily new, they became increasingly prominent in the mid-2000s in the context of unpopular wars in Iraq and Afghanistan (Basham 2013: 23–7; Millar 2016: 10). The UK witnessed a proliferation of invocations and opportunities to support the troops, whether by donating to charities like Help for Heroes, buying certain branded products (Tidy 2015b), attending events like Armed Forces Day, or simply by avoiding criticising wars in which British soldiers are deployed. The British government has specifically encouraged this visible and participatory public engagement with the military as a way of contending with low public support for British overseas interventions (Gee 2014: 93–100). These 'support the troops' practices are closely tied into broader processes of national military commemoration, such that the purchase and display of red poppies in November has become a near ubiquitous practice that is increasingly concerned with the 'veneration of serving military personnel' (Basham 2016a: 885). As Katharine Millar argues, these practices, powerfully positioned as private and altruistic, play an important role in depoliticising or even legitimising ongoing conflicts (2016: 22).

Beyond those which explicitly concern the military, a wide range of social practices are implicated in banal militarism. Films, video games and TV programmes reproduce and normalise militaristic narratives and rationalities, often in a form saturated by and generative of affective pleasure in and desire for militarism (Robinson 2016; Gee 2014: 42–79).[7] Contemporary fitness culture, exemplified through organisations such as British Military Fitness, trades on the cultural resonance and affective pleasures of military discipline and the martial body (McSorley 2016).[8] Youth education is militarised through 'military ethos' initiatives which normalise and sanitise the role of the military while constituting children as 'potential future soldiers or as disciplined, martial subjects' (Basham 2016b: 270; see also Gee 2014: 102–6). And universities are (and have always been) also sites of militarised practice, with military and arms trade recruitment on campuses, military funding directing research and knowledge production, and teaching priorities oriented towards military needs (Stavrianakis 2006; Howell 2018).

In these practices and others, we see how different spaces, subjects, bodies, desires, moral codes and value systems are bound up within militarism. As before, the particular militarised politics of these practices is determined by their relationship to other social hierarchies. Victoria Basham demonstrates how practices of remembrance in Britain normalise certain narratives about violence and heroism while erasing histories of both British imperialism and colonial subjects who fought in the British empire's wars; these narratives also rely on 'gendered and racial geopolitical logics, where sacrifice becomes a regrettable but necessary burden for the white, muscular, masculinist British state, threatened by irrational enemy others' (Basham 2016a: 885). Those practices also place uneven burdens of expectation, with acts of commemoration by non-white (and especially Muslim) subjects treated with particular suspicion (Basham 2016a: 890). Elsewhere Basham argues that the militarisation of youth and education should be understood through a class lens, as fundamentally concerned with the production of a militarised, disciplined and productive workforce (Basham 2016b).[9] The militarisation of entertainment is a highly gendered and racialised process, a site for the production and normalisation of tropes about militarised masculinities and black and Oriental others (Robinson 2016; Šisler 2008; Shaheen 2015). And the militarisation of higher education is shaped by a neoliberal context wherein universities are in thrall to commercial interests and where the technological expertise of science and engineering departments has become integral to the development of capital-intensive warfare (Stavrianakis 2006).

This circulation of militarist values and practices is, of course, not total or absolute. The importance of political context, alongside the manifold points of failure and resistance which accompany all of the examples given above, trouble any attempt to provide a straightforward account of what or where militarism might be. Nevertheless, the examples here demonstrate both that sites of militarised power are manifold, and that militarism is deeply bound up with who we are, what we value, how we think, and what we desire. Such a perspective has significant implications for resistance. Merely targeting institutional arrangements is insufficient; contesting militarism means coming to terms with the ways in which the very fabric of our selves cannot be thought outside of militarism. The general account of militarism given here informs the analysis that follows in this book. Each chapter adds to it, reshapes it, and identifies contradictions or challenges that emerge from this conception.

White Poppies, Blue Hoodies

To close this chapter, I want to introduce two groups for whom the work to challenge everyday and banal militarism happens in a relatively focused manner. One of the most well-known and most visible forms of opposition to banal militarism in the UK is the wearing of white poppies (in contrast to the near-ubiquitous red poppies) in the run-up to Remembrance Day. White poppies were first distributed by the Co-operative Women's Guild in 1933, but it is the Peace Pledge Union (PPU), which has sold them from 1934 onwards, that has been the organisation most closely associated with the campaign.[10] The intended meaning of the white poppy has three elements: 'remembrance for all victims of war, a commitment to peace and a challenge to attempts to glamourise or celebrate war' (Peace Pledge Union undated). The last of these reflects the critiques of remembrance practices identified above:

Many of the activities around Remembrance Day are detached from any meaningful attempt to learn the lessons of war. Arms companies allow their staff to pause work for two minutes' silence. Politicians who plough billions into nuclear weapons lay wreaths at the cenotaph. Arms dealers sponsor Remembrance events even while their work makes war more likely. (Peace Pledge Union undated)

The PPU Co-ordinator made this argument in somewhat more forthright terms to me:

> they say we are remembering the dead, [yet] we march up and down waving the symbols of the system and the practice that led to their death; and I find that as repugnant as claiming to remember people killed in car accidents by walking up and down waving bits of broken car covered in blood. (Interview M)

Red poppies are as notable for their hegemony as for their militarism; not only are millions sold each November, but the act of *not* wearing one is frequently read as a political statement (Snow 2006). In this context, the wearing of white poppies stands as a very public refusal of the militarised spectacle of remembrance. It has consequently attracted the ire of establishment figures, not least Margaret Thatcher (Hetherington 2015: 49–50), and remains popular amongst (particularly older) anti-militarists – over 100,000 are sold each November.

Another notable source of resistance to the role of militarised ritual in public life is Veterans for Peace (VfP). VfP was founded in the US in 1985, with the UK chapter forming in 2011. Membership is composed exclusively of ex-service personnel who commit to raising awareness about the causes and costs of war, and to work towards the abolition of war (Veterans for Peace 2016). The group runs campaigns, stages dramatic interventions and gives talks, all of these targeted towards challenging ideas about the heroic nature of warfare and armed service. Particularly striking is their annual remembrance ceremony at the Cenotaph in London, which takes place immediately after the 'official' Royal British Legion parade. In contrast to what VfP see as the militaristic nature of the British Legion's approach to remembrance, which masks 'the brutality and stupidity of warfare' (Griffin 2013), VfP members walk (not march) to the Cenotaph without berets or medals, wearing blue hoodies bearing the slogan 'War is Organised Murder', behind a banner which reads 'Never Again' (ReelNews 2016). Then, amongst the host of red poppies, they lay a wreath of white poppies.

Interventions like this constitute very public refusals of the kinds of political roles that are usually expected of former soldiers, these being to represent military service as both noble and non-political. They are powerful largely because VfP members are able to call on the social legitimacy and public support that is afforded to military personnel, but twist these against their conventional purposes (often in a manner which arouses considerable anger from the press, public, and other service personnel). There are, of course, dangers here, insofar as turning repentant former service personnel into 'heroes of the antimilitarism movement could unwillingly perpetuate exactly the sort of masculinized privilege that nurtures militarism' (Cockburn and Enloe 2012: 553; see also Tidy 2015a). Nevertheless, VfP's alternative practices of remembrance unsettle near-hegemonic militarist representations of soldiers within British public life.

In recognising how everyday life is conscripted through a series of apparently routine or banal practices which shape the ideational contours of national life, the PPU and VfP call attention to some of the most visible manifestations of militarism in British society. They also subvert these, mimicking their aesthetics and embodied practices while turning them to another purpose. They therefore serve as important examples of how militarism is contested on an everyday level by anti-militarists. However, it is notable that such examples engage with contexts and spaces that are already widely comprehended through a military frame, even as they reconfigure their meaning. While these are important processes, it is also important to account for how anti-militarists contend with less apparent dimensions of militarism, with social relations and subjectivities which are not so obviously connected into the production of organised political violence. It is on these terms that the following chapter considers the role of feminist and queer politics within anti-militarism.

Notes

1. Understanding the role that these institutions (and the political economy within which they are situated) play in determining the particular nature of militarism has been central to the historical sociological literature on militarism (Mabee 2016; Mabee and Vucetic 2018; Mann 1987; Shaw 1991; Stavrianakis 2010).
2. This phrase was subsequently picked up and used by CAAT.
3. The example of DSEI in this context is interesting, insofar as there is some debate amongst activists on the question of localisation. A number of activists and groups, amongst them East London Against Arms Fairs, an anti-militarist group based near to ExCeL, expressed discomfort with CAAT's preference for targeting government support for the arms fair (and so holding demonstrations at Parliament and at various government offices). They have insisted that the arms fair is, for them, a *local* issue, and that to focus only on the government is insufficient. Whilst CAAT have agreed (and ExCeL has, over time, become the main focus of protest), the extent to which attention should focus on different locations is a matter of continual debate. Such frictions are not new; during the first wave of the anti-nuclear movement in the 1960s there was disagreement over the extent to which action should be targeted against particular and dispersed military bases, or focused on the government in London (Randle 1987: 138-40; Walter 2011: 87-9).
4. I am talking about militarism, with the implicit understanding that this involves an ongoing process by which social life is implicated in the production of violence. Other scholars, especially Enloe, use the concept of militarisation to describe such a process, with militarism understood more straightforwardly as an ideology (2004: 219-20). Alison Howell has criticised the concept of militarisation, and uses thereof, which imply a before-and-after process, a transition from not-militarised to militarised. Such conceptions obscure the always already violent nature of liberal politics, often in a manner which conceals violence directed against marginal subjects. Instead, Howell offers the concept of 'martial politics' (2018). I am sympathetic the critique of militarisation, but feel that the concept of militarism (rather than militarisation) is well able to respond to such a challenge. Nevertheless, in Chapter 7 I outline how dominant conceptions of militarism within anti-militarist movements also tend to conceal violence directed against marginal (racialised) subjects.
5. For further discussion on and development of this list, see Bernazzoli and Flint (2009: 400-2).
6. See Butler (2016a); hooks (1995); Inwood and Bonds (2016); Razack (2004, 2014); Thobani (2014)
7. A number of authors have identified a series of institutional relationships underpinning the militarisation of entertainment, including close collaborations between military organisations and popular culture industries. For more on the military–entertainment complex, see Der Derian (2009); Löfflmann (2013).
8. On the militarisation of sport, see Kelly (2013); Mangan (2003).

9. The militarisation of youth is clearly also determined by racial categorisations which militarise young people of colour in entirely different ways (Miah 2013).
10. The PPU is an explicitly pacifist organisation that was established in 1934, merging with the No More War Movement in 1937. Its members all affirm the following pledge: 'I renounce war, and am therefore determined not to support any kind of war. I am also determined to work for the removal of all causes of war' (Rigby 1999).

CHAPTER 3

Feminist and Queer Anti-Militarism

The most developed accounts of the everyday and banal politics of militarism have tended to emerge from feminist and queer politics. In their work to explore the multifarious relationships between gender, sexuality and militarism, scholars working in these areas have gone further than most in recognising the complex entanglements of subjects, rationalities, ideas, practices and institutions which constitute militarism. At the same time, feminist and queer anti-militarists have played a central role in the development of contemporary anti-militarist politics. These theoretical and historical contexts give compelling reasons to suggest that resistance to militarism is not possible without a corresponding encounter with heterosexism and patriarchy. However, these positions are not often explicitly articulated in anti-militarist spaces or discourses. For many anti-militarists, questions of gender and sexuality might be important, but they are a broadly separate issue to matters of war and peace. Such attitudes allow for the reproduction of patriarchal and militarised gender orders within anti-militarism.

This chapter looks at how the militarised politics of gender and sexuality are dealt with in British anti-militarism. I begin with an account of how the relationship between militarism, gender and sexuality has been theorised in academic work, before outlining the relative absence of such conceptions within contemporary British anti-militarism. The main part of the chapter looks at three cases where gender and sexuality *have* been centred by activists. In different ways, these cases demonstrate how anti-militarists are able to contend with the interweaving of militarism, gender and sexuality, while also revealing certain tensions and dilemmas that emerge in the process. They also highlight the importance of understanding how militarised social relations can be reproduced within movements as much as beyond them – a fundamental insight for understanding the relationship between militarism and resistance.

Feminist theorists have identified a complex and co-constitutive series of relationships between militarism and patriarchy, wherein particular hierarchies of masculinity and femininity are intimately entangled with practices of warfare and militarisation. Much of this work has focused on the gender politics of military establishments. Feminists have long recognised militaries as 'quintessential sites of hypermasculinity' where '[s]uccess in war is presumed to demand a constellation of qualities long considered the exclusive province of men: superior physical strength, incomparable male bonding, heroic risk taking, extremes of violence, and readiness to sacrifice one's life for the cause' (Spike Peterson 2010: 23). They have examined how the constitution of effective military forces has proceeded through the mobilisation of different kinds of masculinity (themselves produced through hierarchies of class and race), in a manner which has shifted but not been fundamentally unsettled by the introduction of women into forces (Higate 2003; MacKenzie 2015). They have also outlined the ways in which militaries depend on gendered labour carried out by women, whether as wives, mothers, nurses, or sex workers on military bases (Enloe 1989, 2000; Horn 2010).

Beyond this explicit focus on military establishments and practices of warfare, feminists have identified how a series of gendered rationalities, ideologies and performances are integral to the normalisation and legitimisation of organised political violence. These include the valorisation of aggressive forms of masculinity, the belief that war is a natural expression of masculinity, and the idea that true masculinity is realised through defence of the nation (Hutchings 2008), as well as the deployment of masculine frameworks of rationality which serve to normalise mass violence (Cohn 1987). A consistent narrative underpinning modern political violence has been the idea that 'just' violence is carried out by men or masculine subjects in the name of protecting or saving women or feminised others, if only from themselves (Elshtain 1995; Stiehm 1982). These narratives were instrumental to colonial violence, the interventions of European powers legitimised with reference to the need for rational and advanced masculine nations to 'civilise' primitive, feminised others (Said 2003; Stoler 2010). They have also been central to the US-led War on Terror, which has exemplified the 'militarist concern with competing masculinities', the 'civilized, moral, and benevolent masculinity of the West' set in opposition to the 'barbaric, backward, oppressive, and deviant masculinity of the "brown man"' (Khalid 2015: 644). Different figurations of femininity are also highly productive here, with the idealised, free, white Western woman a symbol of Western superiority, contrasted with the oppressed, agentless 'brown woman', a symbol of the barbarity of the Other and a potential target for Western saviours (Khalid 2011; Kumar 2004; Nayak 2006). The normative superiority of masculinity over femininity runs throughout these conceptualisations and plays a primary constitutive role, such that the feminisation of perceived enemies – whether through rhetorical or more embodied practices – is a 'normal' feature of conflict (Skjelsbæk 2001), and the attempt to avoid (the perception of) feminisation is a primary motivation for violence (Jeffords 1989). In these ways and others, feminists have revealed the 'manifold linkages of patriarchal society and aggressive (or hegemonic) masculinities with violence and militarism' (Wibben 2018: 142).

Queer theorists have built on this work to show how regimes of sexuality are also central to the deployment, reproduction and specificity of militarism (Richter-Montpetit and Weber 2017). This has involved demonstrating the heterosexist foundations of military masculinities, as well as how such masculinities also involve (and must work to conceal) a range of homosocial, homosexual and feminised practices (Belkin 2012; Higate 2012), and how increased LGBT inclusion in militaries confuses (without straightforwardly subverting or reproducing) such foundations (Bulmer 2013). Research has also shown how queer subjects are often positioned as strange or dangerous in ways which legitimise warfare and militarism (Pratt 2007; Amar 2013), are particularly vulnerable in situations of conflict, and are routinely excluded from peacebuilding initiatives (Hagen 2016; Jauhola 2010). In recent years there has been a substantial focus on how some states and actors have mobilised queer subjects, issues and rights within an exceptionalist and liberal militarist framework, justifying foreign interventions and military chauvinism by tying these to a rhetoric of queer inclusion and liberal progress. These discourses tend to fold in and enlist 'acceptable' (liberal, capitalist, patriotic) queer subjects, opposing these to anti-modern, monstrous and racialised queer others.[1]

The recognition that militarism is reliant on and constitutive of particular orders of gender and sexuality has led many to insist that militarism cannot coherently be opposed without also working to resist patriarchy, heterosexism, and racialised configurations of queer inclusion/exclusion (Cockburn and Enloe 2012). Contending with the ways in which militarism is produced through value systems, practices, rationalities and subject positions must involve accounting for how these are always, in multiple and fluid ways, intimately constituted through particular configurations of gender and sexuality. It is on these terms that feminist writers have studied anti-militarist politics through lenses which interrogate how militarised gender orders are deconstructed and/or reproduced by activists. This frequently involves placing critical attention on the maintenance of patriarchal gender relations within anti-militarist campaigns, insofar as such dynamics 'reproduce the privileges and subordinations that underpin militarism' (Tidy 2015a: 454).[2]

Feminist Anti-Militarism?

Raising the question of gender in relation to UK-based anti-militarism inevitably draws activists to recall Greenham Common Women's Peace Camp, and the explicitly feminist anti-militarist politics of the 1980s that it came to represent.[3] Women have played a major role in the peace movement from at least the early nineteenth century (Liddington 1989), but Greenham Common was the first time that gender was acknowledged as a serious anti-militarist concern on a large scale (Cockburn 2012: 23–42). And while the separatist politics and often essentialist analyses of Greenham were not uncontroversial amongst activists, it was a significant challenge both because it insisted on the importance of feminist politics within anti-militarism, and because it challenged the assumption 'that men in [the peace movement] are somehow different from other men and therefore exempt from oppressive behaviour and sexism' (Cockburn 2012: 44). Cynthia Cockburn cites one activist's reference to the Greenham year as a 'good learning time' for activists working at the intersections of gender and militarism (2012: 41–2).

Despite this legacy, the argument stressed by feminist anti-militarists – 'that transformative change in gender relations, and particularly in forms of masculinity, is necessary work for peace' – is not widely accepted within British anti-militarism (Cockburn 2012: 16). Activists are often supportive of feminist politics, and may even self-identify as feminists, but this is frequently conceived as politically distinct from their anti-militarism. That distinction sits alongside a fair amount of sexist (and homophobic, transphobic) behaviour in activist spaces. In my interviews, every single non-male interviewee described experiences of being ignored, patronised and humiliated by men in the movement. They also called attention to the prevalence of the 'alternative machismo . . . which assesses people's commitment on the basis of how often they resist arrest or go to jail' (Feminism and Nonviolence Study Group 1983: 44–5), and to the tendency of meetings and organising spaces to become dominated by male voices in what one interviewee referred to as a 'look at my huge dick of arms trade knowledge' contest (Interview G).

The exclusion of gender from many activists' conception of militarism was demonstrated in a difficult encounter that took place while I was attending a Peace News Summer Camp in 2011, during which there was an all-male workshop on 'militarism and masculinity'.[4] The purpose of the workshop was to explore the relationships between gender and militarism, and to think about whether and how men might organise to challenge militarised forms of masculinity. The workshop opened with an exercise in which we were invited to express our feelings about feminism, standing somewhere on a line from positive to negative. The majority clustered in the middle. When asked to explain their position, participants expressed their suspicion of the 'extremes' of feminism; more 'moderate' varieties were briefly acknowledged, but brushed aside in the rush to emphasise 'cultish' and 'matriarchal' tendencies and to eschew the 'by women for women' nature identified in much of feminist politics. A palpable sense of paranoia ran through the discussion, that I sensed would not have been present were the exercised focused on anarchism or socialism and their unacceptable 'extremes'. One participant, raising the subject of women-only spaces, suggested that they are no longer necessary because women had surely by now built up enough confidence to join with men – 'at least, men like us'. Set in this context, the following conversations in the workshop with regards to the intersections between masculinity and militarism were muted and confused, with many participants wholly unconvinced that the subject merited consideration. The suggestion that people might form an all-male feminist group to explore possibilities for anti-militarist masculinities was met with uncomfortable glances and sniggers.[5]

This example is not necessarily representative of the entire movement, or even of everyone present at the workshop. Conversations afterwards revealed that several others had felt deeply uncomfortable with how the conversation had developed, and the two male facilitators who had designed the workshop looked pained throughout the session. However, the particular attitudes which dismiss suggestions of a relationship between militarism and masculinity, and which presume the benign or innocent nature of 'men like us', are not uncommon. Insofar as militarism operates through gendered subject positions and rationalities, the declarations of good conscience contained in such claims limit the scope of anti-militarist politics by closing down questions of subjectivity precisely when they need to be kept open. As Enloe reflects, 'patriarchy needs men in peace movements who think they know best' (Cockburn and Enloe 2012: 554). It is precisely here that a prefigurative imaginary is productive; prefigurative politics begins from the understanding that we as subjects are implicated in the social relations of what we are opposing, and uses this as a starting point for attempts to construct alternative political formations. Claims to innocence or exemption close down these processes, often (as in the case here) precisely where work is needed.

What is perhaps most notable about the gender and sexuality politics of contemporary British anti-militarism is the conspicuous absence of campaigns and actions which make visible the entanglement of militarism, gender and sexuality. While many activists are highly active in feminist and queer politics, and place great emphasis on challenging sexist or homophobic conduct in more private anti-militarist spaces, few feel the need to make the connections with militarism a visible part of their actions – and certainly not to the extent seen at Greenham and other contexts in the 1980s. There are, however and of course, exceptions to this trend.

Three Cases

24 June 2012. Central London. Sparkles Not Shrapnel
Eight activists, all women and non-binary, walk into the National Gallery wearing military helmets and fabulous sequin tops. They enter a busy room, take a deep breath, and then seven of them collapse to the ground in mock death. The eighth begins to read Carol Ann Duffy's anti-war poem *Last Post*:

> *In all my dreams, before my helpless sight,*
> *He plunges at me, guttering, choking, drowning.*
>
> If poetry could tell it backwards, true, begin
> that moment shrapnel scythed you to the stinking mud ...
> but you get up, amazed, watch bled bad blood
> run upwards from the slime into its wounds;
> see lines and lines of British boys rewind
> back to their trenches, kiss the photographs from home –
> mothers, sweethearts, sisters, younger brothers
> not entering the story now
> to die and die and die.
> Dulce – No – Decorum – No – Pro patria mori.
>
> (Duffy 2009)

As they read the poem, which tells the story of war in reverse, and so of soldiers coming back to life from their grotesque final moments, those on the floor slowly and silently rise to stand up straight. As a piece of theatre it is striking; they attract quite an audience. A security guard approaches one of the activists and asks whether they have permission to be doing this. 'Yep!', they reply confidently, and he leaves them to it as they hand out leaflets explaining who they are and what they are doing. They repeat the performance five times around the Gallery, by which point the guards have realised that this is 'more of those bloody protestors'. They leave before they can be apprehended.

These activists were part of Sparkles Not Shrapnel (SNS), a queer anti-militarist group who were active between 2011 and 2013. This particular action saw SNS taking part in the Disarm the Gallery campaign introduced in the previous chapter, which successfully pushed for the Gallery to end its sponsorship relationship with Finmeccanica. The group was formed in the run-up to DSEI 2011 with the intention of increasing queer visibility at anti-militarist demonstrations. In part, this was as a means by which to create safer spaces for queer activists, as one member explained:

> Everyone in the founding group of some six people were 'experienced' protesters but had found protests surprisingly unpleasant at times: it may seem odd but people can be 'right on' when it comes to peace, but can be (to put it kindly) thoughtless or (at worst) actively oppressive when it comes to trans or gay issues. The police are especially hostile, and Sparkles experienced that first hand during the DSEI action, and was nearly shattered by the heavy handed approach from the police [who harassed, detained and searched SNS while ignoring many others]. (Interview J)

SNS had decided to carry out an action in the National Gallery to highlight connections between queer (in)visibility in the art world and the worlds of both militarism and anti-militarism. However, SNS's aims went beyond simply increasing visibility; they sought (in my interviewee's terms) to 'bring the gay' to protest actions, to embody a form of 'tactical frivolity' where joy and fun are used 'as a tactic and strategy to resist war – because these are too often absent from anti-war protesting, and "camp" has always been a way to clown around with the stuff that society takes seriously' (Sparkles Not Shrapnel 2011). It is on such terms that SNS demonstrated outside Clarion's Holiday & Travel Show wearing holiday outfits and wielding glitter guns, and outside the National History Museum (which was hosting a reception for arms dealers) with an inflatable 'genderqueerosaurus'. As the SNS website states, 'queer is not an adjective, it is a verb: queerness is about disruption of ordinary ways of doing things, of patriarchy, and of oppressive structures, while war is both oppressive, and the means by which this oppression is reproduced and perpetuated' (Sparkles Not Shrapnel 2011). SNS were a small group and stopped organising under that banner after a few years. However, they were an important (and highly visible) intervention who brought often marginalised narratives within anti-militarist spaces.

3 May 2016. Henlow, Bedfordshire. Sisters Against the Arms Trade
It's 5 a.m., and fifteen members of the newly formed Sisters Against the Arms Trade are crammed into a minibus and driving down an innocuous-looking country road, waiting to arrive at a factory owned by the European missile producer MBDA. Activists target MBDA for a number of reasons, not least that the Royal Saudi Air Force has been using MBDA-produced weapons in its assault on Yemen. However, the particular focus of this action is the British government's bombing campaign in Syria, and MBDA's Brimstone II missile that has not only been used, but the alleged superiority of which was central to David Cameron's argument for the 'value-added' of Britain's involvement in the coalition (Hambling 2015). The activists, all of whom are women and non-binary, are well organised, and within a minute of their arrival there are chains around the factory gates and two people obstructing the driveway in arm tubes.[6] All access to the factory has been blocked.

There is a large MBDA sign at the entrance to the facility, which is replaced with a banner which states that 'No Missiles Will Be Produced Here Today'. The factory is indeed closed, and a steady stream of workers arrive, see the protest, and turn around. Some seem pleased to have the day off, others more disgruntled. For the next few hours the Sisters hold the space, singing and dancing together. They adapt a chant popularised by the Occupy movement and Movement for Black Lives in the US:

Back up! Back up! We want freedom! Freedom!
All your racist killer bombs, we don't need'em, need'em!

The police maintain an uneasy presence, but do not intervene to stop the protest. It is virtually impossible to move people in an arm tube safely without a specialist cutting team, and while in metropolitan areas cutting teams are usually nearby, that is not the case for unexpected rural blockades. After about eight hours, once it has become clear that the factory will not have the opportunity to open, the Sisters leave the site and head to the pub to debrief.

There were a number of reasons behind the decision to form an explicitly all-women and non-binary anti-militarist group, and to organise this action under its banner. One of these was the desire to highlight the gendered politics of the arms trade. As one of the participants noted, 'there's often a lot of policy work done around the impact of war on women and things like that, but that very rarely translates into things people actually *do*' (Interview L). While many anti-militarists do have a gendered analysis of militarism, that analysis is often absent from public-facing campaign communications and actions. The MBDA action explicitly centred such an analysis, primarily by building solidarity relationships with Syrian women affected by the conflict.

The activists worked closely with a Syrian-led group called Women for Syria, whose members included a number of women who had been forced to leave Syria after having been involved in resistance to the Assad regime. They attended Women for Syria meetings, sought feedback on their messaging, and arranged the action so that it fit into the wider timetable of Women for Syria's campaign.

> I think that at that stage, all of the Syrian women involved with that weren't on secure UK visas . . . that was an example of [when] it's really not safe for people to take arrestable direct action, but because we have citizenship we have greater power, so we're going to use that to break the law here, as part of that campaign. (Interview N)

During the action itself the Sisters read out testimony by Syrian women and filmed a solidarity statement in Arabic to send to the women's council in besieged Darayya. They also made the following statement:

> Syrian women are the forgotten protagonists in the Syrian struggle for self-determination. It is the call of Syrian women that we echo today for

dignity, self-determination, and food not bombs. The only people who have benefited from the UK's decision to bomb Syria are weapons manufacturers. MBDA have seen record profits from their deadly business.[7]

These moves were part of an explicit effort on the part of those involved to avoid a solidarity politics which assumes the needs, desires or interests of affected groups, which presumes to speak for them, and which therefore reinforces objectifying, hierarchising and colonial relations (Mahrouse 2014; Mohanty 2003).[8]

The decision to organise an all-women and non-binary action was also seen as a way to contend with sexist dynamics within British anti-militarism, and in particular to avoid an all-too-familiar gendered division of roles in which men do the action and 'women end up doing a lot of the care and emotional labour' (Interview K). For some participants, this involved learning skills that are predominantly held by men, such as the construction of blockading equipment. A number of members called attention to the differences between planning this action and planning others:

> I just think people were just more sensitive to each other, and less sort of cavalier . . . more talking about our feelings. It sounds so stereotypical but . . . I felt we were kind of softer and kinder to each other and people didn't have anything to prove. (Interview O)

Women for Syria itself formed as a subgroup of a broader Syrian-led solidarity campaign because of issues with intimate partner violence, opening spaces for recognising common experiences between the groups:

> I guess it sort of brings together that 'militarism fucks you over, the patriarchy fucks you over' . . . I've had so many intensely sexist experiences in the antimilitarist movement and I think organising in a women and non-binary group, you don't necessarily erase all of those but it's a good way to say, 'We are powerful, we will do this for ourselves, and we will find commonality with other women who are resisting in this way and we'll share tactics, we'll share strategy, we will try and speak as directly to each other as we can.' (Interview N)

While the action itself was most explicitly targeted at both MBDA and UK government policy, it was therefore also a response to the internal politics of these movements. In making a highly visible statement about the gendered politics of the arms trade, in forming solidarity relationships with women affected by conflict, and in forming an anti-militarist community that is less shaped by 'cavalier' attitudes, sexist conduct and gendered divisions of labour, Sisters intervened in a manner that paid close attention to the co-implication of multiple sites and forms of power in the constitution of (gendered) militarism.

25 June 2016. Central London. No Pride in War
I'm standing on the pavement on Piccadilly, leaning against a metal barrier while trying to hold together a large banner that's bending and tearing in the wind. Around me is a group of about forty activists, comprising in equal parts queer activists and members of VfP. Behind us a large and brightly coloured crowd mills with drunken cheer, while in front of us, on the other side of the barrier, runs the parade route for London Pride. Forty thousand strong, the parade is winding slowly through London's streets, showcasing organisations ranging from Kings Cross Steelers Rugby Club and Macmillan Cancer Support to PriceWaterhouseCoopers and the Metropolitan Police. We are partly here in order to be a visible presence, but we are also waiting for two particular events. A distant roar alerts us to the first of these, and in the sky over Trafalgar Square appear the Red Arrows, flying in their familiar V-formation. The jets speed towards us, along Piccadilly, and down towards Buckingham Palace, streaming red white and blue smoke in salute. Our jeers are drowned out by the thunder of their engines, so we wave our banners and placards instead. These read 'No Pride in War'.

Once the flyover is complete, we go back to chatting, chanting, looking for friends in the parade, and giving leaflets to passers-by. We cheer when Lesbians and Gays Support the Migrants march past, stay mostly silent for the corporate floats, and wait for the arrival of BAE Systems. It is the flyover by the Red Arrows and the presence of a BAE Systems corporate bloc in the parade that have provoked today's protest, and while our presence was easily (and dispiritingly) invisible from the skies, the parade is much closer. Eventually, around thirty BAE staff approach, holding aloft a banner which proclaims 'PROUD OF WHO WE ARE, PROUD OF WHAT WE DO'. Unfortunately for them, the march comes to a halt immediately in front of where we stand behind the barriers. Most of our group remain on the pavement, chanting, 'No Pride in War! No Pride in War!', but seven of us climb into the road and stand in front of the BAE bloc, holding up placards. The response from the crowd is mixed. Some cheer in support, others boo. In front of BAE (and so behind us as we face them) is Ritzy Picturehouses, and those on their float signal dislike for our action by throwing water over us. After about five minutes the parade starts to march again. We move back behind the barriers and allow it to pass.

This was not the only action in recent years to challenge the transformation of Pride marches from protests against police and state violence into corporate events through which NGOs, businesses and state institutions are able to position themselves as gay-friendly (Greer 2012: 145–53; Abraham 2017). The involvement of BAE Systems and the Red Arrows in Pride is an example of what has become known as pinkwashing, understood as the glossing over of militarised violence by shifting attention to questions of LGBT inclusion (in a manner which tends to portray Western companies and states as always more tolerant, enlightened or progressive than non-Western states) (Puar and Mikdashi 2012a; Schotten and Maikey 2012). In calling attention to this pinkwashing, No Pride in War (NPIW) were not only opposing the actions of BAE Systems and the Red Arrows, but were challenging an assimilationist attitude within the wider queer community, where issues around militarism are primarily framed through the question of inclusion (Tatchell 1995). That position was neatly summarised by one activist's reflection in an article about the protest:

> Dani Singer of LGBT+ Against Islamophobia told us, 'with hindsight, I feel like my reaction to the announcement of BAE Systems, [and the] Fly Over was driven by something outside me – I felt intense anger and a sense of betrayal from those who claimed to be representing me, and my community. In researching the wider community's response to the announcement, I found nothing but celebration and positivity – the support of the Air Force, which for years has ostracised and outlawed gay

recruits, meant so much to the wider community, and I was shocked, but not by them; by my reaching, by my own ability to ignore and belittle the sentiments of the community, on whose behalf I briefly believed I was angry. (Rasmussen 2016)

Both the practice of corporate/state pinkwashing and the assimilationist politics which enable it should be understood through the concept of homonationalism (Puar 2007). Homonationalism refers to the processes by which progress towards certain liberal models of LGBT rights are allowed to signify the tolerance, enlightenment and legitimacy of some (predominantly Western, liberal, capitalist) societies while also demonstrating the backwards and illegitimate status of other – mainly Islamic – states, societies and cultures. As Jasbir Puar has argued, homonationalist rationalities have permitted the alignment of apparently progressive LGBT positions and movements with Islamophobic, anti-immigrant, militaristic, and peculiarly homophobic politics (Puar and Rai 2002; Puar 2007).

In challenging the ways in which Pride is complicit in the reproduction of homonationalist frames, NPIW is potentially on unsteady territory. A key part of their challenge to BAE Systems was to point out the self-serving hypocrisy of the company presenting itself as a paragon of LGBT rights for its employees, while also being (in one activist's terms) 'a major trading partner with governments who are explicitly opposed to any form of gender and sexual liberation and equality' (Rasmussen 2016). While this narrative was by no means the only element in their opposition to BAE Systems, it featured prominently. For instance, in a YouTube video of an action in which activists blocked the entrance to BAE Systems' office in London, text appears stating: 'BAE Systems is the world's third largest arms producer. One of its main clients is Saudi Arabia, where it is illegal to be gay and punishable by death' (Taylor 2016). On the one hand, this is a smart way to call attention to the highly uneven way in which BAE Systems' support for LGBT rights operates. However, such accounts are themselves reliant on the same logical structure at work in homonationalism, framing international legitimacy in a manner 'that accord[s] civilizational status to "gay-friendly" nations, cultures, and religions' (Puar and Mikdashi 2012a).

Opposing arms sales because the recipient regime has a poor record on LGBT rights is an argument that risks feeding into and reproducing the legitimising strategies of Western and liberal militarism, while reinforcing racist and colonial attitudes about the kinds of people who should be allowed access to weapons. It accords with a discursive conjunction which renders the violence of 'gay friendly' actors as *a priori* more civilised, pacific and legitimate than other actors (while of course obscuring such actors' homophobia and their reliance on strategies of queer endangerment). It is on similar terms that Puar and Maya Mikdashi argue that 'one should query the accusation of homophobia as a political whip' (Puar and Mikdashi 2012a). I raise this critique not in order to undermine NPIW's position, but to show how homonationalism has become a deeply pervasive discourse which reproduces militarised rationalities even through critique:

> Like modernity, homonationalism can be resisted and re-signified, but not opted out of: we are all conditioned by it and through it. Arguing that some pinkwatching rhetorics reproduce the queer exceptionalism of homonationalism is simply to note that we are subjects formed through apparati of state, consumer, and legal recognition that are engendered by the historical advent of what we can now identify as homonationalism.
> (Puar and Mikdashi 2012b)

The point here is most usefully developed through the lens of homonationalism. However, in Chapter 9 I argue that critiques of the arms trade which at some level serve to legitimise Western and liberal militarism while reproducing colonial and racialised discourses can be found across much of the anti-arms trade movement.

NPIW was organised by a collective that included both queer activists and members of VfP. As with Sparkles and Sisters, an important component of the campaign and action was to signal to the wider anti-militarist movement about the importance of taking feminist and queer liberation politics seriously. However, NPIW differs from the other two insofar as it explicitly involved organising across particular identity boundaries within the movement. Alongside the major action described above, the campaign involved a number of smaller actions, as well as meetings, banner-making sessions and pub trips, most of which involved both VfP members and queer activists. The working relationship here was generally very positive, shaped by a common experience of co-option and objectification within the service of militarisation. Both veterans and queer subjects are subjected to a process whereby a partial and often unfamiliar account of their identity is mobilised to legitimise armed forces and foreign military intervention. This provided a strong foundation to recognise shared experience and build solidarity across lines of difference.

*

These three cases are strong examples of how feminist and queer anti-militarists seek to contend with the banal or everyday dimensions of militarism while also targeting particular institutions. They also demonstrate the need to recognise how militarised social relations can be reproduced within movements as much as beyond them – a point stressed by generations of feminist anti-militarists. That recognition is important analytically for how we think about the relationship between militarism and resistance. The idea that anti-militarism and anti-militarists are innocent of participation in militarism, or that there is some stable boundary between militarism and anti-militarism, cannot hold when we think about the micropolitical processes through which militarism operates. The values, ideas, practices and rationalities which serve to normalise, legitimise and shape the conduct of organised political violence are just as likely to be found within movements as beyond them. The focus here has been on how feminist and queer anti-militarists call attention to such dynamics; later chapters will explore other contexts through which anti-militarists attempt to contend with the everyday politics of militarism, work to prefigure alternatives, and yet also serve to reproduce militarism. The next two chapters engage with the politics of security, a central framework through which contemporary British militarism operates. I examine how anti-militarists attempt to formulate alternative practices of security, to negotiate their status as subjects and objects of security, and to resist the conceptual and political terrain of security.

Notes

1. See Agathangelou (2013); Agathangelou et al. (2008); Manchanda (2015); Puar (2007); Puar and Rai (2002); Rahman (2014); Richter-Montpetit (2014); Weber (2016).
2. See Alexander (2010); Cockburn (2012); Conway (2012); Eschle (2013, 2017).
3. See Frazer and Hutchings (2014b); Laware (2004); Roseneil (1995); Young (1990).
4. Peace News camps normally take place once a year, and are discussed in more detail in Chapter 6. The idea for this particular workshop had been raised following a workshop on gender and militarism at the previous year's camp, where participants had discussed possible reasons for the absence of an all-male feminist anti-militarist group.
5. Here, I am inclined to agree with Enloe's account: 'Perhaps many men in anti-war movements feel as though it already takes "guts" in a patriarchal society, as a man, to challenge militaristic beliefs and values, since accepting those is a common measure of being a "real man". So to go the next step, to actually challenge masculinized privilege itself, may appear a risk they think they can't afford to take' (Cockburn and Enloe 2012: 554).
6. Arm tubes are one of the principle pieces of blockading equipment used in the UK. They are usually cylindrical in shape and made for two people. Activists slide their arms inside and clip (or handcuff) themselves to a bar running through the middle, and then sit or lie down. Once attached they cannot be pulled out, cannot be moved without risking injury, and can only be cut out with great (and time-consuming) caution.
7. There was some ambiguity in the target and message of this campaign. Some of the Syrians with whom the Sisters worked were not opposed to British military action against the Assad regime, and there were substantial differences of opinion about what the response to the civil war should be. The 'food not bombs' narrative was one able to generate consensus.
8. The racialised politics of solidarity within anti-militarism are engaged in more detail in Chapter 7.

CHAPTER 4

Agents of Security

In 2009 the words making up the acronym DSEI were quietly changed, from Defence *Systems* and Equipment International to Defence and *Security* Equipment International. In 2015 DSEI hosted its first 'security zone', with exhibitors focusing on terrorism, border security, cyber warfare and policing. In 2017 a 'security theatre' seminar series further signalled the growing importance of security for the event. These shifts are emblematic of the proliferation of security as a dominant political category within contemporary liberal societies. While state leaders have long proclaimed national security as their primary objective, the past thirty years have seen an unprecedented expansion of the spaces, social domains and subjects which are to be rendered 'secure'. These are, the story goes, under threat from a plethora of hostile forces: terrorists, Islamists, Russia and/or China, nuclear proliferation, illegal immigrants, cyber-criminals, gangs and, of course, anti-militarists and other political activists. Those actors, posing a sustained threat to the security of the nation, economy, society and family, necessitate ever-increasing expansions of the state security system.

Security and militarism are intimately connected political formations. The promise to achieve security, or to minimise insecurity, are powerful claims which have the capacity to legitimise vast exercises of power while concealing their politics and their violence. Core institutional practices of militarism, such as foreign military interventions, arms sales, and the continued possession and deployment of nuclear weapons, are all justified with reference to the myriad threats faced by the nation and its people, to the need for security in an insecure world (Basham 2018). In the context of liberal militarism, the rhetoric of perpetual insecurity plays a central role in justifying intervention in illiberal spaces, 'as a means to fostering liberal identity' (Mabee 2016: 250). Some have even suggested that there is something specifically militarising about the very language of security, arguing that its force as a political discourse lies precisely in its evocation of emergency and exception, of threat and defence, of existential challenges requiring martial response (Wæver 1995). Certainly, the post-9/11 security environment, characterised by an intensified concern with the (in)security of domestic Western populations, has been one in which security concerns slide easily into military and militarised action.

These connections become more apparent when we reflect on the role of militarised practices in more quotidian and domestic security governance. The rapid expansion of security discourses, practices and industries is accompanied by the growth of a wide range of technologies of control, as integral to the conduct of global economic and political violence. As Swati Parashar argues, 'it is security as conceptually amorphous and easily invoked that enables militarism to percolate into and govern the everyday lives of people' (2018: 126). It is on these terms that police forces, border agencies and private security companies make increasing use of military equipment, tactics and rationalities in processes of population management and repression (Feigenbaum 2017; Fekete 2013; Wood 2014).[1] National security discourses have always been just as concerned with managing domestic populations as containing external threats (Campbell 1998), and the internationalisation of security governance provides ample opportunities for the extension of large and militarised security regimes (Abrahamsen 2018). In *Empire* Hardt and Negri note with concern that a central dimension of contemporary global capitalism has been war's shift from a grand imperial project 'to the status of police action' (2003: 12–13). This 'banalisation' and routinisation of war creates fertile ground for the militarisation of security practices. In such a climate it is unsurprising that events like DSEI increasingly focus on catering to the security sector. It is therefore important to situate the political apparatus of security as an important component of contemporary militarism, while also recognising how militarism is underpinned by the conceptual apparatus of (in)security.

As we identify these close connections between security and militarism, so might we also recognise a specific set of relationships between political activism, resistance and security. Activists try to reveal and challenge the insecurity experienced by marginalised subjects. They demonstrate that established security systems are better recognised as networks of privilege and violence, and often precisely productive of insecurity. They work to imagine and fashion alternative security practices and narratives. And of course, in the wake of these interventions, they are themselves framed as disturbers of the peace, bringers of chaos, images of that which demands the security gestures of the state. Political resistance thus always involves some contention with one's status as a subject, agent, and object of security (Rossdale 2016).

In the following two chapters I outline several ways in which we can see anti-militarists contending with the militarised politics of security. In this first chapter I argue that we might view activists as responding to the colossal insecurity produced by state security and military practices by working to produce alternative, less militarised forms of security. As they resist a security politics rooted in militarism (and indeed intertwined with racist, patriarchal, colonial and neoliberal forms of governance), anti-militarists function as agents of another kind of security politics. This alternative security politics is not only one which recognises militarism as a perennial source of *in*security for most people, but also one which prefigures a politics of agency that does not rely on or turn towards hegemonic and sovereign political formations as the self-evident agent of security. The chapter first looks at how the relationship between resistance and the politics of security has been framed by the Critical Security Studies (CSS) literature. I argue that while resistance has been given a role in producing critical and emancipatory narratives around security, that role is circumscribed by an ontology of agency which reinscribes the state as the natural agent of security. In the second part I draw on the account of direct action developed in Chapter 1 to argue that we might recognise anti-militarists not only as petitioning for an alternative form of security, but precisely as agents of that security. Through several case studies I show how interpreting activists in this manner opens spaces to think about the relationship between security and resistance which develops in anti-hegemonic and anti-sovereign directions.

The third part of the chapter introduces three vignettes which demonstrate how understanding anti-militarist direct action as a practice of security agency can lead to productive interpretations of activist encounters with security politics. The first of these shows how this assertion of agency can be read as a form of security contestation; the second looks at how these practices should be understood as a negotiation with, rather than escape from, extant frameworks of security; while the third examines how these attempts to enact alternative security politics can themselves end up reproducing surprisingly conventional forms. In the next chapter, I develop these discussions to suggest that we might think not in terms of alternative forms of security, but in terms of a more fundamental resistance to the political and conceptual terrain of security. I will argue that it is on those terms that security's status as militarism's metaphysics can be more substantially challenged.

Critical Security Studies and the Politics of Agency

Post-Cold War developments in the politics of security have been accompanied by a lively literature in the field of CSS. In broad terms, CSS has served to challenge the idea that security is a straightforward social good or a neutral political technology. Instead, writers within CSS have revealed the militarised, violent, racist, Eurocentric, statist, gendered, neoliberal and ultimately self-defeating politics (to list but a few) involved in contemporary practices of security (Booth 2005; Browning and McDonald 2013; Peoples and Vaughan-Williams 2010).[2] One of the common threads which unite the diverse theoretical landscape of CSS has been the challenge to state-centric conceptions of security. Numerous authors have pointed out that secure states do not necessarily mean secure people, that the security of states is often won at the expense of the security of people, and that for many people their primary source of insecurity is in fact their own state (Booth 1991; McSweeney 1999: 45–67). On such terms, CSS scholars have sought to conceptualise 'non-statist' forms of security, including 'human security' (Wibben 2016), emancipation-as-security (Booth 1991; Nunes 2012), 'ecological security' (McDonald 2013) and cosmopolitan security (Burke 2013), which prioritise the well-being of individuals, social groups and ecosystems over the often violent abstractions of states.

Social movements and political activism have often been identified as fruitful sites for the development and mobilisation of these alternative conceptions of security. They are seen as a means by which political pressure can be exerted on governments to adopt policies more in tune with the actual needs of their citizens, insofar as they 'destabilise the government's central security narrative' by making space for 'alternative (and marginalised) security voices' (McDonald 2005: 186).[3] In the face of statist and militarist narratives which dominate official security discourses, social movements produce critical counter-narratives which invite other understandings and practices of security.

Anti-militarists can be seen to intervene in this fashion, demonstrating how militarism is underpinned by particular understandings of security. Ken Booth makes this clear in his seminal article on security and emancipation when he uses the example of Greenham Common:

> Thatcher demanded Cruise and Trident as guarantors of British sovereignty. In the opinion of the prime minister and her supporters the main threat was believed to be a Soviet occupation of Britain and the overthrow of the Westminster model of democracy. It was believed that British 'sovereignty' and its traditional institutions safeguarded the interests of the British people . . . The Greenham women sought denuclearization. The main threat, they and anti-nuclear opinion believed, was not the Soviet Union, but the nuclear arms build-up . . . People could survive occupation by a foreign power, they argued, but could not survive a nuclear war, let alone nuclear winter. (Booth 1991: 320)

For anti-nuclear activists, any conception of security which legitimises nuclear proliferation is one which radically endangers ordinary people. Similar arguments are made by CAAT with respect to the arms trade; in response to a government narrative which insists that the production and export of arms is good for 'national security', they argue that a conflation of security with military means 'can decrease security by prioritising military solutions to problems, increasing the likelihood of armed conflict' (CAAT 2016c). CAAT has challenged the dominance of military issues in government security discourses, submitting responses to consultations on the National Security Strategy and Strategic Defence and Security Review while also inviting members of the public to share their own perspectives on what security means for them. They have also participated in Rethinking Security, a network of organisations that have sought to develop a critique of the current, militaristic approach to national security, while producing alternative understandings of security that are 'grounded in the **wellbeing of people** in their social and ecological context, rather than the interests of a nation state as determined by its elite' (The Ammerdown Group 2016: 3; original emphasis).

There is clearly value in an analytic which interprets social movements as generating counter-narratives which displace statist and militaristic formulations of security – and many of the examples in this book would fit squarely into such a frame. However, my interest here lies not with particular counter-narratives, but with how the question of agency is framed and understood in these debates. As it positions social movements as generators of (some kind of) democratic pressure and as producers of counter-narratives, and even as it does so with attention to how these counter-narratives are less state-centric in their referent objects (that is, whose or what's security is to be prioritised), CSS has remained heavily state-centric in how it has conceptualised security agency. Whilst a non-statist form of security is the goal, the assumed agent of this security remains the state, and non- or sub-state actors are of interest largely insofar as they can influence state policy or enhance state capacity (Rossdale 2010). As Matt McDonald and Lee Wilson argue, despite the proliferation of referent objects beyond and beneath the state, 'we are limited, it seems, in our capacity to conceptualise security agency in anything other than statist terms' (2017: 243).

How we theorise agency matters. Security studies, in both its traditional and critical forms, has generally focused on what are called great powers, those actors who are apparently self-evidently the principal agents of global politics. While critical scholars have challenged more traditional approaches' indifference to those harmed by the actions of these great powers, this often happens in a context wherein 'the weak are of interest but primarily as bearers of rights and objects of emancipation, that is, for their normative value in Western political theoretic terms' (Barkawi and Laffey 2006: 333). The ways in which the marginalised are themselves involved in shaping global politics are obscured in a manner which further embeds the narrative of the powerful (whether 'the West', men, or the entrepreneurial) as the sole (and, therefore, inevitable) progenitors of history. Other critical scholars have challenged this closure by uncovering how 'marginal' actors profoundly affect the functioning of international relations (Enloe 1996) and by exploring how a 'great power' narrative relies upon and sustains particular narratives of what it is to be powerful. As R. B. J. Walker suggests, we might want to examine marginalised social groups (for him, as here, social movements) 'not in terms of some timeless notion of what power is but in terms of their capacity to alter our understanding of what power can be' (1987: 146). In this sense agency should not be seen in conventional terms, as a property that is (or is not) held by an actor who is (or is not) agential. Such conceptions are always already political performances which prioritise particular understandings of power. It is more useful to view attributions of agency as ontological representations that reflect and produce imaginaries of capability and political possibility, through interpretations of responsibility, legitimacy, capacity and coherence. It is on these terms that the enduring statism of CSS might be critiqued and transcended.

Viewing security agency in purely statist terms is problematic for a number of reasons. First, it depoliticises the state, representing it as a pure or unproblematic presence, rather than an 'intrinsically contested, always ambiguous, never completed construct', and one that is 'always in the process of being imposed in the face of never-quietened resistances' (Ashley 1988: 231). CSS ostensibly eschews statism, with repeated acknowledgements that, far from being security providers, states are frequently the primary source of insecurity for their own citizens (Booth 2007: 203). However, the reflexive recourse to statist agency as the fundamental means of achieving security means that this anti-statism is only ever partial. More fundamentally, CSS's commitment to statist agency draws on and reinforces certain binary logics, positioning these as the condition of possibility of meaningful political action in a dangerous world. Most notably, a hierarchy of sovereignty over anarchy is at play. As Richard Ashley writes,

> modern discourses of politics, upon encountering ambiguous and indeterminate circumstances . . . recur to the ideal of a sovereign presence . . . as an originary voice, a foundational source of truth and meaning . . . a principle of interpretation that makes it possible to discipline the understanding of ambiguous events and impose a distinction: a distinction between what can be represented as rational and meaningful (because it can be assimilated to a sovereign principle of interpretation) and what must count as external, dangerous, and anarchic. (Ashley 1988: 230)

In positioning states as the fundamental agents of security (i.e. as sovereign presence), and routing the activities of non-state actors through the state, CSS reproduces a political imaginary rooted in the distinction between sovereignty and anarchy. While it may advocate or expect less antagonistic relationships between selves and others than found in more traditional approaches to security, its theory of agency holds fast to the principle of sovereignty. The sovereignty/anarchy hierarchy is deeply implicated in contemporary forms of militarism, predominantly through the figure of the state. The subordination of anarchic threats to the sovereign order is the highest function of statecraft, and the use of violent and military means in order to do so is a celebrated (if frequently counter-productive) manifestation of sovereign power.

This statism on the part of CSS also imposes an interpretive closure. In routing all agency through the state, it circumscribes the possibilities that might be found when considering practices which develop in more anarchic, anti-hegemonic, anti-sovereign directions. In the following section I argue that interpreting anti-militarist activists as themselves agents of security can unsettle some of these closures. This is politically valuable, insofar as it offers strategies for disrupting the politics of sovereignty and hegemony and opens spaces for prefigurative politics. It is also analytically useful, insofar as it permits a more nuanced account of how security is practised, negotiated and reproduced by a wider spectrum of actors than a statist account permits.

Doing Security

As they take action against institutions related to the security industry, and criticise militarised framings of security, anti-militarists do more than outline or imply alternative ways in which security might be understood. In the widespread use of direct action tactics (and the sentiments that underpin such tactics), we can see an encounter with security that situates activists as *agents* of security. They are not simply petitioning for a better conception of security; they are putting it into practice themselves. Against the expectations to appeal to the proper authorities, anti-militarists are prefiguring a security politics based on the participation and creative energy of ordinary people.

In Chapter 1 I introduced direct action as form of political action where subjects seek to impact directly upon a situation. It was contrasted with more liberal frameworks which claim that political change should emerge through demands made upon representative institutions, usually the state. Direct action privileges what Day calls a 'politics of the act' over the 'politics of demand' (2005, 2011), and is concerned with encouraging and even prefiguring a 'society of participants' (Ward 1982: 26). I introduced several examples of anti-militarist direct action in which activists have sought to halt or disrupt the normal functioning of militarist institutions, including the destructive action of the Seeds of Hope women and the obstructive actions of DSEI protestors. In what follows I argue that we can view such direct actions as precisely a performance of security agency. I begin with another important contemporary example of British anti-militarist direct action, the EDO Decommissioners.

At midnight on 17 January 2009, Harvey Tadman, Elijah Smith, Tom Woodhead, Ornella Saibene and Bob Nichols broke into the EDO MBM factory in Brighton with the aim, in Smith's words, to 'smash it up to the best of [our] ability'. EDO were involved in manufacturing a VER2 mechanism for the F16 fighter jet, which was at that time being deployed by the Israeli Air Force as part of Operation Cast Lead in Gaza. In a documentary made by Press TV, one of the Decommissioners described the action:

> Well we smashed what we could, we broke manufacturing equipment, we threw computers out the windows, we broke hard drives, anything we

could get our hands on actually, we tried to smash, because we wanted to stop the factory from working completely. We then put our hammers down and waited peacefully to be arrested. (Press TV 2010)

Machinery used to make release mechanisms (which carry and eject missiles from fighter planes and unmanned drones) and an assembly area for electronic components were put out of action. Over the course of an hour and a half, the five caused around £200,000 of damage, halting production at the facility for a number of weeks. This was not just a symbolic action, but a self-conscious desire to actively intervene and halt the production of military equipment, to break the supply chain which ended with the Israeli military.

They were all arrested, along with several supporters who were outside the factory. Throughout the action and the resulting court case (in which all of the defendants were acquitted, though not until several had spent considerable time in prison) they claimed that their actions were legal, and that they had acted after normal democratic means had failed. Saibene justified her actions by stating that 'if the law and the police can't do anything about it, it's about time somebody else did' (Press TV 2010). The action came on the back of (although distinct from) the long-running Smash EDO campaign at the factory which, alongside weekly vigils, had been 'complemented by peace camps, marches, mass demonstrations, direct action, sabotage, roof occupations, street theatre and petitions calling for the closure of the factory' (EDO Decommissioners 2009: 3). In court, the Decommissioners used what is known as an affirmative defence, arguing that, as they had sought to prevent a greater crime, their actions were legal. To the surprise of many, the jury accepted this defence, and they were acquitted.

The Decommissioning is one amongst a number of actions in which activists have sought to physically dismantle equipment that might otherwise be deployed in conflict; other UK-based examples include the two Seeds of Hope actions and the Raytheon 9's destruction of Raytheon's Derry offices in 2008. They take influence from the Plowshares movement, which popularised the strategy of using small 'affinity groups' to disrupt military production or emplacement at military bases and weapons factories through the 1980s and 90s (Laffin 2003; Nepstad 2008; Tobey 2017). The 'directness' of the Decommissioner action, 'the hallmark of a really successful action' according to one interviewee, has earned it a reputation as one of the most significant contemporary moments of UK-based anti-militarist activism (Interview C). Whilst in many ways exceptional, and unlikely to be specifically mimicked by many, the use of simple tools grounds the action in opposition to the grand narratives of the state form; in Plowshares founder Philip Berrigan's terms, '[t]he hammer . . . confines us within human limits – we are not superpeople nor do we embody the fantasies of Hollywood or Washington plutocrats' (cited in Laffin 2003: 7).

The EDO Decommissioners' actions were, most straightforwardly, an attempt to directly disrupt the Israeli state's capacity to wage war, and EDO MBM's capacity to facilitate and profit from this war. They recognised both that the factory was connected into a network that was productive of major harm and insecurity, and that the British government was either unwilling or unable to do anything about this, and thus opted for direct action. In so doing, they also signalled and enacted an important rewriting of the politics of security agency. Having viewed statist and representative politics as either unnecessary or insufficient to the task of limiting the insecurity caused by EDO MBM, they intervened in a more immediate and tangible manner. In this respect, they were 'doing' security politics in a more substantive form than CSS allows when it interprets activist practices through a statist lens. This dynamic can be seen both in terms of the action itself, and at the broader level of stirring popular imagination about the role of ordinary people in the context of security practice. The Decommissioners practised and preached the realm of security politics as the *agentic* concern of ordinary people, not solely in the traditional context of political representation (in various forms) but as a direct and practicable normative concern (Rossdale 2010: 498). Traditional political structures were shown to be insufficient and/or ignorant to the task of acting to prevent (or at least limit) the assault on Gaza, and 'direct' alternatives were employed.

In provoking a reimagination of the politics of agency, the EDO Decommissioners were not calling for people to join their group, to unite under their banner as a platform for challenging militarism. The group itself was not a sovereign presence which would permit such a reading, nor was it an aspiring hegemon; it was a temporary collective defined by a common task, united by its action and through the resulting court case and media attention. In an interview with one of the participants, he told me that the group only came together over three days (with the initial idea arising on the Monday, and the action taking place on the Thursday), and derived from nothing but the common urge to do 'something' (Interview E). It was a group constituted through the affinity of action whereby shared ethical and political commitments form the basis of intervention and community. In this case, the affinity was temporary and, as my contact went on to explain, limited – tensions emerged within the group as they progressed through the court case. Other affinity groups might endure through time and undertake multiple actions and campaigns together. Both disrupt statist or hegemonic forms of agency, seeking and enacting direct interventions whilst displacing the imperative to sovereign presence.

Another example of anti-sovereign organising can be found in the Spies for Peace, a group of activists who, in 1963, broke into a secret government bunker and photographed and copied documents which revealed for the first time the government's plans for how it would fight a nuclear war, and to govern in its aftermath.[4] As Colin Ward recounts, it was illegal to publish the information which had been uncovered, 'yet all over the country it appeared in little anonymous duplicated pamphlets within a few days, providing an enormously interesting example of *ad hoc* federal activity through loose networks of active individuals'. Such practices exemplify a contingent attitude towards organising action, 'coming rapidly into being and if necessary disappearing with the same speed, but leaving behind innumerable centres of activity, like ripples and eddies on a pond, after a stone has been thrown into it' (1982: 52). Membership in the dispersed networks through which the information spread was not granted, or applied for, but taken and used by those who felt an affinity of purpose. This made it very hard to break down (1982: 57–8).

These organisational principles move beyond the tactical advantages of being difficult to police or regulate (although this is clearly not unimportant). They also function as an *invitation* through their refusal to assert sovereign presence. Anyone can take part in this kind of action; no membership or mediation is required, nor should it be. One does not need to join a party, the government, or other traditional, (counter-)hegemonic platform in order to intervene, and one's participation does not imply a totalising performance. When read in this manner, direct action of the sort practised by the Decommissioners and those reproducing the Spies for Peace material embodies a very different sort of security politics to that envisaged by much of CSS. In refusing to act through (or seek to establish) sovereign authority, but in intervening nonetheless, these activists helped to reimagine the possibilities for ordinary people to act within security politics.

This is clearly an ideal-type analysis, which has placed to the side several important issues; in particular, the ways in which these acts of resistance are situated within and constituted by existing relations of power, and the fact that 'anti-hegemonic' interventions are always to some extent, and perhaps inescapably, marked by hegemonic and sovereign claims, aspirations, and ethical and political foundations. As I explore in more depth in Chapter 8, that the Decommissioners were compelled to frame their action (and intentions) in legalistic terms at some level troubles the anti-hegemonic quality of their intervention. However, my argument is not that direct action of this sort is '*non*-hegemonic' or '*non*-sovereign' – it is difficult to envisage how any political intervention could be entirely innocent of hegemonic or sovereign gestures. Instead, the point here is to call attention to the *anti*-hegemonic qualities of such actions, to avoid automatically framing them within a statist framework or disciplining them through a sovereignty/anarchy hierarchy, and to recognise the specifically disruptive potential of leaving open these narratives. This is, then, a question of interpretation, based on the understanding that remaining open to how actors challenge or subvert hegemonic political imaginaries provides space for a more radical account of security politics.

That this is a question of interpretation manifestly does not mean that interpretations should rest with the assumption of a break with hegemony, or with the belief that such acts of direct action straightforwardly transform security politics; it is simply to suggest that a starting point which allows for a rewriting of the politics of agency allows for a more substantive critical encounter.

In the second half of this chapter, I discuss three vignettes which demonstrate how understanding direct action as a subversion of security agency can help us to think about different encounters with the politics of security. The first demonstrates how these assertions of agency occur in tension with others; the second looks at how these practices should be understood as negotiations with, rather than straightforward escapes from, existing frameworks of security; the third looks at how attempts to enact alternative security politics are always liable to reproduce logics of security.

Negotiating Agency

Summer 2012. Brighton. The Citizen's Weapons Inspection
In entertaining the idea of anti-sovereign assertions of security agency, it is important not to lose sight of the fact that the 'official' agents of security command significantly more resources, and possess far more capacity and inclination to deploy force, than the activist groups working to challenge them. Indeed, in targeting infrastructure that is seen as crucial to national security, anti-militarists situate themselves as security risks for the state to manage. This has a number of implications; one is that anti-militarists often find themselves in conflict with police officers and security guards. At these moments we often see a struggle to articulate precisely who the 'real' agents of security are, and what the 'real' nature of security is. McDonald and Wilson have framed such struggles as sites of 'security contestation', arguing that

> security can ultimately be viewed as a site of contestation between different actors attempting to advance particular visions of the values and scope of a particular political community (referent); the core threats to those values and that community (threats); the tools and actions to achieve or advance security (means); and the actors responsible for advancing or protecting it (agents). (McDonald and Wilson 2017: 245)[5]

Here again, agency emerges not as the property of an actor, but as a particular representation of power and legitimacy, which exists in competition with other representations. The struggle over particular concepts and political systems tends to involve some contestation over agency. One example of this struggle emerged during an attempt to carry out a citizen's weapons inspection at the EDO MBM factory in the summer of 2012, as part of the Smash EDO Summer of Resistance.

Dressed in white boiler suits (mimicking the attire of 'official' UN inspectors), around sixty of us gather in Brighton in order to carry out the weapons inspection. After marching as a bloc from the town centre to the factory, we find the narrow road to the gates blocked by a heavy police presence. Whilst we are not contained (or 'kettled'), the police have positioned themselves in such a way that it is impossible to reach the factory and carry out the inspection. However, in doing so, the police have also effectively blockaded the factory, erecting a large mobile wall and preventing all deliveries. Had the situation ended here, it might already have provided a good example of the often self-defeating nature of security gestures. However, a group of six activists takes things further by revealing that the dummy missiles several of them have brought as props are in fact well-disguised arm tubes. Refusing to allow the police's surprising show of force to define the situation – even though the situation has already become a blockade of sorts – they chain themselves together and lie in the road in front of the police barricade.

On the one hand, there is little reason for this action – the factory is no more or less impaired as a result. On the other hand, this is less about the blockade than the performance of agency, the signification that the police are playing *our* game. Certainly the atmosphere changes quickly; on first arriving at the barricade there had been an air of frustration within our group, a sense that we had little answer to the forceful physical presence of the police. The activists' own blockade reverses this to some extent, and introduces a more affirmative dimension (not least because it demonstrates the absurdity of the police's securing gesture). The police appear to feel the same, and move quickly to untangle this inversion. Within around ten minutes of the activists' counter-blockade forming, a section of riot police has arrived, forced the rest of us away from the barricade, and proceeded to arrest the six. It takes around an hour to complete the arrests (which are hindered as far as possible by the rest of the activists), and for the situation to revert to the original, police blockade.

Both the police and the activists might coherently claim success in this context: the police stopped the activists from carrying out their stated aims, while the activists stopped the factory from functioning as usual. My suggestion here is that we might see the situation as precisely a contestation over who is 'enacting' security (and so, of course, what security in such a situation would be). For the police, allowing activists to attempt to gain access to private property, with no official permission, would be anathema. For the activists, conventions of law and order function not to provide security but to mask the normalised insecurities of the state and militarism. What is at stake is not just whether or not the factory is open for business, but a struggle over what kinds of political action are to be seen as effective and legitimate – that is, over what story about agency is to be performed. Much of anti-militarist resistance represents at some level this discursive struggle. That the police were eventually successful in clearing the activists' blockade in the example given here is perhaps, in this context, not particularly relevant; the irony had performed its task and opened up these questions of agency.

Summer 2015. Shenstone. Block the Factory
At the same time as activists are engaged in a series of contestations with the police around the question of agency, they are also negotiating their way through different security discourses, which variously enable, shape and constrain their interventions. To read them as performing agency is not to suggest that they are able to step outside of dominant security frameworks; they are still (also) objects of security. However, they are able to use tactics which occupy and subvert their object status. The second vignette here explores these dynamics with reference to how anti-militarists take advantage of regulations which relate to police use of force. I argue that we can see a series of complex negotiations around questions of security on the part of activists, and that the limits of these tactics demonstrate something of the instability (and privileged space) of these negotiations.

Many activist tactics in the UK involve taking advantage of the ways in which the police (and to a lesser extent other actors), at certain times and under certain conditions, will take their obligations to use *reasonable* force seriously, and will refrain from causing harm to activists. This is particularly true for tactics which aim to cause obstruction, such as the use of superglue, arm tubes and tripods;[6] in all of these cases, the activists are not difficult to move, but are very difficult to move safely, often requiring specialist equipment and trained personnel, both of which may not be immediately available. Activists use these tactics to blockade or occupy spaces for long periods of time, relying on the hope and expectation that the police will respect their obligations not to cause avoidable harm. In what follows I show how these processes played out during a specific demonstration that took place in 2015, a mass blockade of the Israeli arms company Elbit Systems' factory in Shenstone near Birmingham. Looking at this case shows how these tactics capture and subvert security systems, while also revealing their limits and contradictions.

The blockade has been called to mark the one-year anniversary of the July 2014 assault on Gaza. Hundreds of activists from across the UK are to take part, with coaches scheduled to arrive throughout the morning. Our plan is to occupy the road outside the factory and use the space to hold workshops and other creative actions. Three smaller actions at the other Elbit factories in the UK will take place simultaneously. In order to shut down the road such that the space can be occupied, at 5 a.m. six of us (myself included) lie down in the road, in three groups of two, attached to concrete arm tubes. These arm tubes are really heavy, meaning that the few police who are present at this early hour are unable to move us safely to the side of the road. They have no other option but to turn all traffic away from the site. Recognising that they can't move us without specialist equipment, the police leave us to our own devices (with the exception of their photographer, who is understandably keen to take our photos). Crucially, this means that they don't stop other activists from congregating in the road and setting up gazebos and stalls. By 8 a.m. over a hundred people are gathered outside the factory, which has consequently halted production for the day.

Eventually, the 'cutting team' arrives. Cutting teams are police officers with the training and equipment needed to safely extract activists from arm tubes. However, in order to begin that process they first need to clear the area around us (which is, by this point, thick with activists, most of them chatting, eating breakfast and getting ready for the day's activities). Starting from one end of the road, a line of police forms and tries to move forwards, pushing activists back. However, the activists resist this advance. It is an emotionally charged space, with memories of last year's bombardment firmly in people's minds and more than a few Palestinians in the crowd. People are aware that, if the police are able to remove those of us in arm tubes, it will be far easier for them to clear the rest of the road and for the factory to reopen. The crowd therefore sits down, links arms, and attempts to stop the police from pushing through.

What follows is a melee. Over the course of around forty minutes, the line of police moves slowly towards us, forcefully pulling activists out of the front line and sending them back up the road. The air fills with cries of pain as the police get more and more physical, twisting arms, bending fingers and pushing pressure points.[7] Eventually the police line reaches the area where my partner and I are lying in our arm tube. Around us is a sprawled mass of activists, who are holding onto each other and us. Some are sitting in front of our arm tube and linking their arms around straps wrapped around it. This changes things a bit. Whereas up to this point the police have been pulling people out of the crowd with minimal assessment, they begin to use more caution. This is because, as we point out loudly and clearly, attempting to move people who are holding onto us could cause us serious injury.

That this shifts the dynamic does not mean that the police are not still using painful levels of force; only that they are using it more slowly and carefully. They slow down even more when someone throws a long coil of rope into the fray. Before the police can react, we coil the rope around our hands, arms and legs, winding ourselves into a web. Moving one activist might now mean tightening the rope around another a few paces away and causing very real harm, and the (infuriated) police recognise that they need to be more methodical in their approach.

As they come closer to my partner and me in the arm tube, and clear more people away from around us, the police begin to pay us particular attention. They meet my eyes and check that I am OK. Our cries of pain (occasionally exaggerated) get a quicker response than those of others. Whilst the entire crowd is placing themselves in a vulnerable position, the concrete tube places us more squarely as objects of some kind of care. At one point I am pulled sharply and shout out in (real) pain – an officer checks that I am OK, and asks if I would like him to put my rucksack under my head so that it is better supported. One other person is receiving similarly exceptional treatment; an elderly white woman, in a folding camping chair, is sitting just behind us. She has been there for some time, chatting to us before the police began their assault, and appears to be unfazed by the fracas, despite activists clinging to her chair to avoid being pulled out of the road.

After some time, the crowd of activists who were surrounding us are gone; the police line has pushed them back, so that there is now just us in the arm tube, the lady on her chair, and the cutting team with their equipment. The police come to inspect the tube, and then try to speak to us. They ask if we are comfortable, and suggest that we unlock ourselves and go to join the rest of the protest. We ignore them, continuing to talk amongst ourselves. After a short while the officer in charge returns and gives us a choice: unlock ourselves and go free, or be cut out and arrested. We ask her to give us a few minutes to confer, and she withdraws out of earshot so that we can talk.

We hadn't expected to be given a choice. At this point, we've been in the road for five hours. My feeling is that blocking the road for that long and then escaping without arrest is a pretty good deal. My partner thinks that it's worth being as obstructive as possible; another coachload of activists is due to arrive at any moment and the extra time could be vital. We decide to split up. I unclip myself and slide through police lines, leaving her locked onto the arm tube. This leaves her with the police, the woman on the fold-out chair, and a few photographers who have managed to slip onto that side of the police line. At this point, the police could easily reach into the end of the arm tube that I vacated and unclip her; it has become even easier to remove this blockade. However, it is still not possible to do so without risking causing her injury (not least because she lies and tells them that she is superglued to the inside). Instead, they are forced to go through the laborious process of cutting her out. After providing her with protective eye-wear the police team get to work, beginning by using a pneumatic drill to cut through the concrete. It takes them nearly another hour before she can be unclipped from the inside. However, she remains an obstruction, refusing to move to the side of the road and forcing the police to physically move her themselves. As is explained at so many activist training sessions, by letting your body go limp you become very difficult for the police to move you safely; it takes far more effort, and more officers, to lift an activist who has 'gone floppy'. Even after being cut out of the arm tube, then, my partner is using these particular obligations to their maximum disruptive potential.

By recognising that the police would adapt the level of force they use in accordance with the harm that would be caused, we were able to hold the road and shut down the factory for most of the day. Variations on this tactic lie at the heart of many obstructive direct actions in the UK. Several features of the tactic are worth highlighting. The first is that it can be a disorienting experience. You have watched friends and comrades being grabbed and kicked and thrown, and suddenly those same police officers are apparently keen to ensure your well-being. The particular props (alongside legal observers and photographers) place a different set of imperatives on the situation and on your body. By making oneself vulnerable in a particular manner, and thus making it impossible for the police to use 'reasonable' force, the care of the state suddenly appears; this shift offers substantial opportunity for manipulation.

This is clearly a transient experience; the police's care is temporary and limited. As the officer leans down to tell me that 'right now, my primary concern is your safety', I can hear the shouts and screams of friends only ten feet away, the police line pushing further forwards in order to reach the third arm tube. It is a deeply ironic set-up and we are under no illusion that the police are truly concerned with our well-being. However, by placing ourselves in such an insecure position we have managed to short-circuit their securing processes. As a tactic it is tense and unstable, but surprisingly (and consistently) effective.

The tactic relies on the police respecting certain regulations and acting with the appropriate degree of restraint. The photographers and legal observers are essential to the process, as might be a nominated liaison person who will explain to police officers the nature of the situation and the potential harm which could be caused they are not careful. The X-factor here is private security guards, who are far less likely to have an active sense of their duties with respect to reasonable force. At the Block the Factory action, the closest I came to real physical harm was not when facing the police, but an hour or so later, when a private security guard employed by Elbit Systems threatened to 'take me out' when the police weren't looking. More than one activist has expressed their relief at the arrival of the police to a situation where private security guards were losing their cool (as well as their clear discomfort with this sense of relief).

While the tactic is often effective on its own terms, its subversive qualities are limited in a manner which signals the logics through which contemporary systems of security operate. This point can be developed with reference to two further dimensions. First, that the activist is, in a particular way, an object of care, clearly does not mean that the police are not also videoing, cataloguing, collecting evidence. One remains an object of the state's security gaze. Indeed, the activist using the tactic becomes particularly vulnerable in this light, having rendered themselves easy to photograph and arrest. The tactical scrambling of particular security processes thus fits squarely within, rather than in challenge to, broader state security apparatuses.

The tactic also specifically relies on *passive* bodies, which allow the police to do them harm in the hope and expectation that they will not. When facing more active resistance, the calculation of reasonable force made by the police shifts dramatically and the particular subversions in play here are likely to cease (although others may come to the fore). The ability to use the tactic thus also depends on the assumption that the police will read and respond to one's body as passive, an assumption more likely to be attached to some bodies than others. Most clearly, racialised forms of privilege are involved in the expectation that the police will view you as non-threatening – a context that was underlined with some force on this particular occasion, as the police directed special levels of hostility and aggression towards Palestinian members of the crowd. The tactic is far more likely to be used by white activists, and while people of colour do use it, they do so in a climate where this carries extra risks.[8] On a slightly different tack, bodies which fit into narratives of fragility receive extra dispensation. At an action involving arm tubes in 2013 I was surprised to see the police take extraordinary levels of care, only to find out that one of the activists lying in the road had informed the police that she was arthritic. Another activist with whom I have carried out many actions delights in noting that she is able to get away with far more mischief than most, her status as a retired woman meaning that she is rarely viewed as threatening. A pensioner sitting in the road claiming to have a dislocated shoulder can cause a surprising amount of chaos.

The subversive dimensions of this tactic are therefore contoured by those practices of control through which contemporary security apparatuses are most effectively able to govern and limit political action; that is, through surveillance and calculation, through the production of passive bodies, and through the distinction between more and less dangerous subjects. Even as they prefigure alternative forms of security agency, then, activists remain objects of and situated within the dominant security system.

Summer 2011. Shropshire. Peace News Summer Camp
As well as conducting their action within particular frameworks of security, activists can also find themselves engaging in fairly traditional securing processes. I have suggested that the anti-sovereign qualities of anti-militarist action contrasts with the statism at work in CSS. However, this does not mean that activists cannot also reproduce sovereign gestures. Defending selves and spaces against challenge can quickly raise the spectre of security, the organisation and constitution of the subject against the image and imposition of insecurity. In the final vignette here, I consider a particular moment at a peace camp when I was involved in evicting a number of fellow activists, in order to explore the ways in which boundaries were (and were not) performed in familiar ways.

I've been staying at the Peace News Summer Camp for about three days when around eight people from a nearby anti-coal protest camp come to visit the site and hear music from the activist band Seize the Day, who are to play this evening. They are clearly very drunk upon arrival and the atmosphere, which was previously relaxed and friendly, becomes quite tense. One of the new arrivals has a dog with him; there are a lot of children at the camp and so the 'safe space' policy states that dogs are not allowed. He is therefore asked to take it off the site, which he does at first. Shortly after their arrival, one of the organisers of the camp approaches a friend and me to ask whether we will help out by staying with the welcome tent at the entrance to the site. She acknowledges, quietly, that she and the other organisers feel that they may have to remove the newcomers at some point; a number of people are coming to her to express discomfort about their intimidating behaviour.

Standing by the welcome tent, my friend and I spend the next hour confronting and turning back the owner of the dog, who is by this point very drunk and determined to bring his pet onto the site. Although he is becoming increasingly aggressive we continue to explain that he is welcome to come onto the site, but that he will have to leave the animal at the gate. On one occasion, more physically confrontational than others, he aims sexually abusive comments at a woman standing nearby. It's at this point that one of the organisers begins to arrange transport so that the man can be taken back to his own protest site. During this period, people are becoming really stressed. The laid-back atmosphere has broken down, and uncomfortable conversations about the politics of eviction are beginning to take place.

After the expulsion I step away for a while to calm down and write some notes. When I return, about an hour later, several more of the activists from the coal camp are being evicted. I never learn the precise nature of the final straw, but at the camp meeting the next morning we are told that, after a number of infractions and many complaints, they were given a final warning and eventually asked to leave. The whole story (without personal/individual details) is relayed to the camp and an hour of the day's schedule is given over for those who want to discuss what happened and the processes which led to the eviction.

There is a fairly traditional security politics here. For a short while I was a security guard, policing the borders and upholding the rules (No Dogs!), and providing support to those administering the space through my confident and masculine presence. I was excluding some for the protection of others, maintaining order by demarcating the specific boundaries of disorder. While, as I suggest below, there are differences to traditional forms, it remains that in the exploration of a space which sought to be open and refuse the instrumentalities and authorities of militarism (as further discussed in Chapter 6), we felt compelled to secure the borders and eject those who (over-)disrupted the equilibrium within. The prefigurative aspirations of the space and concomitant desire to experiment with alternative ways of living were called into question by the familiar deployment of rules, borders, police and masculinities.

There were, however, important differences from conventional conceptions of security. The decision and practice of evicting (and so performing the camp's borders and their politics of security), whilst deemed necessary, was not affirmed easily or unproblematically. There was no recourse to a juridical logic whereby the fact that the rules had been broken justified the eviction without question. Discussing the matter with other attendees, I was struck by the extremity of the discomfort on the part of most (albeit not all) campers; whilst everyone seemed to feel that the least bad option had been chosen, the situation was still experienced as an indictment of a purportedly libertarian and open space, as a tragedy of the camp and its politics.

There was an atmosphere of profound uncertainty within the certainty, probably in no small part fuelled by the well-targeted insults shouted by those evicted as they left the camp: 'middle-class wankers!', 'you're no better than Tesco's!' The point is that despite the closure, the affirmation of the border and the delineation of the limit through which the ontology of the camp was constituted, the *question* of the limit remained open (Dillon 1996: 26–7). In looking inwards at how the moment constituted (and corrupted) the camp, and at the uncomfortable experience of bordering practices (not insignificantly, bordering practices targeted against those whom many considered *allies*), the impulse to secure the gesture of security was deferred. I suspected that, were a similar situation to arise, the camp would have gone through the same ordeal again, rather than carry out a more efficient bordering practice against a stabilised image of insecurity.[9]

This example is one amongst many others; evictions from such spaces are not uncommon. The purpose here is not to condemn or vindicate, but to highlight some processes through which logics of security re-emerge, and to further suggest that their re-emergence does not necessarily signify parity with traditional, state-sovereign practices. I would tentatively suggest that the commitments to non-exclusion, consensus decision making and non-hierarchy in operation can work precisely to maintain openness in the light of the (conceptual and spatial) bordering often demanded by and performative of situations of security/insecurity.

*

Recognising anti-militarist activists as agents of security unsettles some of the closures of CSS. It disrupts the statist account of agency and opens spaces to think about anti-hegemonic practices of security, of direct action as an invitation to an anti-sovereign political practice. It also allows us to think about how activists contend with and are situated within security in different ways. The three vignettes here demonstrate how activists-as-agents are engaged in contestations, negotiations and reperformances of the politics of security. These interpretations are important for thinking about how security is understood, performed and negotiated, but they are also somewhat constrained by the fundamental idea that, ultimately, security is a social good, albeit one which should be thought and practised very differently. The vignettes started to touch on the limits of such an account. In the next chapter, I argue that we can go further by interpreting activists not as agents of security, but as resisting the very orderings of security.

Notes

1. My argument here is not that police, borders and private security have suddenly become militarised in the contemporary age of security, but rather that their always already militarised status is shaped and legitimised through particular frameworks of security.
2. CSS has had an ambivalent relationship with militarism. While the study of security has to a large extent crowded out the academic study of militarism, some writers within CSS have explicitly linked a critique of militarism and security. This has been a particularly prominent feature of critical feminist approaches to security (Åhäll 2016; Cohn 1987; Masters 2014; Wibben 2018). Others have made more oblique or nominal connections, arguing that excessive

'securitisation' of issues may lead to 'militarisation', which will tend to be counterproductive (Eastwood 2018: 51–2; see also Bigo 2002; Wæver 1995: 64–5). Elsewhere, while acknowledging the dangers of unnecessary militarisation, CSS scholars have been happy to acknowledge the role for state military actors in pursuing security (Eastwood 2018: 52–3; see also Booth 2007). Indeed, the foundations of the apparently 'alternative' forms of security developed within CSS have proven perfectly compatible with – if not constitutive of – contemporary forms of militarism (Abrahamsen 2018; Frowd and Sandor 2018; Gilmore 2015).

3. See Dunne and Wheeler (2004); Hwang (2018); Kaldor (2003); McDonald (2012); Wyn Jones (1999: 161).
4. Nicolas Walter, whose identity as one of the Spies for Peace would remain a secret until after his death, provides an in-depth (if carefully de-personalised) account of the action (2011: 93–123).
5. McDonald develops this concept in more detail elsewhere (2012: 10–26).
6. Tripods are tall structures composed of three poles, connected together at the top. Someone perching on top of the tripod cannot easily be taken down, and the tripod cannot be moved without risking serious harm.
7. After the event, many of those present remarked that they had not seen such levels of police violence in the UK used against activists using passive resistance tactics; we will later learn that this particular police force have only recently received counter-terrorism training, and have been keen to put it into practice.
8. There was one person of colour using an arm tube in the Block the Factory action. In 2016 activists from Black Lives Matter (BLM) used arm tubes and a tripod to shut down the runway at London City Airport to highlight the racialised politics of climate change. While BLM actions primarily involve black activists, this action was notable because most of the nine activists who blocked the runway were white. Given the sensitive target and particular security context, the potential dangers that would be faced by black activists taking part in such an action were felt to be too great; instead, white allies took on this role.
9. This is, of course, conjecture, and in danger of marginalising the difficulties experienced by many of those involved in organising the camp, who experienced the situation more acutely than I did. It would be difficult to condemn an instinct towards further closure on their part.

CHAPTER 5

Resisting Security

In the previous chapter I argued that anti-militarists can be read as not simply petitioning for an alternative or non-militarised form of security politics, but as agents of that security. Moving beyond the politics of representation, they intervene directly in order to limit the production of militarised insecurity. In so doing, they open spaces for an anti-hegemonic, anti-sovereign ontology of security agency (although not, as the second half of the chapter made clear, without complications). This interpretation is valuable for thinking about how direct action politics relate to the politics of security. Nevertheless, it also retains the idea that security is fundamentally a social good, albeit one which should be understood and produced very differently. In a world saturated with militarist and statist formulations of security, the move to imagine and enact more emancipatory frameworks is understandable. However, such moves fail to adequately contend with the depths to which images and technologies of security structure our political and conceptual landscape, give ground and energy to militarism, and entrench statist and hegemonic political forms. In this context, we might look not for a better approach to achieving security, but for a more substantive form of resistance to security. In this chapter I show how we can read anti-militarists as resisting the politics of security.

The first part of the chapter draws on poststructural theories of security in order to argue that the conceptual foundations of security are too intimately tied into political rationalities of authority and mastery to serve as a productive basis for political transformation. I therefore consider what it might mean to resist, rather than rehabilitate, security, suggesting that we can see this as taking place both through the evasion of state security practices, and (more substantively) through disruptions of the security/insecurity binary. The rest of the chapter looks at how we can view these forms of resistance in anti-militarist practice. I begin by examining a series of activist practices which demonstrate the first order of resistance, focusing on strategies and counter-conducts of refusal and evasion through which activists seek to make themselves unsecurable. Tactics used here include the wearing of face masks, the cultivation of 'security culture', and organised non-compliance. These practices enable activists to resist coercive and invasive state/corporate interference, and create spaces for effective campaigns and actions. They also defy principles central to the constitution of hegemonic security narratives. However, whilst these practices are essential, they also to some extent retain the fantasy and metaphysics of (an other) security.

I therefore turn to a more deconstructive reading, looking at how activist practices scramble logics of security. The argument is built around two examples, one involving the attempt by the Space Hijackers to auction off a tank outside the 2007 DSEI arms fair, and the other involving a mass direct action against the EDO MBM factory in Brighton in 2010. While there are significant differences between these actions, they both subvert the politics of security in disruptive and creative ways. The chapter ends by casting some critical reflection on these spectacles of resistance. Whilst they play an important role in provoking a reimagination of the limits of security and militarism, they are also unstable, ephemeral, and vulnerable to recuperation within discourses of security. I therefore finish these chapters on security by suggesting that these practices of resistance should be thought alongside more banal, everyday and prefigurative practices of resubjectification. Such will be the focus of the following chapters.

Deconstructing Security

Security is often understood as a kind of value, the particular meaning of which is to be determined through political contestation.

However, it is perhaps more appropriate to view security as a *political technology*' (Burke 2007: 28; original emphasis), or 'a principle of formation' (Dillon 1996: 16), which shapes political life in particular ways. Security is not a variable within a wider order, but a series of logics which are intimately involved in the continual (re)production of that order. My argument is that the particular logics, codes and images that are involved in security politics render it a dangerous candidate for rehabilitation. The ordering of social and political life into continually proliferating images of threat, danger and response, grounded in desperate but impossible fantasies of control and mastery, tends towards authoritarian political formations, militarist rationalities, and the *de facto* legitimacy of dominant power relations (Campbell 1998; Edkins 2003; Neocleous 2008).

To understand how the pursuit of security reproduces political authority, it is important to recognise the dependent relationship between security and insecurity. Ideas and technologies of security can only function in a context of *in*securities, which they may identify and seek to pacify, but which they also *need* (and for which, of course, they are frequently responsible). As such, the legitimacy of institutions which purportedly exist principally to provide security – most significantly the state – are also deeply dependent on the persistence of insecurity. As David Campbell notes,

> [s]hould the state project of security be successful in the terms in which it is articulated, the state would cease to exist ... Ironically, then, the inability of the state project of security to succeed is the guarantor of the state's continued success as an impelling identity. (Campbell 1998: 12)

Or, in Michael Dillon's more general terms, 'it is only because it is contoured by insecurity, and because in its turn it also insecures, that security can secure' (1996: 127). The nature and content of any particular designation of security depends on its specific relationship with insecurity, through which particular exceptional and routine responses become possible. This regulative binary of security/insecurity interweaves with others that have similar effects, such as sovereignty/anarchy, order/chaos, inside/outside. All of them regulate politics in a manner which cements the place of political authority and hegemonic political imaginaries (Ashley 1988; Edkins and Zehfuss 2005; Walker 1992).

I opened the last chapter by arguing that the conceptual and political apparatus of security plays an integral role in contemporary Western militarism. This is not an accidental conjunction; the particular motivations and imperatives at play in logics of security/insecurity tend towards the legitimisation and institutionalisation of organised political violence. This becomes clearer when we read the security project within the wider context of Western metaphysics, where the task has been one of contending with existential anxieties by constructing and securing foundations, discovering (rational) certainties (Dillon 1996: 14–19). Security emerges as the Archimedean position from which the edifice of modern politics has been constructed, as a project fundamentally concerned with mastery and management; 'our (inter)national politics are the municipal metaphysics of the Western tradition' (Dillon 1996: 30). The need to render ourselves secure in the face of insecurity has become a primary political (and existential) imperative, one which can justify a terrifying array of practices. The violence this engenders is most obviously and destructively directed against those who are cast as sources of insecurity, but it also encompasses those who are supposedly to be rendered secure, and who therefore have to be made into the kinds of subjects who can be secured. They must be made vulnerable to calculation, categorisation and conduction, must learn particular combinations of docility and compliance, must adopt certain value systems (Dillon 1996: 123; see also Der Derian 1995; Walker 1997). The processes which accompany such transformations suture violence into the everyday politics of contemporary Western societies.

I have previously outlined several ways in which we can interpret anti-militarists as enacting alternative, anti-hegemonic and anti-militarist security politics. The discussion here makes clear that simply seeking a better form or practice of security carries limitations, insofar as it leaves intact the authoritarian and violent tendencies at work in the concept of security/insecurity. This is not to argue that there is no value in those interpretations, but that at a certain level the politics and metaphysics of mastery which are expressed through security politics are reinforced when we assume their totality. We might therefore consider what it would mean to resist, rather than ameliorate, the politics of security.

The particular understanding of security that I am advancing here is one predicated on contradiction; that security is reliant on both the presence and absence of insecurity, and therefore both resists and engenders violence, renders the concept fundamentally unstable. It is from this instability that we might explore practices of resistance. Anthony Burke uses Jacques Derrida's conception of aporia to reflect on security's contradictions:

> An aporia is an event that prevents a metaphysical discourse from fulfilling its promised unity: not a contradiction which can be brought into the dialectic, smoothed over and resolved into the unity of the concept, but an untotalisable problem at the heart of the concept, disrupting its trajectory, emptying out its fullness, opening out its closure. (Burke 2007: 30)

Burke further argues that

> it is important to open up and focus on aporias: they bring possibility, the hope of breaking down the hegemony and assumptions of powerful political concepts, to think and create new social, ethical and economic relationships outside their oppressive structures of political and epistemological order – in short, they help us to think new paths. (Burke 2007: 30)

Burke invites us to think and to create new paths, but to do so whilst remaining at the impasse. To do otherwise, to maintain fantasies of escape or rehabilitation, leaves too much intact. Instead, 'the aporetic stranger "does not simply cross a given threshold" but "affects the very experience of the threshold ... to the point of annihilating or rendering indeterminate all the distinctive signs of a prior identity"' (2007: 30, citing Derrida 1993: 12–35). A disruption of security/insecurity must therefore remain at the impasse, neither choosing between grand visions of security nor affirming any escape from the discourse, and instead occupying, politicising and playing with the ambiguous terrain of *in/security*.[1]

Resistance to security might then be understood in terms of an occupation of the contradictions and internal tensions – the aporias – at the heart of security. Such a resistance does not seek to articulate counter-hegemonic visions of security, nor to collapse into nihilistic images of insecurity, but to make playful and productive the borders and contours between security and insecurity. This can operate to deconstruct the totalising gestures of security, to politicise that which security depoliticises, and to hold open anti-hegemonic political possibilities. My argument in this chapter is that there are two ways we can conceptualise resistance to security at play in British anti-militarism. The first lies in strategies of evading, subverting or straightforwardly refusing those processes through which official forces seek to assert order over chaos, sovereignty over anarchy, and security over insecurity. These actions can be both radically subversive and a prerequisite for radical politics. The next part of this chapter looks at how anti-militarists engage in resistance on these terms.

The second approach to resistance concerns a more deconstructive series of moves, wherein the binary logics of security/insecurity are displaced in a manner which reveals their violent fictions and defers (or even reflects) their threats and ever-proliferating dangers. A disruption of security/insecurity might be seen to occur through a positive rejection of the former and an ironic subversion of the latter. Expected images of security (such as those associated with regularity, hegemony and legality) are refused, ignored and violated, while those practices and institutions through which narratives and promises of security are produced and guaranteed are cast as illegitimate, insufficient, undesired and counter-productive. This refusal, however, does not then produce the insecurities which might be anticipated; these are deferred, and in their place we see contingent but productive explorations of affinity and solidarity: relationalities and subjectivities which, in their refusal of foundations and their affirmation of possibilities in the spaces exposed, expose a productive fracture at the margins of security/insecurity. Thinking resistance in these terms moves beyond fantasies of rehabilitation, but does not entertain the illusion that we can somehow escape from security. Instead, it seeks to occupy and make playful the aporia of in/security, and in so doing perhaps open pathways for the imagination and cultivation of alternative political formations. The chapter will go on to look at a series of examples which demonstrate this second understanding.

Unsecurability

Anti-militarist activists routinely find themselves marked as security threats by corporations, government and the security services. Monitoring and surveillance of anti-militarist activity is routine. Police evidence gatherers are a familiar sight on demonstrations, and activists have found themselves identified and catalogued on the police database of 'domestic extremists'. At DSEI in 2005, police officers were even equipped with spotter cards displaying the faces of particular troublemakers (Thomas 2009). Anti-militarists are also subjected to covert forms of surveillance. Undercover police officers including Mark Kennedy have befriended activists and collected information, and in 2003, CAAT's national campaign and events coordinator Martin Hogbin was exposed as a corporate spy working on behalf of BAE Systems. The consequences of these practices are significant, undermining campaigning activity while causing considerable harm to activists themselves. Hogbin was a close friend of many in the movement and the secular godfather to one activist's son; the practical and emotional fallout still resonates (Thomas 2007b).

Anti-militarists go to significant lengths to resist being made objects of security, or at least to make this objectification process as slow, inconvenient and inaccurate as possible. Central to these efforts are tactics of anonymity and non-compliance. Saul Newman argues that we should read such practices as forms of resistance to security:

> Freedom must be discovered *beyond* security, and this can be achieved only through practices of political contestation, through forms of resistance, through modes of collective indiscipline and disobedience. For instance, the refusal and subversion of surveillance, and even the surveillance of surveillance, become part of a new language of resistance that expresses the desire for a life that no longer seeks to be 'secured'. (Newman 2010a: 171; original emphasis)

Common tactics of anonymity used by anti-militarists include the use of fake names, 'burner' phones used to organise one action and then discarded, and the use of encrypted messaging apps like Signal. Activists tend to turn off their mobile phones when planning actions (usually placing all phones in a different room), and wherever possible make detailed plans in person. These practices serve the dual purpose of providing some insulation from the securing gaze of the state, and pre-empting attempts by the police to gather information which may disrupt plans to carry out illegal or semi-legal action.

One of the most visible practices of anonymity mobilised by anti-militarists is one that has become familiar in the post-Seattle era; the use of face masks and bloc tactics. The use of masks and clothing which obscures the identity of individuals within a crowd is common on demonstrations and actions where some form of direct action is anticipated. These practices exemplify the refusal Newman identifies; when indistinguishable from those around you, and thereby (to an extent) freed from the disciplinary gaze of the police, one is in an important sense unsecurable. Police strategies oriented around identifying and arresting troublemakers, or collecting intelligence on particular individuals, are blunted.

The act of wearing a mask also constitutes an act of solidarity with those around you. Even if you yourself are not concerned with being identified, it is insofar as one blends with the crowd that these tactics of anonymity function. This is a collective refusal of security. It allows for a simultaneous expression of the individual and the collective, whereby the collective produces and makes possible the actions of the individual, and the individuals together mobilise a collective anti-security. Later in this chapter I recount the story of one action in which around 200 participants wore face masks and all-black attire, making use of the Black Bloc tactic popularised through the anti-summit actions of the early-2000s; the leaflet handed around before the action stated: '[w]e cover our faces not to threaten and intimidate, but to represent the faceless victims of the arms trade and to protect ourselves from intrusive surveillance. We will not be numbered, catalogued or controlled.'

The masks are not, however, just means of hiding. They are affirmations, gestures towards forms of solidarity and subjectivity beyond the state's images of security. Graeber recalls seeing a particular series of masks during the alter-globalisation protests in Québec City in 2001:

> A fair number of people in fact are already masked up: not so much for security reasons (there seem to be no police anywhere) as because they have, by far, the coolest bandanas ever: which, if folded in half, cover the bottom half of your face with a life-size picture of the bottom half of someone else's face. I start noticing them everywhere: they come in red, orange and yellow.
>
> Ben already has one, in orange. He proudly displays it: one side is the happy side, with a big smiling face; the other has a face with its mouth taped closed behind barbed wire.
>
> [...] Inscribed on the margin, in French and English, are the following lines:
>
> > We will remain faceless because we refuse the spectacle of celebrity, because we are everyone, because the carnival beckons, because the world is upside down, because we are everywhere. By wearing masks, we show that who we are is not as important as what we want, and what we want is everything for everyone. (Graeber 2009: 147–8)

Such masks, of course, differ significantly from the more familiar images of Black Bloc outfits. Indeed, as I argue below, Black Bloc aesthetic might be criticised as in some ways reproducing spectacular logics of security. It is important to note, however, that the advantages and transformations which might occur through the use of indistinguishable blocs are not consigned to the colour black or the somewhat tired image of the Black Bloc.

The Clandestine Insurgent Rebel Clown Army (CIRCA), a very loosely organised movement whose members attend demos dressed half as clowns, half as soldiers and whose conduct actively subverts militarist imaginaries, stand as one important example here. As they state,

> [w]e are **clandestine** because we refuse the spectacle of celebrity and we are everyone. Because without real names, faces or noses, we show that our words, dreams, and desires are more important than our biographies. Because we reject the society of surveillance that watches, controls, spies

upon, records and checks our every move. Because by hiding our identity we recover the power of our acts. Because with greasepaint we give resistance a funny face and become visible once again. (CIRCA undated; original emphasis)

Another example comes from the Italian Tute Bianche, who attended alter-globalisation protests in white overalls and inflatable body armour (so that they could withstand physical assault from the police and, in many cases, literally roll through police lines). In the citizen's weapons inspection described in Chapter 4 we all wore white overalls and chemical masks, rendering ourselves anonymous while adopting an aesthetic more commonly associated with UN officials, ambiguously mobilising their legitimacy.

Alongside these tactics of anonymity, anti-militarists engage in concerted strategies of non-compliance and even active disruption of police security measures. Groups like Smash EDO and Disarm DSEI take the explicit position that they do not negotiate with the police (Stavrianakis 2010: 176), and while actions often involve a designated 'police liaison', their role is primarily one of slowing things down and buying as much time as possible through rounds of discussion, negotiation and relentless double checking. When groups like Green and Black Cross (GBC) run legal briefings for activists ahead of actions, they will always insist that there is 'no such thing as a friendly chat with the police', stressing that the friendly faced Police Liaison Officers who mingle and chat with activists are doing so for the explicit purpose of collecting intelligence. In response to the activities of Police Forward Intelligence Teams (who attend demonstrations with surveillance equipment), activists often engage in the practice of 'FITwatching', holding up banners, flags, umbrellas and other equipment to prevent the police from gathering data.

These practices of anonymity and non-compliance fit within a wider series of practices and attitudes that activists call 'security culture'. Security culture refers to those measures taken in response to attempts by state or corporate actors to monitor, control and repress resistance. Christine M. Robinson points out that, while such practices have been commonplace for some time, they have become essential in the post-9/11 security environment where, in the face of increasingly invasive surveillance, 'meaningful resistance is predicated on the strength and organization of the community's security culture' (2008: 235). More a sensibility than a clear or well-defined set of rules, security culture operates as a 'strategy of collective resistance to a regime of social control that reinforces the need for deviant groups to avoid scrutiny and sanction' (2008: 248).

It is clear that some level of security culture is essential in a social climate of intensified surveillance and infiltration, particularly when engaging in some form of illegal direct action. Care and caution on these fronts can protect activists from legal reprisals and preserve the element of surprise when conducting actions. Some of the most significant anti-militarist actions simply could not have taken place without having been planned and carried out with the utmost secrecy. To this day, the names of those who carried out the 1963 Spies for Peace action remain undisclosed (with the exception of Nicolas Walter, whose participation was revealed posthumously (Walter 2011: 93–122)). However, security culture also carries potential drawbacks. Practices of secrecy and evasion can operate as forms of exclusion, enacting closures within movements and generating troublingly familiar discourses of security and insecurity. One does not spend long in activist spaces before finding out what kinds of questions should not be asked (particularly concerning past experiences of activism), or learning to guard against careless talk. Whilst there is obvious merit to such caution, it can also make participation unattractive or inaccessible, and bring suspicion (surely not always incorrectly) onto those who breach these codes.

Activists tend to explain their attitude towards security culture and possible infiltration with reference to three interconnected concerns. First, they frequently acknowledge the trauma that has been experienced within the movement as a result of undercover surveillance. Recent revelations about state and corporate agents who have posed as activists, befriended activists, engaged in long-term and sexual relationships with activists, and even fathered children with activists have sent shockwaves throughout the British radical left (Lewis and Evans 2013). This translates into an intense experience of vulnerability, as activists struggle to contend with the knowledge or expectation that someone they know, like, trust, even love, might not be who they seem. Everyone works in an organising context 'where people have been traumatised by relationships with police spies' and where activists recognise that, at some point, they are likely to find out that 'there will be people who I've organised very closely with who are police spies' (Interview K). As one activist put it, 'our relationships are our source of strength and solidarity, and also . . . our most vulnerable point' (Interview O).

In the light of this trauma and vulnerability, the second thing that activists will often highlight is the importance of taking precautions to prevent or limit the possibility of infiltration and surveillance. While acknowledging the virtual impossibility of any kind of certainty, people generally abide by the principle that, when organising secret or illegal actions, or handling sensitive material, it is advisable to work within circles of trust. At the start of a covert organising process, participants will usually set out the principles of secrecy by which they will operate – discussing who can be included in the process, what information (if any) to share with which outside people, and what security precautions should be taken when working on the project. More risky actions are likely to involve more closed processes. In special circumstances, further measures can be taken. The legal support project GBC hold a large amount of data on thousands of activists who have been arrested. To ensure the safety of that data they run a rigorous vetting process to verify the identity of anyone who will have access to it, which includes talking to friends and family members, so that it would be impossible for undercover agents to pass through 'without having a support cast' (Interview P).

These levels of secrecy are exceptional, and most movement spaces, including meetings, workshops, actions and even social spaces, remain relatively open. However, even in these more open spaces activists are attentive to the possibilities of infiltration. Certain behaviours and attributes will mark people out as suspicious. If you turn up to a meeting knowing no other attendees, with an apparently awkward grasp of the political terms of the movement, and right away suggest dramatic or illegal action, then people will immediately assume that you are some kind of infiltrator.[2] Even more so if you are a middle-aged white man – activists have a very clear profile on this front. Those who fall into these categories are rarely explicitly excluded from spaces without very concrete evidence, but their participation will be carefully managed. Certain conversations will not take place in their presence, their name might be 'accidentally' left off e-mail lists, and cautionary gossip will circulate. People might also engage in gently provocative behaviour to test the waters. At an organising meeting of around a hundred people prior to DSEI 2015, one man closely fit the profile set out here, and the word had spread to avoid discussing illegal activity in his presence. Towards the end of the session, one activist approached the man to strike up a 'friendly' conversation, asking him about what other groups he was involved with and whether he had enjoyed the day. The man's scowling awkwardness was read as confirmation of our suspicions.

The third aspect of security culture that activists tend to raise is the importance of *not* allowing security concerns to dominate and close down spaces. It is notable, in a context where people recognise that undercover surveillance is not only possible but likely, that they continue to take risks with one another, to welcome newcomers, to organise in a highly participatory manner, and to put active care and attention towards not allowing suspicion and paranoia to become a feature of everyday practice. Activists are attentive to the potentially self-defeating nature of attempts to secure their spaces against surveillance:

> If you get into a mind-set of not trusting each other, not telling each other what you're doing in case it gets back [to the police/state/companies], being suspicious, trying to guess who's to blame, [then] BAE or the police or whoever will have already had a substantially negative impact on your organisation or campaign, even if they haven't got a spy. (Interview M)

Secrecy and suspicion can have a deeply corrosive effect on movements and groups, prompting mistrust, pushing activists to internalise the disciplinary gaze of the state, and precluding democratic and accountable forms of organisation. One activist reflected critically on a high-profile action in which she had occupied the rooftop of an arms factory, noting that the secrecy with which a small group had planned the action caused problems later, when members of their wider group felt frustrated by the ways that that secrecy led to the emergence of a hierarchical insider/outsider dynamic (Interview O).

For these reasons, activists tend to adopt a somewhat defiant position, recognising the harm that would come from allowing a general sense of paranoia or suspicion to pervade the movement; 'most of the way we deal with [infiltration] is by carrying on, by doing the stuff that we wanted to do ... we can't stop trusting each other or we lose our entire movement' (Interview N). This attitude is often difficult to sustain in the wake of continual stories about the extent of monitoring and the harm caused by undercover policing. At demonstrations police are fond of addressing activists by their first names when they are able, passing off the gesture as a sign of friendly policing while reminding subjects that they are seen and known. Activists recognise that remaining open and trusting in these conditions is challenging, but view it as a task worthy of careful work. One former CAAT staff member reflects on the response when it emerged in 2007 that BAE Systems had employed a corporate spy to investigate CAAT, and that this spy had passed legally privileged internal CAAT documents on to BAE:

> What was really, really, really important, I think, was that we didn't get all paranoid. Because, especially when we thought there might be a physical spy in the office, as soon as you started to think, 'Well I wonder who it is' or 'Could it be so and so?' then you're going down the path that can end in disaster ... And I'm really glad we managed to avoid that mostly ... but it took some effort to avoid it, it took some mental effort on the part of all of us. (Interview M)

The experience of vulnerability and potential trauma, as well as the desire to protect the movement, mean that remaining open in the face of infiltration demands sustained and active effort.

Out of these three concerns (vulnerability, precaution and openness) comes a general consensus that movement spaces should try to find a balance, taking some cautious measures without rendering participation inaccessible or descending into paranoia. However, within that general consensus can be a certain amount of frustration, where some feel that too much emphasis is placed on security culture, while others, too little. One activist complained:

I'm not saying don't be cautious, I just find some things that activists do, whereby you have to switch your phone off and put it in the fridge and stand on the roof and refer to people by code names ... I just wonder whether it's actually that they really still want to be in the Famous Five; you know, firstly it's over the top and secondly ... you get the impression that [some people] just find it all quite exciting to be secretive. (Interview M)

While the Seeds of Hope activist Needham reflects: 'I rather liked the codenames in the same way I liked sneaking around in the dark at Wharton; it was fun, like playing spies but with a serious purpose' (2016: 66).

The end result of these various positions, balancing needs, and frustrations, is an approach to security culture that is relatively uneven and often somewhat contradictory. We might recognise this less as a problem than a (sometimes awkward) tactical negotiation, wherein oscillations between openness and closure signal the dual imperative to resist state or corporate surveillance and to avoid ceding to suspicion, the totalising or self-defeating gestures of either alone demanding a ceaseless interrogation of the security politics at work. Both attitudes might be framed as practices of resistance to security. On the one hand, activists work to resist the securing actions of state and corporate forces. On the other, they do so while deferring the fantasies of mastery and control that run throughout dominant conceptions of security. In an insecure environment with very reasonable grounds for paranoia, the refusal to become immobilised or to efface one's vulnerability, to internalise one's status as an object of in/security, should itself be understood as a form of resistance.

In activists' resistance to the securing gestures of the police, we can identify two levels of refusal. The first concerns the *particular* order of security operative within the political environment. In this order, the force of the law protects property and defends militarist institutions (these being essential features of a secure polis), and targets threats to these as sources of insecurity. In the first level of refusal, we can read the alternative security practices explored in Chapter 4 as prefigurative explorations towards alternative, more emancipatory or ethical, forms of security. However, the resistances outlined here can be understood more generally, not as resistance to a particular sovereign order of security, but as disrupting security *as* a sovereign order. This is the second level. In their resistance to being secured and their practice of direct action, anti-militarists are refusing core tenets of security: order, legality, statism, hegemony. In so doing, they move beyond notions of 'other' and 'better' securities to provoke alternative political imaginaries. This is not to argue that they are somehow operating outside the logics of security. As the discussions in the second half of the previous chapter made clear, such claims risk obscuring the depths of our entanglements. However, it is to suggest that they may be mobilising a disturbance at the boundaries, a contestation which denaturalises, ridicules and subverts the will to mastery or hegemony involved in any concept of security. The next section expands on this possibility, looking at how anti-militarists mobilise these refusals and resistances in a manner which deconstructs the politics of security. I discuss two contrasting examples: the first concerns the attempt by the Space Hijackers to sell a tank outside DSEI in 2007; the second is a mass demonstration held by Smash EDO in October 2010.

Politics of In/Security

11 September 2007. East London. The Tank Auction
On the morning of 11 September 2007, during the DSEI arms fair, the Space Hijackers attempt to leave their storage yard in an 8.5 tonne tank. Rumours that this will happen have been widespread, and there's a significant police presence outside. After negotiations and a small scuffle, the police agree to let the Hijackers onto the road, and to escort them to ExCeL. However, soon into their journey, they are pulled over by police and subjected to a roadside inspection that is clearly intended to halt their action:

> Time for plan C!
>
> Bristly [Pioneer[3]] informed the police we had an important announcement to make, and that we would have to delay the inspection. Leaving them by the roadside, he clambered onto the bonnet of the tank, and was passed a microphone through the gun turret by agent Hardcastle. Craig connected him to the sound system and turned down the music.

> 'Ladies and Gentlemen, I'm afraid I have a sad announcement to make. It seems the Police are doing everything in their power to delay us today, and prevent our perfectly legal vehicle from driving on the road. It basically looks to us like they are going to prevent us at every turn, and doubtlessly find some odd reason as to why our vehicle isn't able to drive. Basically Ladies and Gentlemen, we don't want to hold you up any longer as the world's largest arms fair is happening, and the police seem more interested in stopping legitimate protest than stopping some of the most corrupt and nasty people on the planet.'
>
> 'Ladies and Gentlemen, we have just had a very important phone call from two of our agents who couldn't be here today. Apparently our SECOND TANK, a great big tracked 60 tonne tank has just left its location and is rolling towards the fair as we speak. We suggest you follow our agents and go to meet it.'
>
> Cue chaos! The shock on the faces of the assembled police at this point was a picture, as they reached for radios and dived into their vans the scene was amazing. Within 2 minutes 90% of the police had flown off down the A12 in a bid to find our second tank, the Hijackers quickly pedalling along too and the various press hailing cabs to join the chase. (Space Hijackers 2007)

The surprise second tank is able to get to ExCeL, where the group attempt to auction it off:

> We proudly announced that after years of struggling against the arms dealers and police, we had seen the error of our ways. That the government's £400,000 support for the fair, not to mention the £4,000,000 worth of police provided, was obvious support for a business which has no regard for human life, and certainly takes no responsibility for its actions. If arms dealers can come to London and sell weapons to regimes regardless of how these weapons are going to be used, then why shouldn't we follow suit? We therefore announced to the assembled crowd that we would be auctioning off our tank to the highest bidder, regardless of their intentions. If they so chose to drive it through the police lines and into the fair itself, we would be taking no responsibility. (Space Hijackers 2007)

This action is remembered by many anti-militarists as a particularly creative and audacious intervention, an example of what it is possible to get away with if you dare. It can also be read as a form of resistance to security.

Anarchists in a tank might, for many, signify an archetypal situation of insecurity; the abject and public failure of the security forces to prevent the tank from moving around London even more so. Nevertheless, the situation is clearly an ironic performance, an inversion of two forms. In one, the absurdity of the auction outside the exhibition serves to highlight what the Space Hijackers felt to be the deeper, 'ordered' absurdity within. In another, the time and resources spent by the police attempting to stop the tank stands in contrast to the privileged status of those they were protecting, the attendees at the exhibition. The decision to use a tank was a clear invitation to the police to intervene, but again, in two different ways. For the police, it was an invitation to secure, to redraw the lines of order and chaos, to assert sovereignty in the face of anarchy. For the Space Hijackers, it was an invitation to play a game, to subvert easy narratives of security and insecurity and revel in the (tragic) comedy, in absurdity. In this absurdity, the terms of insecurity are politicised as the state's role in guaranteeing security is rendered partial – both insofar as the target of their securitising gesture is ridiculous, and because they failed even in this partial attempt to secure. The state's 'order' is mocked by a gleeful and ironic chaos, which reveals the constitutive (and political) *dis*order at the heart of the state's security system – specifically, in this case, the international arms trade. We see not a competition of visions of security, but a competition of (ridiculous) insecurities, in the face of which either one can choose the self-defeating attempt to re-secure (both ill-fated and indicative of the militarist politics at work), or one can choose to play games in the interstices. The logics of security/insecurity are thus rendered strange and contingent, and yet simultaneously a serious and important site of intervention. Whilst the police play a hapless game of cat-and-mouse, genuine arms dealers are selling weapons systems legally and with the full protection of the state.

The action is a good example of how playfulness can operate as a subversive practice that reveals and exploits the instabilities of apparently stable concepts without imposing new ones. It is notable that the invitation to play the game includes the police, avoiding drawing stable lines of friend and enemy. While the police are the baddies of the tale, and the anarchists the goodies, there is a wry contingency which takes the ethical disruption and intervention seriously but avoids easy closures of identity and role. That invitation should not be read as a call to the police force itself, as a desire for more effective, well-targeted policing. Few if any anarchists would follow this path. However, it might be read as a call to individual officers, both to question their prescribed role in the game, and to have fun. Of course, this is both an invitation and a dare; the police can have fun, but know that in so doing, they become complicit in the ridicule of precisely that on which their authority depends. This is the 'keeping in play' that deconstructive thought urges in response to 'a security simply ordering to order' (Dillon 1996: 25); a play that demonstrates the violence of the state's (dis)order and (in)security while affirming a creative politics of dis/order and in/security. Such playfulness is not necessarily unproblematic; as later chapters explore in more detail, it can conceal its own militarised dynamics. Nevertheless, it can be a powerful means by which to unveil the immanent absurdity of apparently serious practices.

13 October 2010. Brighton. Hammertime
My second example here differs in several ways from the first; however, despite obvious dissimilarities, it too can be interpreted as mobilising disruptions of the security/insecurity binary. It concerns a mass demonstration against the EDO MBM factory in Brighton in 2010, during which I joined about 300 other anti-militarists in an attempt to 'besiege' the factory (as Gaza has been besieged) and shut it down. The action was named Hammertime in jubilant reference to the action of the EDO Decommissioners and their recent acquittal.

I arrive in Brighton on the evening of the 12th and make my way to the Cowley Club, a social centre that sits at the heart of radical politics in Brighton. There, to a packed crowd, activists from Smash EDO explain the purpose of tomorrow morning's action, confirm the plan, and provide logistical and legal information. They stress that participants in the action should dress in black and wear face masks. After the briefing, the bar in the Cowley Club opens. I have a few drinks and chat to people, before getting into a minibus and heading to the 'convergence space' – a local squat where activists from outside Brighton, about sixty of us, can sleep ahead of the action.

I wake in the morning to find the squat surrounded by several lines of riot cops. We assume that we are about to be arrested, but the ranking officer explains that they plan to escort us to a designated protest zone in a field nearby the factory. There is a brief standoff while the police insist that we all remove our face masks and we, for a time, refuse. Eventually we relent, and walk slowly down the road, tightly encircled by officers who are focused on preventing us from escaping into the woods adjacent to the factory. We arrive at the field and are met by a big group of activists who had not stayed at the squat. For some reason the police leave us alone for a few minutes; when they start to reform around our (now much bigger) group we turn and run, up a large hill and into the woods which separate us from the factory.

We walk quickly through the dense woods with police officers following us at a moderate distance, and emerge into another field. A line of police is moving uphill towards us from the direction of the factory. Most of our number run away from the police, but I join a group who are moving downhill with a reinforced banner attempting to break through police lines and reach the factory. This is unsuccessful, and we are quickly surrounded by police and held in the field for over an hour. Eventually we are (once again) escorted back to the designated protest zone, from which we are told we will be able to come and go freely.

The police take us to a fenced area 100 metres from the factory, where a large number of other activists have also been taken. After a few minutes we realise that the police are attempting to form a perimeter around us. In response, we jump over the fences and scatter. At this point, a chaotic situation emerges, small groups of activists running around the nearby roads and housing estate, the police attempting to surround as many as possible. I am contained a number of times, and immediately 'uncontained' as the officers surrounding the group I am with decide on a different target. Whilst remaining in the same place, exhausted and content to watch the situation unfold, I am contained and freed, secured, unsecured and re-secured, several times over a twenty-minute period. Cries of 'Stay together!' and 'We're stronger united!' by protesters are ignored and followed variously and spasmodically, with similar police instructions – to activists and one another – being equally ineffective. With attempts to reach the factory itself rendered impossible by a large portable wall (of the type ironically blockaded in the citizen's weapons inspection described in the previous chapter), groups of activists try to move back towards Brighton town centre. There, several people have superglued themselves to Barclays Bank, citing Barclays' considerable arms trade investments. However, few are successful and, finally, the police manage to get hold of about fifty activists, all of whom are arrested (and, a short while later, 'de-arrested').

This mass action was, clearly, very different from the Space Hijackers' more playful intervention; more confrontational and, in different ways, more and less participatory. My focus here lies in the politics of the 'insecure' situation. As with the Space Hijackers and their tank, the image of several hundred black-clad anarchists wearing face masks attempting to shut down a factory fits neatly into any conventional understanding of insecurity. The corresponding refusal to submit to the attempts by police to secure the situation, to restore order and facilitate 'legitimate' protest, reinforces this perspective. This interpretation, whilst valid, is only partial. In one sense, this is for similar reasons to the tank action; the police expended considerable resources in their attempt to control and limit the protest in the name of protecting a factory which might be said to be itself a considerable source of insecurity. There is, however, a more substantial reason why straightforward narratives of security and insecurity are insufficient in this case. Beyond grand narratives, whereby the police invoke the insecurity manifested by the activists, and the activists the insecurity caused by the police and the arms trade, we instead see a productive confusion of in/securities, which are multiple, contingent, and crucial for understanding the creative disruptions enacted. There are a number of moments which might be taken from the action to draw out this point. Several were made apparent when I was contained in the field after trying to break through police lines down the hill.

I join a group of about twenty-five activists, who are gathered behind a reinforced banner and trying to push through police lines to reach the factory. As we push, the police push back, aggressively.

One person falls, shouts in pain, and is arrested. Some of our number attempt to de-arrest her – to literally pull her back into the mass – but unsuccessfully. The police then form a tight ring around us, two officers deep, and prevent us from leaving. A few people attempt to escape but the police outnumber us, and have become quite physical. Behind us, up the hill, another group is in a similar situation, while many more continue a cat-and-mouse game with the police.

After a few minutes, an officer attempts to tells us that we are in breach of a Section 14 order, which he hands out.[4] People sing loudly while he talks, and refuse the pieces of paper.[5] The police then tell us they will escort us to the designated protest zone (now about a mile away). We all sit down immediately and link arms, ignoring threats of arrest. For the next hour, we sit together on the grass. During this time a spontaneous community arises. We sing and tell jokes, eat, drink, smoke and talk. Some people take the opportunity to relax and read a book. Attitudes towards the police vary; a few people talk to them in a friendly manner, some tease them, while others direct angry comments, apparently genuinely furious that the police are more concerned with us than with the arms factory itself. Most ignore them. The police keep offering to escort us down to the protest zone. Eventually, they promise that they will let us keep our face masks on, will not film us, and will give us freedom to come and go once we reach the site. Feeling that we have little choice, we reluctantly agree to be taken back.

There are a number of noteworthy dynamics here. The instinctive attempts to de-arrest the person who was arrested, and the insistence on keeping masks on, are important forms of solidarity, as well as examples of the strategies of unsecurability introduced earlier in this chapter. The instinctive singing and linking of arms are indicative of the community which arose. During the hour I chatted, shared what food, water and tobacco I had, and joined in protest songs. This was an entirely temporary community; I could not tell who the people sitting around me were, knew only their eyes and their voices, and knew that the comfort we provided one another was transient. This fact, however, did not stop people within the group from placing their fates in the hands of one another for a few short moments.

A casual reading of the situation might signify a very traditional security situation: an insecure force pacified by official authorities. It is notable that, for some, the day was viewed as something of a failure precisely because the police were relatively effective in holding people and preventing them from reaching the factory. Without wishing to fall into simplistic narratives of what it means to 'succeed' when the terms are so opaque, we might think about what these failures offer; as Jack Halberstam makes clear, failure can be a potent political space from which to think critically:

> Under certain circumstances failing, losing, forgetting, unmaking, undoing, unbecoming, not knowing may in fact offer more creative, more cooperative, more surprising ways of being in the world . . . failure allows us to escape the punishing norms that discipline behavior and manage human development with the goal of delivering us from unruly childhoods to orderly and predictable adulthoods. Failure preserves some of the wondrous anarchy of childhood and disturbs the supposedly clean boundaries between adults and children, winners and losers. (Halberstam 2011: 2–3)

Despite the surface simplicity of the situation, the 'successful' security gesture, and in the context of those failures, a closer look reveals multiple and competing frameworks of security and insecurity, the terms rendered contingent and deeply political. The affinities which were generated in this short time are not predicated on a will to conquer, to enact a counter-hegemony to the police's narrative of security, but rather show an openness to come together as a unit for a temporary set of purposes. There is a rejection of hegemonic and statist conceptions of security, refusing to submit to the instructions of the police on even basic terms, but the supposed social disintegration of insecurity is also deferred; instead, we see indications of a positive politics of anarchy, a productive series of affinities, political possibilities articulated beyond and against the terms of hegemony and mastery. Another part of the action, which occurred when we were being escorted from the squat at the beginning of the day, serves to further emphasise this point.

We have reached the edge of the field which contains the designated protest zone, and have been made to wait for a few minutes, before being told to continue walking. In the context of collective dispirit at having followed police instructions thus far, our group spontaneously sits down and refuses to move. There is no particular strategy or reason; merely the desire to do the opposite of whatever it is that the police instruct us to do. Rather than simply dig in, however, the space is used creatively. After a few awkward minutes, one activist stands up and begins talking about anti-militarist campaigns he has organised. After he finishes, another stands and speaks about her visit to Palestine, describing the repression she witnessed. Another follows. For around twenty minutes we sit, listen, and share stories; the police, awkwardly, stand by. Again, this moment arguably occurred within the context of failure, but signifies a response which transformed the space, and affirmed a collective spirit which would, even in a partial and transient sense, unsettle the terms of security/insecurity.

The concept of spontaneity is potentially misleading here; these relations of affinity were not formed in isolation. The work of organising actions like these involves building the social relations that make possible such encounters. This includes the presence of 'action medics', trauma support centres, and the use of squats and social centres as communal bases (whether for preparation before, sanctuary during, or debriefing after actions). During most large-scale direct actions, including Hammertime, activists run an arrest support centre, noting where the police have taken arrestees, contacting friends and solicitors, and making sure that witness statements are taken. They may also organise police station support, ensuring that people are met by friendly faces when they are released from the cells. Another familiar sight on actions are 'legal observers' – activists wearing high-vis jackets, taking copious notes, and advising people of their legal rights when necessary. Several activist groups (including GBC and Activist Trauma Support) exist for the sole purpose of organising and training people to play these support roles. Others organise to ensure that activists have food and water, with the Nottingham-based Veggies a particularly welcome sight on demos. The affinities within the kettle are indissociable from these contexts; they make possible the risks taken and connections made, and are themselves important examples of affinity-based direct action.

The forms of resistance being highlighted here are not accidents; they are carefully facilitated.

Christine Sylvester makes a similar series of points with reference to the Greenham Common Women's Peace Camp, which became 'the bustling point of energy for a good anarchic system where in the absence of rule-governed expectations, there was room to change what and where one was properly supposed to be through actions at the fences of assigned place', and to do so in a manner which affirmed difference, 'refusing to interrupt or to force conformity on others in the name of "the" cause' (2002: 260–1). We might then read the Hammertime action not as advancing a counter-hegemonic vision of security, but as subverting the foundational logics of security/insecurity, mobilising a politics of anarchy that reveals the regulative dimensions involved in any narrative of sovereignty. We see both an inversion of conventional binaries, and a disruption which robs these binaries of their totalising force. In this disruption, spaces for exploration and creativity are revealed.

In the use of face masks and all-black attire, the Hammertime action draws heavily on the Black Bloc tactic most commonly associated with the alter-globalisation movement. Reflecting on the tactic, which he considers to be the most 'spectacular example of a creative direct action to impede the flows of state and corporate power',[6] Day makes arguments not dissimilar to those mobilised here. He argues that it offers a challenge

> to the monopoly on invisibility and silence, with its active ignorance of the command not only to behave well, but to be available to be *seen* behaving well. In refusing to follow the rule of transparency which guides the societies of control, Bloc subjects represent glaring exceptions within the domesticated and privileged strata of the global North. Not only has the system of cybernetic regulation failed to modulate their behaviour properly, but they also seem to be immune to self-discipline, fear of physical punishment, and verbal and physical attacks by other activists and academics. (Day 2005: 29)

Bloc subjects refuse to adhere to hegemonic understandings of security, whether those expressed by 'official' sources or by other activists. Instead, they create their own temporary terms, and act in accordance with them for as long as might be necessary and/ or desirable. Through general misbehaviour, occasional property damage and a refusal to submit to the police (or indeed the authority of would-be counter-hegemonic forces), the Bloc exhibits an approach which fails to accord with most dominant conceptions of security, which avowedly refuses to be secured. However, this does not necessarily entail a descent into 'insecurity'.

As Graeber makes clear, the Bloc cannot be adequately explained through the appeals to nihilistic confusion or chaos often invoked when discussing it. Contrary to media representation, Black Bloc activists at the 1999 alter-globalisation protests in Seattle were mostly 'fastidious about their dedication to nonviolence', even in the face of physical violence from other activists angry with the Bloc's window-smashing tactics (2009: 497):

> Still, for those who have taken part in [Black Bloc] actions, the really critical thing is the sense of autonomy created by an emphasis on solidarity and mutual defense. When you join a Black Bloc, you render yourself indistinguishable from all other participants. You are in effect saying, 'Any act done by any of us might as well have been done by me.' At the same time, you know that each one of those other participants is looking out for you, watching your back, that while everyone is trying to avoid arrest, the one situation in which most will be willing to risk arrest will be to save you from being arrested. It's precisely this that, for so many, makes Black Bloc tactics feel so liberating: it is a way to create one, fleeting moment when autonomy is real and immediate, a space of liberated territory, in which the laws and arbitrary power of the state no longer apply, in which we draw the lines of force ourselves. (Graeber 2009: 407)

In this sense, the Bloc exploits the aporias of security/insecurity, rendering both concepts arbitrary, contingent, liable to be discarded and replaced with another reading at any moment. It constitutes a challenge to hegemonic conceptions of political action and legitimacy, and a construction of modes of intervention and self-discipline founded in the affinity for affinity.

We can see these disruptions of security/insecurity throughout the examples discussed in this book. As anti-militarists reject particular narratives of security, they also move beyond that which is supposed to constitute order and security: obedience to the law, respect for property, a demand-making polis. Their organisation is not predicated on hierarchy or sovereignty, and celebrates disobedience, dissent and diversity. They run from the police, drive tanks through London, break into military bases and damage equipment. Traditional narratives of security are not subverted to demonstrate the truth of an *other* totality, but to render the concept of security insecure. Nevertheless, this rejection of order and of security, this collective indiscipline, does not rest at the level of transgression or inversion. We do not find a collapse into chaos and insecurity (the terms of which are often merely images shaping what we recognise as order and security). Instead, we encounter moves to fashion something more affirmative and exploratory in the margins; relations of affinity, solidarity and responsibility, prefigurative experiments, a politics of the act. In these moments we see anti-militarists contesting the politics of security in ways which refuse to be confined within the binaries, and which signal ruptures, openings, possibilities beyond the totalising and hegemonising logics through which much of political life is conducted.

The point here is not that, in the face of such performances, the concept of security suddenly unravels, that the existential anxieties and promises it conceals lessen, that its incitements to violence subside. The extent to which contemporary Western militarism is constituted through the conceptual and political apparatus of security is a good indication as to the depth and force of these frameworks. Nevertheless, it would be entirely self-defeating to assume their totality. The logics of security/insecurity are powerful, but they are also absurd and partial, and must work hard to mask those features. And, perhaps, the ridicule of that absurdity and exposure of contingency is a political intervention that can disrupt or defang those logics and the militarised politics they mobilise.

Spectacular Resistance

In this chapter I have argued that we can read anti-militarist direct action as a form of resistance to the politics of security. I have outlined a number of examples, suggesting that they reveal the violences which accompany predominant conceptions of security, order and sovereignty, occupy and subvert the contours and content of security and insecurity, and gesture towards non-totalising, anti-hegemonic paths forward. However, this optimistic assessment should be tempered insofar as it engages insufficiently with how discourses of security operate to capture and regulate political mobilisation. The binary logics of security/insecurity, order/chaos and sovereignty/anarchy function very effectively to incorporate challenges within their constitutive framework; the terms shift quickly, either to recuperate resistance within the higher ideal (the human security framework sits neatly here (Neufeld 2004; Grayson 2008)) or, more pertinent for these discussions, to subordinate it within the lower, to emphasise its chaos, its anarchy.

Richard Gilman-Opalsky argues that a particular image of anarchism, 'a kind of spectacular anarchism', has operated in such a manner, helping

> to acculturate widespread acceptance of the 'normal person,' the 'citizen-subject' who is 'upstanding' and law-abiding at all times ... The idea of anarchy is abused and deployed as an epithet, not only to discredit anarchism as such, but to reinforce the acceptance of its opposite – the existing state of affairs and its promises of security, and a more moderate political consciousness. (Gilman-Opalsky 2011: 15)

In this sense, the interventions explored above are in danger of reproducing the terms of security, of helping to constitute a narrative wherein resistance is either welcomed and incorporated into a celebration of liberal democratic principles, or constructed precisely as the image against which this liberal democracy legitimises itself. The Black Bloc tactic is particularly vulnerable to critique here, on the charge of having been sufficiently folded back into the spectacular logics of security/insecurity, as conforming and falling too neatly into completed narratives and images of insecurity to function as an effective disruption.[7] The tactic arguably reproduces those narratives which underpin the state form; as Jamie Heckert argues, the 'character of the dangerous outsider is a necessary figure in state storytelling. What would police, politicians and demagogues do without the promiscuous woman, the queer, the paedophile, the terrorist, the potentially dangerous activist who crosses borders and defies laws?' (2011: 203). This is not to claim that the Black Bloc tactic has never had this subversive quality, nor that it has no subversive quality, but that these subversions are vulnerable to recuperation.

There are two ways in which we might respond to this challenge. The first is to acknowledge, indeed insist, that disruptions of the sort envisaged here, these attempts to provoke 'guerrilla movements of the imagination' (Gilman-Opalsky 2011: 106), must not rely on formulaic, predictable and secure narratives and tactics. As Stevphen Shukaitis argues, paraphrasing Alexander Trocchi, 'the act of having a set definition of an insurgent practice is very much [a] necessary part of the process of containing it', thereby, whilst guarding against over-cynicism, there is a need to recognise how 'conventions of dissent (for instance marches, sit-ins, sloganeering, civil disobedience, street theatre) both make forms of social action more readily recognizable, but also through the easy recognition can make them more easily containable by that very definition' (2009: 214). Gilman-Opalsky makes a similar point, before suggesting that

> [a]t mass demonstrations in the US and Europe, the much maligned Black Bloc is actually on the right track, if only they could come back each time in a manner too unusual to make them immediately identifiable *as the Black Bloc*. (Gilman-Opalsky 2011: 107; original emphasis)

The point can also be made with reference to Michel Foucault's approach to security, which consists in the management, regularisation and conduct of political life, and which (to proceed with Dillon's interpretation) relies upon the securing of human beings' 'indexicality' (Dillon 1996: 31), enacting 'the detailed knowledgeable strategies and tactics that effect the constitution of life and the regulation of the affairs of populations' (Dillon and Reid 2001: 48; Foucault 2007a). As Newman argues, the unpredictability of dissent is a crucial feature in disrupting the operation of such knowledge strategies (2010a: 173). The imperative, then, is towards a perpetually evolving, mobile and imaginative series of resistances which continually seek to outflank narratives of security/insecurity, to displace the discipline of the order/chaos binary, to recognise and evade the knowledge strategies through which dominant (and dominating) political technologies are operating. Resistance is never complete, nor is its form finally determined. In affirming this, and taking on the associated challenges, lies the possibility to resist incorporation within discourses of security. Here, the Space Hijackers' actions are especially important; as the example above and those in later chapters serve to show, their imaginative resistances served precisely to resist such codification, to confound simplistic characterisations of anarchy and insecurity.

The second response to the question of incorporation concerns the politics of the 'everyday', the concept used here in a manner similar to its use by the Situationists, who saw it as a space of political resistance which was not instantly subject to the spectacular logics of capitalism. As Shukaitis makes clear, their concern was to develop 'a model of resistance based on submerged networks of invisible connections that would elude the constantly becoming-image of capitalist development and its ability to integrate forms of resistance to its image array' (2009: 194). In thinking about how dominant political imaginaries might be disrupted, it is important to give space to those less visible spaces, inspirations and relations which are often the site of more successful and less-readily incorporated transformations. This does not mean that more dramatic, visible moments do not have any importance, 'particularly in the generation of new dramatic and mythical imagery', but Shukaitis rather cautions against 'the tendency to reduce the entire and much larger process of social transformation to these particular moments' (2009: 15–16). It is in this vein that the following chapters looks at how creative transformations are prefigured in less spectacular, less visible spaces of anti-militarist action.

Notes

1. Derrida argues that attempts to escape, that is '[t]o decide to change terrain, in a discontinuous and irruptive fashion, by brutally placing oneself outside, and by affirming an absolute break and difference', are deeply problematic. About such strategies, he notes, '[w]ithout mentioning all the other forms of *trompe-l'oeil* perspective in which such a displacement can be caught, thereby inhabiting more naively and more strictly than ever the inside one declares one has deserted, the simple practice of language ceaselessly reinstates the new terrain on the oldest ground' (1982: 135).

2. In the longer term, this can include a disinclination to share details of your past; never having allowed people within the movement to meet your non-activist friends, family, or partner; disappearing for periods of time and then suddenly reappearing; being curiously well-resourced; and asking people lots of detailed questions about plans, or about their own previous activist experiences.
3. Each member of the group had their own agent name.
4. Section 14 of the Public Order Act 1986 allows the police to impose conditions on public assemblies, including the number of people who may take part, the location of the assembly, and its maximum duration.
5. The singing is an effort to make the officer's reading of the Section 14 order inaudible, such that its legal force is weakened.
6. The term 'spectacular' is ambiguous in this context. As will be discussed below, there is reason to be sceptical of spectacular action, which is particularly vulnerable to incorporation within the images of security and the state.
7. One interviewee dismissed the Black Bloc as 'a sport rather than a political tactic' (Interview P).

CHAPTER 6

Contestations

Thus far, this book has drawn on examples of highly confrontational political practices. Activists have blocked roads, broken through police lines, damaged property and shouted at BAE Systems employees: in a variety of forms, both militarism and 'militarists' have been confronted. There is, however, something inadequate about the concept of confrontation in this context. Confrontation draws a line, invokes a binary opposition between forces, between power and its resistance. Such oppositions obscure the ways in which spaces and practices of resistance are always already constituted by and, potentially, reproductive of precisely that which is resisted. They close down spaces in which to explore complicities and responsibilities, and tend to fix the place of power by drawing lines of ontological differentiation which obscure the role of subjectivity and moralise or render innocent the politics of resistance (Butler 2005: 45–6).

I raise these concerns not only as a means to set the terms for a critique of anti-militarist practice, but in order to demonstrate the need to view these apparently confrontational situations beyond the lens of confrontation. Whilst they undeniably have a certain confrontational spirit, there exists within them a generalised refusal to establish a clear opposition between militarism and resistance. Throughout much of anti-militarism we can identify a clear sense that anti-militarists are neither immune to nor innocent of participation in militarised social relations, and therefore that the methods used to oppose militarism should not draw on militarised forms of organisation and contestation. This moves them away from a politics of confrontation towards something more subversive.

Anti-militarists have long understood that militarism cannot only be understood as a network of institutions and elite practices, an external force to be assaulted and overturned. When understood as the social relations which underpin and reproduce organised political violence, militarism must be seen to operate in far more intimate ways. In Chapter 2 I argued that militarism can be understood as a complex of value systems, rationalities, social practices and subjectivities, which are themselves shaped by and implicated in a series of violent social hierarchies. Chapter 3 outlined how feminist and queer anti-militarists have theorised those relationships by interrogating how multiple and ever-adapting assemblages of gendered identities and rationalities are bound up in the formation and legitimisation of political violence. Out of these accounts emerges an understanding that militarism is deeply, unnervingly intertwined with the very fabric of who we are and how we relate to one another.

Critics of militarism have called attention to how a host of apparently banal social roles are entangled with militarism. We are enlisted in our capacities as citizens, workers, consumers, students, parents, fitness enthusiasts, charity supporters, movie lovers, and so on. Beyond these more specific subjectivities, others have argued that some very basic qualities of social relation should be scrutinised for their role in reproducing militarism:

> militarism is not just war as such. It is a social hierarchy of order givers and order takers. It is obedience, domination and submission. It is the capacity to perceive other human beings as abstractions, mere numbers, death counts. It is, at the same time, the domination of strategic considerations and efficiency for its own sake over life and the willingness to sacrifice oneself for a 'Great Cause' that one has been taught to believe in. (Landstreicher 2009: 85)

In these accounts, militarism is reproduced not only through particular social roles, but through the domination of social relations which privilege obedience, abstraction and strategy. These perspectives raise demanding questions; against our best wishes, even those of us who might think of ourselves as anti-militarists are profoundly implicated in militarism. As Donna Haraway succinctly observes, 'I have a body and mind as much constructed by the post-Second World War arms race and cold war as by the women's movements' (1991: 173).

Viewing militarism in this manner has significant implications for resistance. Merely targeting institutional arrangements is insufficient; contesting militarism must involve recognising and resisting militarised forms of subjectivity, within movements as well as beyond. Failure to do so leaves intact, and potentially even reinforces, central dynamics through which militarism is constituted. As Landstreicher argues,

> destructive attack is a legitimate and necessary response. But to militarize this struggle, to transform it essentially into a question of strategies and tactics, of opposing forces and numbers, is to begin to create within our struggle that which we are trying to destroy. (Landstreicher 2009: 86)

Similar understandings led Philip Berrigan, who himself spent time in prison for breaking into a military base and damaging nuclear warhead nose cones, to view resistance as a process fundamentally concerned with demilitarising the self. For him, '[w]e try to disarm ourselves by disarming the missiles' (cited in Laffin 2003: 3).

In these next three chapters I argue that anti-militarists are engaged in an ongoing process of contending with and subverting militarised forms of subjectivity. As they do this, they also generate and explore counter-subjectivities – alternative forms of being and relating which might not so easily reproduce militarism, and which hold open different political pathways. My purpose is not to identify a singular or totalising anti-militarist subjectivity, an ideal towards which anti-militarists (should) strive. Such conceptions serve to establish their own authorities and oppressions, to replicate the terms of 'The Cause' towards which all rational radical subjectivity must be configured – they are precisely the kinds of militarising gestures to be avoided. Instead, the discussion works to interpret a variety of (messy and incomplete) practices as works in progress in the context of what Simon Critchley calls the contemporary 'labour of politics', that is, the 'construction of new political subjectivities, new political aggregations in specific localities, a new dissensual *habitus*' (2008: 112). These experiments in becoming otherwise, and their failures, limits and contradictions, emerge as potent spaces from which to think about both the nature of militarism and the possibilities for resistance.

I conceptualise these explorations of counter-subjectivities through the lens of prefigurative politics, as attempts to embody the changes being sought in the means used to fight for them. As Luke Yates argues, prefiguration can be understood as a compound of processes, combining 'experimentation, the circulation of political perspectives, the production of new norms and conduct, material consolidation, and diffusion' (2015: 2). A prefigurative imaginary has been central to contemporary understandings of direct action, exemplified by one interviewee:

> I really think you've got to try and model the change you want to be. I think you also end up perpetuating the violence of society if you do not do that. So, for example, we must have an accessible movement, we must try and use a non-hierarchical . . . consensus-based decision-making [method] and try and be the society we want to end up in. (Interview P)

I argue both in this chapter and throughout the rest of the book that a prefigurative framing allows us to see less visible practices and processes as integral to the politics of anti-militarism, while also situating the debates that emerge amongst anti-militarists as contentions with the nature of militarised subjectivity and as spaces to think about the ethical practice of resistance and creativity.

This chapter examines several practices through which anti-militarist action calls militarised forms of subjectivity and contestation into question while also exploring alternatives in both the form and content of contestation. I look at three different practices through which anti-militarists subvert militarised forms of contestation: holding peace camps, working with tactics that rely on vulnerability, and using humour. I suggest that each of these calls different aspects of militarised subjectivity into question, while also embodying a form of contestation which seeks to avoid replicating that which is opposed. In the final part of the chapter, I complicate this account by suggesting that the line between militarised and non-militarised forms of subjectivity cannot (and should not) be so easily drawn, making the argument through autoethnographic reflections on my own experience as a militarised subject. This final section sets the terms for the following chapter, where I move to look at how the constitution and negotiation of more private anti-militarist spaces can also be read through the moves to negotiate militarised forms of subjectivity.

Peace Camps

One of the most iconic forms of anti-militarist activism has been the use of peace camps, their place in the popular imagination firmly established thanks to Greenham Common. Contemporary examples include the Faslane Peace Camp (which, having been running for over thirty-five years, is by far the longest-running existing example of such a project), the Peace News gatherings which take place each summer, and the Occupy camps which were set up outside the gates of the DSEI arms fair in 2013, 2015 and 2017. The generation of autonomous spaces, whether temporary or more permanent, is an important example of the desire in contemporary radical politics to explore and enact alternatives beyond the logics of the state and capital, to conduct 'organic experiment[s] in autonomous politics' (Pickerill and Chatterton 2006: 740; see also Brown et al. 2017; Feigenbaum et al. 2013). As with other prefigurative experiments, one does not find blueprints for an alternative, nor calm utopias; instead we find awkward and ambiguous attempts to glimpse or envisage life as it might otherwise be lived.

Peace camps and similar gatherings can take place in the shadows of military establishments, or in more removed spaces. They tend to perform a dual purpose, serving to facilitate actions targeted at relevant institutions (either as a base of operations, as with the Faslane Peace Camp, or by providing a convergence, training and planning space) whilst also allowing participants to experiment with alternative forms of political community (Routledge 2003). With respect to this second purpose, they demonstrate similarities with other radical convergence spaces including No Borders camps, climate camps and anti-summit camps; indeed, many of these other camps make spaces for anti-militarist training and planning.

In practice, this usually means a lack of formal hierarchy and a commitment to share organisational responsibilities and tasks amongst participants. Decisions about the running of the space are made collectively, usually by consensus, and a significant amount of energy tends to be spent exposing and confronting hidden forms of privilege and exclusion. Time is divided, depending on the specific needs and desires of participants, between the organisation of the space, education, training and workshops, and preparation for and carrying out direct action.

Peace News gatherings normally take place once a year. Up to 200 participants live together for five days, focusing on learning, on forming new friendships, and on enjoying the participatory space. At one gathering I attended in the summer of 2011, I participated in workshops on topics including masculinity and militarism, the development of drone warfare, the relationship between obedience and war, community-based campaigning, effective blockading techniques, and the politics of Harry Potter. I also took part in a session planning for action against that year's DSEI event. In the evenings were films, poetry readings, and a fully stocked bar. Decisions on the running of the camp were made collectively at morning meetings, chores (including gathering firewood, helping in the kitchen, running the crèche and staffing the welcome tent) were shared, and a respectful and collective ethos was built.

These spaces can be understood as attempts to break down those social logics which underpin militarism. Most prominently, the principle 'that hierarchical relations produce effective action', a central pillar of militaristic social relations, is subverted as participants take collective ownership of the space (Enloe 2004: 219), while the near-ubiquitous preference for consensus decision making means that differences are resolved not through exclusion or marginalisation, but through a process which centres listening, vulnerability and change (Sylvester 1992: 168). This emphatically does not mean that such spaces are unproblematic, that hierarchies do not emerge and that exclusions are not performed. With respect to the Peace News Summer Gathering, I have already discussed two examples of this in some detail: in Chapter 3, I outlined how the workshop on masculinity and militarism showcased very traditional and even patriarchal attitudes towards feminism and gender relations, and in Chapter 4 I discussed my involvement in an eviction which served to establish quite firmly the terms of exclusion on which the camp was based.

Arguing that we can view peace camps as concerned with the prefiguration of non- or anti-militarist social relations does not mean ignoring or overlooking these problems; on the contrary, it is precisely in those contested encounters that the prefigurative ethos is most important. It was as those of us involved in the space discussed the difficult politics of the eviction (and whether and how it undermined the purported inclusivity of the camp) and engaged in the difficult labour of interrogating our relationship with militarised masculinity, that we negotiated social relations that are integral to militarism. As Jenny Pickerill and Paul Chatterton argue, it is in the face of emergent hierarchies and exclusions that such spaces may be at their most valuable:

> [w]hile no easy answers to these issues exist, addressing them is the bedrock of making autonomy. Interstitial living can also be a source of creativity, producing hybrid, flexible and transient identities, challenging the norms we live by and creating potent new interactions. (Pickerill and Chatterton 2006: 742)

It is precisely these encounters that a prefigurative ethos works to embrace.

The prefigurative gestures of these spaces can be at their most intense when they occur in tension with more explicitly militarist contexts. The camp at Greenham Common is a powerful example here. Sylvester argues that much of Greenham's force came from the strongly prefigurative nature of the camp, which

> highlight[ed] the ways that subjectivities usually refused place in [International Relations] can become the basis of empathetically negotiated actions that strike at IR's core – realist defense. It also show[ed] that homeless refusers of the protector/protected *raison d'être* can develop a politics of empathetic cooperation that translates into organizational practices unknown to IR. (Sylvester 2002: 260)

It was on these terms that the women at Greenham Common 'eschewed usual political conventions such as voting, designating leaders, and organizing committees, and operated well within anarchy' (Sylvester 2002: 260; see also Cockburn 2012: 37–8; Roseneil 1995: 71–96). However, it was at the tense border between the peace camp and the military base that these prefigurations resonated particularly strongly. As Enloe notes, '[a]ny military base is designed to be secure. By cutting the fences, dancing on the missile silos, challenging charges of trespassing in court, the Greenham women managed to transform the very meaning of a base, and of public security'. A military base so easily upended by a group of nonviolent women was not really a military base, and its security claims could no longer be taken seriously (1989: 79).

As well as penetrating the border between the two sites, Sylvester shows that the women transformed the nature of this border in their relations with soldiers:

> Mutual homelessness around these fences raised the prospect of respectful negotiation as an alternative to life on either side. Moreover, daily negotiations at the fence were usually respectful. Rather than denounce or curse the soldiers or women on the other side, each often engaged in 'normal' banter with the other about family, weather, and mutual conditions of security. Defences came down. Common scripts were (potentially) revealed. (Sylvester 2002: 261)

The prefigurative nature of the peace camp and the exploration of possibilities beyond the expected form of political contestation served precisely to question and undermine the nature of the military base, to reveal its contradictions and expose its tensions. In both their more and less confrontational states, peace camps can therefore be important sites for exploring and challenging militarised forms of subjectivity. However, and with important exceptions, they are relatively infrequent occurrences, and no longer take place at the scale of Greenham Common. As such, in the next two sections I look at two very common anti-militarist tactics, arguing that we can also see the negotiation of militarised subjectivities and forms of contestation in more everyday practices.

Vulnerability

The second example of anti-militarist contestation concerns a particular anti-militarist tactic, the 'die-in'. A die-in is a form of demonstration where participants lie on the floor and simulate death. There are many possible variations. A die-in can be purely theatrical or it can be used to directly blockade something. It can be large or small, and perhaps involve costumes and props (fake blood is not uncommon, and getting into body bags makes you incredibly hard to move). Often a statement will be read aloud during the die-in to explain the situation to the public. Music might be played, or there may be silence. Activists can choose to remain on the ground until removed, or to leave of their own volition. Because they are highly participatory, easy to organise, and visually impressive, die-ins are a staple feature of anti-militarist actions.

Although they are sometimes dismissed as a theatrical accompaniment to more serious action, I want to suggest that we can read the die-in as a prefigurative gesture, one which challenges militarism both by politicising space in certain ways, and by subverting militarised practices of contestation by mobilising a politics of vulnerability. A politics of vulnerability refers to political actions which seek to make the experience of vulnerability – fragility, contingency, dependency – productive. Such mobilisations, examples of which might include the practice of lip sewing amongst refugees, and the Chipko movement's practice of hugging trees to stop them from being felled, cut powerfully through expected narratives of contestation, which very often consist precisely in the masking of vulnerabilities (Edkins and Pin-Fat 2005; Shiva 1988: 64–73). These politics do not automatically subscribe to dominant expectations of how politics is done, instead asking questions about what it means to be powerful, to be successful, and to mask vulnerability. They open spaces to think about the (militarised) onto-politics of contestation. The discussion here will focus on two particular die-ins in which I have been involved. The first took place at the University of Manchester in May 2011.

We have been tipped off that BAE Systems are scheduled to run a one-day workshop in the maths department. Around twenty of us go to the building where the session is supposed to take place and, while several remain outside to distribute leaflets, fifteen of us head inside. In the corridor outside the room that BAE have booked we lie on the ground, large cardboard tombstones resting on our bodies. Each tombstone details information about BAE Systems' arms sales to regimes in the Middle East and North Africa, which are currently in the public eye following the use of British-sold weapons to suppress popular uprisings across the region.

While we had expected this particular part of our protest to end when the meeting began, it becomes apparent that the event has stalled. Those students who were planning to attend the workshop are displaying apparent discomfort about stepping over our prostrate bodies, despite (or perhaps because of) the BAE staff encouraging them to do so. They stand awkwardly around the fringes of our sprawled mass, clearly unwilling to pick their way through. We remain on the floor. This stalemate continues for around twenty minutes, at which point the BAE staff announce that they are cancelling the entire event. Unaccustomed to success, and fearing that they will simply move the event to another room, we follow them as they leave the building, and continue to do so, at a moderate distance, all the way to Piccadilly Station.

We were not expecting such a significant response; die-ins are generally regarded as an accompaniment to more obstructive direct actions. A combination of factors including the well-made tombstone signs, the direct blockade of the room and the current public focus on UK arms sales led to a situation in which the discomfort produced by the activists had surprising effects.

The second example here comes from a demonstration in Nottingham in February 2010, where as part of a Peace News Winter Gathering I spent an afternoon in the city centre raising awareness about the nearby Heckler & Koch distribution warehouse.[1]

There are about twenty of us, and we develop a routine that we repeat continuously around the city centre for about three hours. Around five of us crouch underneath a big tarpaulin, against which is placed a large sign asking, 'What is Heckler & Koch Hiding?' After a few minutes, by which time a number of people have gathered to watch, the noise of gunfire is played through some speakers and we fall to the ground. The tarpaulin is then removed to reveal our bodies. As we do this, other members of the group give out leaflets and talk to passers-by about the company and its presence in Nottingham (about which most people are not aware, and which Heckler & Koch have been keen to hide).

This second example differs in a number of ways from the first. While the former sought to mobilise a direct sense of discomfort or shame in potential attendees, the latter seeks to draw in ordinary members of the public. It is more demonstrative than obstructive, finding its value primarily in the question, 'What is Heckler & Koch Hiding?' The question, and the 'to be revealed' nature of our position under the tarpaulin, catches people's attention and leads to a number of conversations.

In both cases, the die-in itself plays several important roles. The first is to ask demanding questions, explicitly in the case of the latter, but perhaps more insistently in the former. The decision to walk into a room became a political one, and attendees were forced to confront the wider implications of BAE Systems' work in a space where, previously, they would not have had to. In this feature two further, interrelated aspects are revealed. The first is the representative nature of the actions. The die-ins are a mirror of distant and forgotten deaths, and an attempt to represent them precisely at the point at which they are simultaneously produced and effaced. Nottingham city centre is a place for shopping, not for remembering the violence produced by businesses operating nearby; representing those deaths forces discomfort and provokes an examination of this space and the 'normal' politics within it (Stierl 2012). Similar dynamics infuse the die-in in the university; is a workshop focused on solving abstract mathematical problems truly so innocent or apolitical? Within this representation there is also a rewriting of the politics of distance, a mobilisation of the localism observed in Chapter 2 and a blurring of the local/global divide. The die-in functions as a means by which to represent foreign suffering, to reintroduce it into spaces from which it has been erased, to reframe space and challenge the prospective employee or shopper to confront the consequences of political practice without the distance of distance.

There are clearly problematic dimensions here. The legacy of representation in this context is uncomfortable, and claims to be more correctly or ethically representing the victims of Western militarism are in danger of reinforcing logics of superiority and capability. In solely representing them as victims (indeed, as passive victims who call forth only the decision of whether or not to take passage over their immobile bodies), particular North–South global imaginaries are reproduced at the very space in which they might be resisted. Die-ins seek to represent those whose vulnerability is most acutely produced, exposed and exploited within militarism; while attention to vulnerability can open spaces of interconnection, the appeal to a shared and universal vulnerability 'carries its own risks of ignoring differences of power and privilege', obscuring the highly uneven ways in which vulnerability is distributed and imposed (Hirsch 2016: 80–2). Furthermore, these attempts to represent are ridiculous in their inadequacy, in their inability to convey anything but the most fleeting of recognitions and discomforts; the bodies themselves do not intervene, and the brutality they convey is muffled, muted (Muppidi 2012: 11–27). In these senses, while those who suffer at the sharp end of militarism are represented, this representation remains inadequate, and tied to familiar, uncomfortable tropes.

A charge of passivity can also be made. The concern is sometimes raised that die-ins, while occasionally striking visually, are limited in their capacity to make 'real' interventions and effect 'concrete' refusals. In the light of this critique the die-in in Manchester would be cast as a surprising exception, which, to some extent, it was. At the die-ins in Nottingham, some of the participants were clearly uncomfortable with the non-provocative nature of the intervention, and one interviewee, who was arrested following a die-in at the 2011 DSEI arms fair, expressed the concern that he 'gave [himself] away cheaply' (Interview F). Whilst not wishing to dismiss these concerns (the politics of voluntary submission to arrest are taken up in Chapter 8), there is an affirmative gesture in the performance of the die-in. Although the subject is, to some extent, a passive figure, there is an active quality to this passivity.

In expressing vulnerabilities – one's own and others effected by militarism – and insisting on the political potency of those vulnerabilities, there is an assertion of alternative practices of power and resistance. That we felt empowered as we lay on the floor in front of a seminar room, while those who stood and watched felt unable to act as though they otherwise would have done, is a surprising but important inversion of expected political logics. Theories of resistance often assume that vulnerability and resistance are antithetical, that vulnerability implies a lack of agency. While the condition of vulnerability can (and does) become a site of harm, and while resistance frequently operates in response to such vulnerabilities, firm oppositions between vulnerability and resistance can blind us to the mutual dependence and implication that is often the foundation and precondition of political community (Butler 2016b; Butler et al. 2016). Indeed, the desire to deny or banish the condition of vulnerability, principally by displacing it onto others, is a major motivating force in the contemporary politics of security and militarism. There is, therefore, something specifically subversive in refusing to do this, and in experimenting with forms of contestation which intervene through vulnerability.

In the willingness to exhibit vulnerability in a public space, often through lying at the feet of police and security guards, we see a refusal to replicate conventional and expected logics of socio-political contestation, a disavowal of practices which might be associated with militarism, and a determined intervention *despite* these evasions. In short, there is a prefigurative dimension to the die-in. This prefigurative politics of vulnerability can also be seen in practices examined in earlier chapters. The use of blockading tactics that operate by both allowing and prohibiting the police from causing harm (Chapter 4), and the refusal to close down activist spaces in response to police infiltration (Chapter 5) are both practices which recognise the productive politics of vulnerability, without idealising it. None of this is to imply that concerns about capacities, passivities and particular forms of representation are not relevant, or that the mobilisation of vulnerability would overhaul militaristic political imaginaries. It does suggest, however, that there is a productive dimension which should not be effaced, and which signifies attempts to think and act beyond the expected terms of contestation.

Humour

The monstrous absurdities which run throughout militarised rationalities provide rich fodder for subversion; it is therefore unsurprising that anti-militarists make frequent use of humour as a tactic of resistance. In this section I demonstrate how anti-militarists use irony, overstatement and mockery to call attention to both the violent politics of militarism and the relationship between militarism and subjectivity. I also argue that, at their best, there is a prefigurative dimension to these uses of humour, insofar as they subvert normal forms of contestation and celebrate an anti-hegemonic absurdity.

In Chapter 5 I recounted the Space Hijackers' attempt to auction off a tank outside the 2007 DSEI arms fair, a tableau which challenged dominant scripts about the politics of security and insecurity by holding them up to standards which were simultaneously ridiculous and deeply serious. The same group's contribution to the 2011 DSEI protests provides another smart example of anti-militarist satire. Without revealing their true identity or intent, the Hijackers established a false company under the name Life Neutral Solutions, and then marketed themselves both to ordinary families and to the defence industry. In this guise, they claimed to offer a service offsetting the deaths caused by arms sales by funding alternative lives elsewhere.

Space Hijackers members in suits and branded T-shirts advertised the company on the streets around ExCeL where DSEI takes place. Their publicity aimed at the general public encouraged them to sign up to the programme:

> You've heard of the importance of being carbon neutral? Well, being Life Neutral is the same – but with people. For every life lost as a result of the use of products from our member organisations, we make sure that a new life flourishes. Join today and your next child could be a Life Neutral™ child. (Space Hijackers 2011a)

Life neutral benefits include IVF, private education, private health care, nappies and formula, and 'access to top universities'. On their defence industry-facing publicity, they took a slightly different line:

> Join the frontline of an exciting new arena in the Corporate Social Responsibility landscape.
> The information age has created a new landscape of consumer aware-

ness. So it's no surprise that customers are becoming increasingly mindful of adverse publicity that has become associated with some defence products in recent years. **Life Neutral Solutions** offers a unique range of bespoke strategies to respond to this changing marketplace. We harness the needs of an increasingly discerning client-base, to provide opportunities for reputational enhancement.

Become one of a growing number of **life-neutral** (TM) brands. By sponsoring births in Western countries, you can **life-offset** the collateral effects of defence operations in third-world conflict zones. (Space Hijackers 2011b; original emphasis)

A website and fliers were created, and a dummy advert was placed on a large billboard (Figures 6.1 and 6.2). The Hijackers were also invited onto the BBC World Service to discuss the company, where, in response to an incredulous reporter, they revealed the prank.

In this stunt, the claims to ethical responsibility from the arms industry are subverted by following them to an absurd but *almost* believable (neoliberal) excess. The tendency for Western lives (and, as the billboard makes clear, *white* Western lives) to be privileged, ethically and financially, over others is highlighted, and communicated to members of the public simply by approaching them to ask

Figure 6.1 Life Neutral dummy billboard advert. © Space Hijackers, 2011. Reproduced with permission

Figure 6.2 Life Neutral flier. © Space Hijackers, 2011. Reproduced with permission

whether they would consider joining the scheme. As with the tank, the violence of the arms trade is critiqued through a mimicry which successfully conjoins the absurd and the credible; Western lives funded by distant wars.

Mocking and satirising militarism plays an important role in the everyday practice of anti-militarism. Many activists will jump at any chance to dress up in ridiculous pastiche, whether of arms dealers, or soldiers, or government ministers. Some find puns for banners,[2] while others share cartoons (Rooum 2003; SchNEWS undated). The activist-comedian Mark Thomas's writing and shows on the arms trade are hugely popular amongst activists. Thomas's routines rest on the absurdities of the arms trade (told in a manner which evokes anger and amusement in equal measure) and anecdotes about his activism, which has included 'kidnapping' a coach-load of arms dealers by offering them a free ride from their hotel to DSEI, and establishing a fake PR firm which advised military juntas on how to deal with difficult questions from Amnesty International (Thomas 2007a). The possibilities for and impact of everyday subversion have expanded with the rise of social media, where irony and overstatement are often highly successful devices for creating content which will be shared. During DSEI 2015, CAAT uploaded a video to Facebook which shows a 15-second clip of an activist dressed as a grim reaper, having climbed over a fence and into the exhibition centre premises, running away from security guards and police. The video has been slightly sped up and mixed with the *Benny Hill Show* theme tune. It is achingly funny, and was widely circulated.

Another humorous action during that same week also received major attention, first from social media and then from print media. Early in the morning on the first day of the arms fair, activists replaced adverts on bus stops and London Underground trains with their own versions. These alternative posters mimicked and twisted the aesthetics of more official sources, a practice known as 'subvertising'. Some adapted the tagline of the government's 'GREAT' marketing campaign (which, in Union Jack colours, usually states something like 'Business is GREAT') to read 'Bombing is GREAT' and 'Selling Arms is GREAT'. These initially looked like official advertising, but on closer inspection turned out to include text outlining the government's role in selling arms to Israel and Saudi Arabia. Other posters looked like publicity for ExCeL, but with text stating: 'We provide exhibition space for anyone wanting to profit from death. We're proud to be enabling violence, repression and war across the world.' And still others looked uncannily like Transport for London information posters, but again focused on the arms fair taking place only a few stops away. These posters, with their insolent blend of cheek, sarcasm and irony, were again highly popular on social media (Brassett 2009). Their effect was amplified when it became clear that they had been installed in collaboration with Banksy, who was at that time enjoying fresh attention on the back of his 'Dismaland' exhibition. Mass media attention naturally followed, and the posters were featured on the websites of several national newspapers (Halkon 2015; Wyatt 2015).

Activists frequently use humour to call attention to the power imbalance between their position as a plucky band of campaigners and that of militarist organisations embedded within and protected by the institutions of the state. When the Smash EDO campaign was handed an injunction preventing them from protesting on the road outside the EDO factory, they held a 'Carry On Up The Injunction' demonstration, during which activists dressed as a particular security guard (with whom they had been having problems) and chased each other around outside the factory serving injunctions and making Nazi salutes. Following this, and banned by the terms of the injunction from taking pictures of the security guards (which made it more difficult for them to hold these guards to account for assault), they held a life drawing class, painting pictures of the factory and security guards (*On the Verge* 2008).

The power of humour in these examples is well summarised by Marieke de Goede, who argues that comedy functions as a form of resistance by 'making strange' sedimented and depoliticised rationalities, subverting mystical foundations of legitimacy through the process of ridicule (2005: 380–2). She argues that laughter 'is more than a superficial attack or helpless gesture in the face of the power of financial institutions: it has a potential to shake the discursive foundations of modern financial rationality' (2005: 381; see also Brassett 2016; Odysseos 2001). The same is true here: the rationalities on which militarism depends result in the police chasing grim reapers, and claims about the ethical trading of arms. Opportunities for 'making strange' are plentiful. There is also a creative capacity in such gestures, inasmuch as actions of humorous overstatement 'scramble the expectations and normal flow of social life, and thus at least for a second open a possibility for some other form of communication and interaction to occur' (Shukaitis 2009: 71).

It is not only *over*statement which is powerful in this context; as one interviewee argued, simply asking uncomfortable questions, when accompanied by euphemistic, dismissive or uncompromising responses, can quickly become farcical. His specific example concerned the recent BAE Systems Annual General Meeting (a popular event on the anti-militarist calendar, at which single-shareholding activists are legally permitted to attend and ask questions of the board) at which he had been present. One activist asked the BAE Systems chairman about weapons which had been sold to Saudi Arabia, and which had been used when Saudi forces entered Bahrain in early 2011. Amidst laugher, the chairman repeatedly and ridiculously attempted to deflect the question and champion Saudi Arabian sovereignty (Interview B). The activist who (repeatedly) asked the question, another interviewee, told me that she was later berated by one 'real' shareholder for 'making a mockery' of the event (Interview A). In this instance, the role of comedian was effectively offered to the BAE chairman, whose compliant self-caricature reveals the limitations of, and makes strange, the rationalities upon which BAE Systems depends.[3]

Anti-militarists have also used humour in a darker fashion. In 2015 VfP released a video called *Battlefield Casualties* as part of a campaign against the British military's recruitment of under-18-year-olds.[4] Drawing on the aesthetics of 1980s–90s Saturday morning children's television, the video is a mock advert for a new range of Action Man toys: PTSD Action Man (Figure 6.3), Paralyzed Action Man and Dead Action Man. It has an upbeat tempo with eager children playing with the toys, a voiceover performed by the comic actor Matt Berry (famed for his use of inappropriate delight), and exciting music reminiscent of that used for genuine Action Man adverts. This buoyant atmosphere stands in deeply uncomfortable tension with the content of Berry's narrative and with the toys themselves, which seek to represent the reality faced by many veterans. For instance, the 30-second section for PTSD Action Man goes like this:

Berry (narrating): 'For PTSD Action Man danger lurks at every turn!'
Boy (on screen): 'Who's that??' *Shows off PTSD Action Man's anxious side-to-side eye movement feature.*

Berry: 'He never feels safe, not even in his own home!'
Boy walks PTSD Action Man in front of mirror, makes him double take and punch the mirror in shock.
Berry: 'Do what you can to block out the memories!'
Boy: 'Glug glug glug!' *Makes PTSD Action Man drink beer.*
Berry: 'With no support from HQ, it's up to you to find a way!'
PTSD Action Man stands forlornly in the shower. Then camera cuts to boy making PTSD Action Man cut drugs with a credit card.
Boy: 'Looks like we're on our own!'
Berry: 'PTSD Action Man now comes with thousand-yard stare action. With time running out, only you can stop the pain!'
Boy ties a noose around PTSD Action Man's head.
Boy (to camera): 'Let's get out of here!'
Boy flicks the chair from underneath PTSD Action Man's feet and departs, leaving PTSD Action Man hanging.

The sections covering Paralyzed Action Man and Dead Action Man are no less brutal. The video links to a website (and, for a few months in 2015, to a physical exhibition) where the dolls are pictured in their packaging and displayed in more detail. Paralyzed Action Man features legs that 'really don't work' and comes complete with wheelchair, painkillers, colostomy bag and a disabled parking permit; Dead Action Man comes in his own body bag and includes a medal, a union flag, a spade and a wreath reading 'DAD' (Veterans for Peace 2015).

The purpose of the campaign was to call attention to youth recruitment into the British military. Whilst most countries only recruit adults aged 18 and over, the UK is one of the few which accepts 16-year-olds. VfP point out that soldiers who enlisted for the army at 16 were twice as likely to die in Afghanistan as those who enlisted at 18 and above, that they are likely to come from the poorest regions of the UK, and that they have the worst risk levels for mental health problems once they have left the forces (Veterans for Peace 2015). They also claim that young recruits are less likely than others to be able to seriously consider the real-life implications of joining up.[5] The website draws an explicit link between the video and the problem of youth recruitment by highlighting a series of toy soldiers launched by the Ministry of Defence in

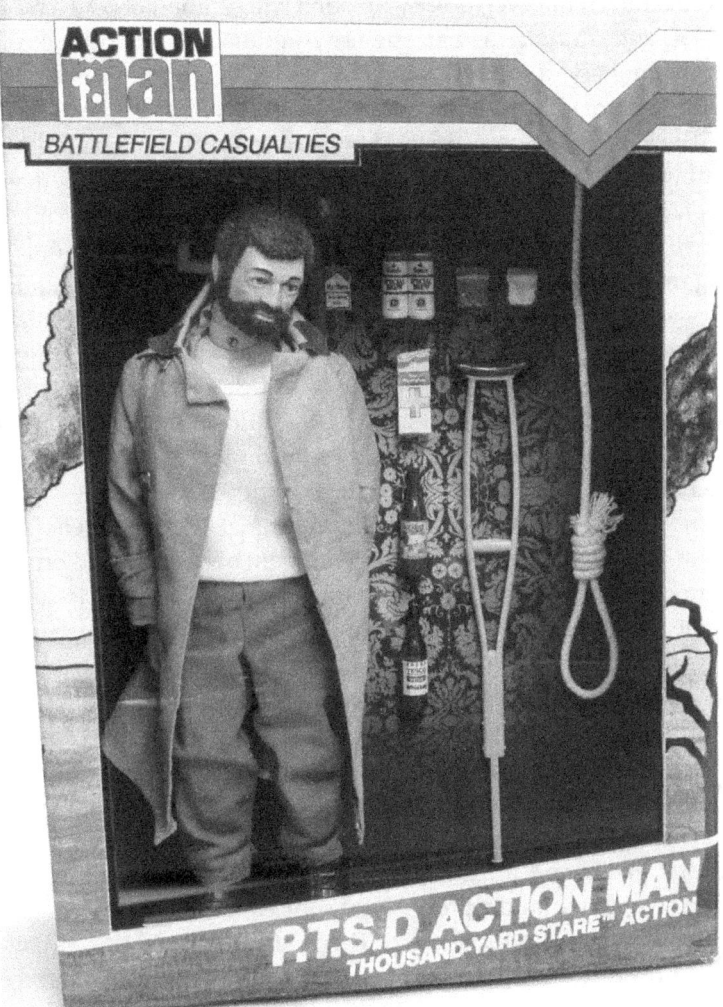

Figure 6.3 PTSD Action Man. © Darren Cullen (spellingmistakescostlives.com).
Reproduced with permission

2009. These toys (which could be bought alongside model drones and radar kits) were aimed at children between 4 and 9 years old and were designed to help improve the image of the armed forces. The Battlefield Casualties website warns that 'not only will [these toys] result in more children growing up and wanting to join the armed forces, but even those who don't will be imbued with a more favourable attitude towards the use of military force and the role of the military in society', a conclusion not significantly at variants with the MoD's own optimistic assessment (Teather 2009).

The Battlefield Casualties project has a very different relationship to humour than the other examples discussed here. It is perhaps even a stretch to call it humour; certainly it does not offer many laughs. Whilst the video is specifically structured as a joke, employing misdirection, ironic juxtaposition and overstatement, its quick escalation towards a cruel reality crowds out what space might normally be left for a wry smile. Available signifiers of delight – the children playing with the toys and Berry's normally infectious enthusiasm – jar, intensifying the discomfort which builds throughout the three segments. It is uncomfortable to watch, an exemplary case of 'painful irony' (Brassett 2009: 230).

In the space of this discomfort, the video makes important points. Most explicitly, it focuses on the recruitment of children and on the hypocrisies of a society that simultaneously leaves veterans to suffer while rendering them heroes in the service of further militarisation. Beyond this, the video calls into question the relationship between recreation and warfare. In mobilising nostalgic tropes of Saturday morning television and Action Man toys, it demands a reckoning with our own complicity in these narratives. It takes what we might have felt to be a relatively innocent form of recreation, whether playing with toys, or perhaps video games and films that follow similar paths, and reveals both the disjuncture between the play and the reality, and the processes of subjectification at work in this supposedly non-political space. The watcher is provoked to consider how their own practices of recreation draw from and reinforce militarised imaginaries.

Humour operates at the more and less spectacular levels to expose and render unstable the rationalities which sustain militarist politics, mobilising a sense of the absurd which is explicit in the resistance (anarchists in a tank, grim reapers on the run, maimed children's toys) and thereby revealed in the militarist target. Beyond this destabilising gesture there is a prefigurative quality, insofar as humour intervenes in a manner which avoids the 'active nihilism' and 'pious humourlessness' which is often the expected (and, as such, always already dismissed) quality of some forms of contemporary protest (Critchley 2008: 124). It does not attempt to mimic expected ontologies of contestation, preferring instead to delegitimate conventional systems of power by revealing their falsehoods, fictions and contradictions. On such terms, the laughter which results is not just relief at the destabilisation; it is a cry of affirmation which refuses to become that which it opposes, which seizes the moment of absurdity in order to mark the desire to be (and contest) otherwise.

These themes can also be read in the manifesto of CIRCA, who have made the comedic subversion of militarism, order and expected scripts of contestation the model through which *all* their interventions (which largely fall within the rubric of the alter-globalisation movement) have taken place. Dressing half as clowns and half as soldiers, they reveal the (tragic) comedy of war and the potency of laughter:

> We are **clowns** because what else can one be in such a stupid world. Because inside everyone is a lawless clown trying to escape. Because nothing undermines authority like holding it up to ridicule. Because since the beginning of time tricksters have embraced life's contradictions, creating coherence through confusion. Because fools are both fearsome and innocent, wise and stupid, entertainers and dissenters, healers and laughing stocks, scapegoats and subversives. Because buffoons always succeed in failing, always say yes, always hope and always feel things deeply. Because a clown can survive everything and get away with anything.
>
> We are an **army** because we live on a planet in permanent war – a war of money against life, of profit against dignity, of progress against the future. Because a war that gorges itself on death and blood and shits money and toxins, deserves an obscene body of deviant soldiers. Because only an army can declare absurd war on absurd war. Because combat requires solidarity, discipline and commitment. Because alone clowns are pathetic figures, but in groups and gaggles, brigades and battalions, they are extremely dangerous. We are an army because we are angry and where bombs fail we might succeed with mocking laughter. (CIRCA undated; original emphasis)

By adopting military aesthetics in order to mock and resist them (while also recognising their attractions and even inescapabilities),

162 / Resisting Militarism

CIRCA occupy and twist militarised forms of subjectivity. Their laughter, and that they evoke, operates as a potent space of anti-militarist prefiguration.

None of the above should be taken to suggest that the use of humour by activists is by any means unproblematic. To acknowledge a prefigurative dynamic that might be productive in destabilising militarised forms of contestation and subjectivity is not the same as suggesting that the *politics* of any particular intervention are necessarily anti-militarist (or anti-hegemonic, emancipatory, and so on). For one last example on this subject, we might look again to the Space Hijackers and to an action they undertook during DSEI in 2005. On this occasion they boarded the Docklands Light Railway (the principal means of transport for arms dealers heading to the arms fair) armed with suitcases full of sex toys (Space Hijackers 2005). These they attempted to sell to those on the train, explaining that dealing in arms may be a sign of sexual repression: 'don't use your rocket to kill, use it to thrill', they urged, while giving out the leaflets shown in Figures 6.4 and 6.5.

The aim here is clearly to make visible the always already gendered

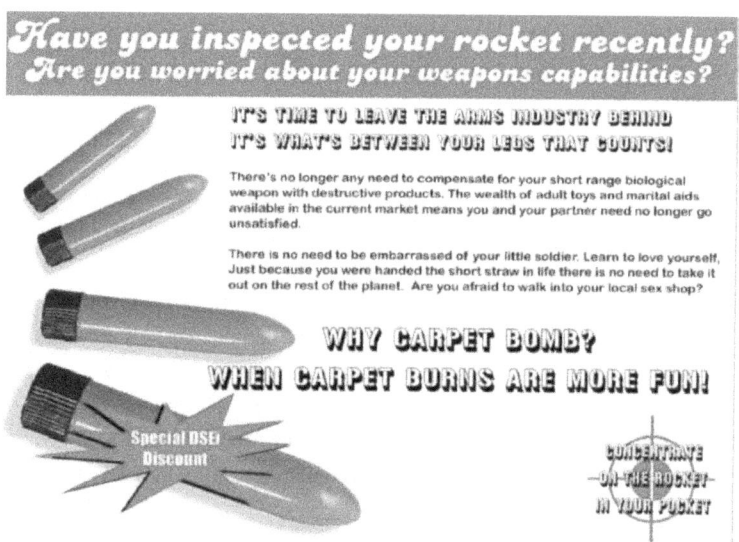

Figure 6.4 Sex toy leaflet – 1. © Space Hijackers, 2005. Reproduced with permission

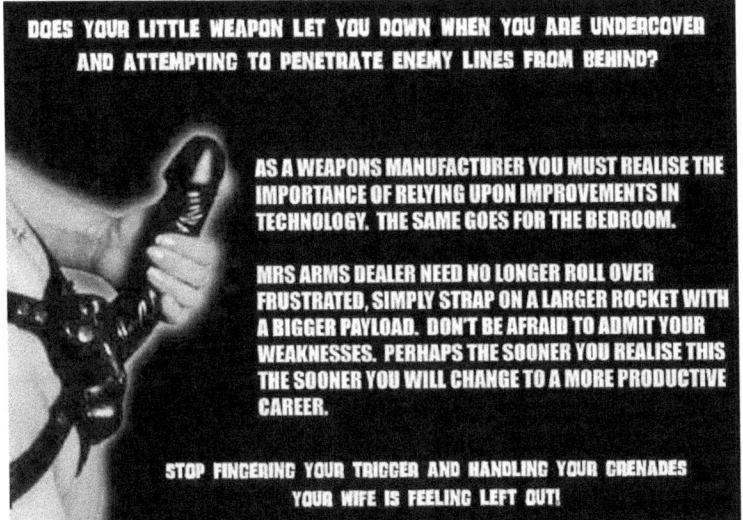

Figure 6.5 Sex toy leaflet – 2. © Space Hijackers, 2005. Reproduced with permission

space of the arms trade, and to situate it in the context of a fragile or insecure masculinity which attempts to displace its vulnerability through investment in militarism. However, as they do this the Space Hijackers also reproduce problematic gendered imaginaries, reinforcing hegemonic and heteronormative standards of masculinity and male entitlement and relying upon narratives which equate successful gender performance with (hetero)sexual prowess. In this frame, the role of the arms dealer's wife, 'Mrs Arms Dealer', is to be receptive, sexual, and to help her husband fulfil his masculinity: peace depends on it.[6] The problem here is not so much that the joke is not particularly funny (as compared with other Space Hijackers examples) than that it relies upon and stabilises images of masculinity and femininity which are themselves implicated in the functioning of militarism.

At its best, humour has an anti-hegemonic quality. It does not impose its alternative, but presents the strangeness of previously stable narratives to the imagination and withdraws, leaving behind a confusion of incoherences. This is not to suggest that humour is by definition anti-hegemonic, anti-militarist or 'emancipatory'. It is often not. It is instead to accord with de Goede's more modest conclusion that 'joking, laughter and carnival *can be* important politics of dissent in an era when . . . political legitimacy . . . depends upon . . . rationality and coherence' (2005: 389; original emphasis). As they direct this energy towards militarised institutions and rationalities, anti-militarists both reveal certain relationships between militarism and subjectivity, and do so in a manner which avoids replicating militarised and hegemonic forms of contestation. This, of course, does not mean that militarism suddenly disassembles as its constituent rationalities weaken. Nevertheless, it is as anti-militarists recognise the social relations that underpin militarism, and as they reveal their strangeness, that cracks appear through which alternative forms of contestation and subjectivity might emerge.

Desiring Militarism

In looking for examples of prefigurative politics, there is a danger that prefiguration is conceptualised as too simple a process, a straightforward departure from militarism and embodiment of some exterior alternative. Such accounts risk the conservatism of good conscience and ignorance of the manifold ways in which we are entangled within militarism. Prefiguration is most powerful as a concept and practice when understood as a ceaseless process of experimentation and critique. One way to think about that process and its challenges is through reflection on the relationship between militarised subjectivity and desire. In Chapter 4 I recounted a series of events from the Block the Factory action in the summer of 2015, during which I helped to shut down an Israeli arms factory near Birmingham by lying in the road attached to a concrete arm tube, facilitated by the ironic operation of particular regulations regarding the acceptable use of force. To introduce the argument here, I tell an earlier part of that same story, as a personal reflection on the ways militarised desire operates in anti-militarist politics.

Summer 2015. Shenstone. Block the Factory
A group of around twenty-five of us spend the night before the action in a house thirty miles from the factory. Over the course of the evening we make and remake our plans, practise with the equipment, and coordinate with the other groups who will meet us

at the factory. Our phones are switched off and kept in a separate room as a standard security measure. The plan is to leave for the factory at 3 a.m. At 1 a.m. we turn off the lights and try to get a little rest. I lie on the floor in an unfamiliar sleeping bag listening to my heart pound in my chest, excitement and anxiety competing for attention. After about an hour I give up trying to sleep and start getting ready to leave. I force myself to eat some jam sandwiches, pull on an adult diaper, and help to lift our heavy props into the van. It's not uncommon for pre-action convergence spaces to be raided by the police, and while that hasn't yet happened the atmosphere is tense. A mysterious car parks up the road from where we're staying, sending us into a small and pointless panic.

Those of us who will form the blockade get into two vans and leave at about 4 a.m., a little later than planned. We drive for forty minutes before pulling up outside a pub on a narrow country lane, just a mile from the factory. Two people jump onto bikes and ride down to the factory to recce the site and check for police presence. The rest of us wait nervously outside the vans, knowing that the plan depends on catching the police off guard by being so early. A couple of people suggest that we should stay in the van, in case someone from the pub sees us and calls the police. Others point out that to any casual observer we look, in our wellington boots and warm countryside gear, like we're about to go orienteering. We get a call from the bikers: it's clear – only a handful of police and perhaps one security guard. Not quite able to believe our luck, we get back into the vans.

Moments later, we're outside the factory. I jump out of the front seat, pull open the side compartment, and help to lift the heavy arm tube out of the van. A second group are doing the same from the back doors, a third from the other van. My partner and I position the tube in the centre of the road in front of the main factory gate, lie down on either side, and slide our arms inside, attaching carabiners to the pole running through the centre. The whole process takes about fifteen seconds, at the end of which we cannot be moved safely or without special equipment. It's 5 a.m., and the factory is blocked.

In Chapter 4 I used this example to show how activist blockading tactics operate through a fragile negotiation with-and-of state security systems. The account I want to give here is more personal, concerning my own affective relationship with the action. That affective relationship is one laced with militaristic codes. This first occurs as I lie on the ground and take stock, realising that our plan to occupy the space has worked perfectly. Adrenaline floods my system. 'This is so fucking cool!' I remark to those around me. 'It's like being in The A-Team!' As the theme tune to the 80s cult classic TV show bounced through my mind, I thought about the different elements of the action which had combined such that my instinctive association was with a reference point so saturated with military themes. These included the clandestine organising, the recon team, the well-timed swoop, the synchronised watches (unnecessary but an old joke between a friend and myself) and, of course, the whole plan coming together.

The image of Hannibal's renegade band of military misfits stayed with me both during and after the action. Certainly, an integral part of the experience of direct actions like these can be the pleasure derived from the intimacy of working as a small group, entering into a space of mutual trust and vulnerability, and taking on the world together. Theories of soldier mobilisation refer to precisely such motivating factors in the constitution of effective military units (Nuciari 2006: 63–7). Similar tropes are also widely used in military hero stories, like *Saving Private Ryan* and *Band of Brothers*, to provide (carefully situated) human context and relatability to the abstraction of war (Wetta and Novelli 2003). The figure of the heroic yet rebellious military subject, who outwits the authorities and breaks the rules in the service of a higher code, plays an important role in these tales. They also carry highly gendered narratives, with The A-Team providing an exemplary case of disaffected (and deeply patriarchal) militarised masculinity (Schwichtenberg 1987).

*

My experience here is not unique. Several interviewees called attention to the propensity to frame and structure activist organising in martial forms. One pointed out that the language of direct action is often explicitly militarised, involving talk of infiltrating, or laying siege (Interview K). Not long afterwards and with that conversation still fresh in my mind, I heard an experienced organiser refer to the critical mass bike riders who slow down traffic around ExCeL as the 'shock troops' of anti-DSEI protests. And this is not only about language; there is a more embodied dimension. For instance, the secrecy, plotting and intrigue which accompany the security culture practices discussed in Chapter 5 are frequently saturated with militarised affect – and often fun precisely on those terms. These aspects of militarised anti-militarism are often conceptualised as somewhat ironic by activists, as cheeky comments and playful inversions of the sort taken to more dramatic heights by CIRCA and the Space Hijackers. Such irony can, of course, help to disrupt militarised imaginaries; it does not, however, straightforwardly efface the desiring relationship they signal.

Jesse Crane-Seeber argues that our critiques are better served by acknowledging, rather than hiding, that part of ourselves that desires militarism. He critiques accounts of soldier mobilisation which focus exclusively on the repressive and submissive effects of power and marginalise the fact that, to put it bluntly, 'war is sexy' (2016: 41). Recognising militarism as something that is both desirable and pleasurable allows for a more nuanced account of how militarised social relations are reproduced. While Crane-Seeber's account focuses on soldiers, McSorley demonstrates that an account of militarism as an embodied and desirable social system which operates through 'shifting imbrications and tonalities of discipline and camaraderie, pleasure and pain, exhaustion and aliveness' is necessary for understanding the popularity of commercial military fitness programmes in the UK. He argues that martial bodies and symbols shape and give particular energy to 'the intensities and feelings of physical achievement and togetherness' and 'the embodied experience of collective effervescence, of however fleetingly feeling like part of something bigger than oneself' that make these programmes so popular (2016: 114). I want to suggest that a similar perspective is necessary here as well, that it is important to be open to the ways militarised desire operates in and is constitutive of anti-militarist spaces. Doing so complicates in important ways the narrative developed throughout this chapter.

This chapter has outlined forms of contestation which serve to subvert militarised forms of subjectivity and open spaces for the prefiguration of alternatives. Whilst these alternatives have been handled with some caution (as speculations and explorations, rather than grand counter-hegemonic visions), there remains the risk that they are read as movements outside of or away from militarism, as escapes or declarations of innocence. Indeed, they are often conceptualised in such terms by activists. However, an analysis rooted in prefiguration resists this move. The political force of prefigurative politics comes from the insistence on an ongoing process of creativity, experimentation and reflection, where subjects recognise the depths and complexities through which they are embedded and constituted within relations of power. On these terms, the response to prefigurative gestures which seek to displace militarised forms of subjectivity must in part be to ask in what ways these same gestures reproduce militarism. How, even (or perhaps especially) in the space of outright resistance, does militarism structure, constitute, and even thrill?

A fuller account of the militarised elements at play in my experience of the Block the Factory action (and others like it) comes when situated in the context of my wider desiring relationship with militarism. It is one that is not insubstantial. While I might prefer to trace my signal moments of political development to marches against the Iraq war in 2003 and a visit to Hiroshima in 2005, it would be dishonest to discount my obsessive watching of the TV show *24* (and accompanying enchantment with Jack Bauer's model manifestation of a highly militarised hegemonic masculinity) over that same period. I have venerated left-wing icons, such as Huey Newton and Leila Khaled, whose appeal and image is heavily militarised, and have a complicated but undeniably desiring relationship with guns.[7] In my spare time away from research, teaching and activism my primary form of recreation is playing videogames, and while I often seek out games which specifically develop critiques of militarism I have also spent many hours playing games which are unmistakably and unremittingly militarist (the *Call of Duty* series being the best-known example), gently and with unnerving ease negotiating the cognitive dissonance required to shift between anti-war critique and recreational slaughter. In these, and many other ways, I cannot otherwise but recognise myself as a militarised subject.

There is a substantial literature on the politics of militarised videogames, which sets out the role these games play in normalising and reinforcing a series of values and common-sense tropes central to the functioning of militarism – particularly those concerning the utility and moral virtue of violence, the desirability and naturalness of conflict, the necessity of certain militarised forms of masculinity, and Orientalised depictions of enemy others (Mantello 2012; Robinson 2016; Šisler 2008). Activists have also called attention to this relationship, with the Drone Wars campaign in particular focusing on how a so-called '"Playstation" mentality' renders the development of drone conflict particularly dangerous (Cole et al. 2010). This is not to say that playing videogames leads to violence in a straightforward sense; rather to suggest that their role in establishing certain norms, rationalities and desires cannot be discounted, and that when we play these games (or watch, listen, and otherwise relate to the world and cultural forces around us) our selves are neither as fixed nor as immune as we might like to think. In Michael Shapiro's terms, 'with the exception of some resistant forms, music, theatre, TV, weather forecasts, and even cereal box scripts tend to endorse prevailing power structures by helping to reproduce the beliefs and allegiances necessary for their uncontested functioning' (1992: 1; see also Weldes 2003).

The purpose of these reflections is not to generalise in straightforward terms from my own particular experience (which has as its very specific context my positionality as a white, British, middle-class man), nor to attempt or encourage any kind of redemptive confession. Even more importantly, it is not to invoke a moral hierarchy which castigates any instinct or behaviour which can be loosely connected to militarism while vaguely gesturing towards an ideal and pure anti-militarist subject. On the contrary, the point is to defer an analytic which might distinguish clearly between subjects and practices which are and are not militarised, and in the place of such heroic categories to remain open to the traces, gestures, instincts and narratives through which militarism operates and becomes both possible and normal. Recognising that we are intimately and ineradicably bound up with militarism does not render moves to prefigure alternatives futile, but it does mean that they are never complete, that there is always more work to do. The very force of prefigurative politics comes from the openness to these dynamics, and from the recognition that because they are constituted within relations of power, practices of resistance can be an important space for exposing those relations.

Such revelations can be read both as challenge and as opportunity. On the one hand, this process challenges the moral status of resistance. In acknowledging the pervasiveness of militarised social relations, resistance loses any hope of innocence, and is instead consigned to a ceaseless negotiation of complicities. On the other hand, this shift also opens up myriad spaces for action. The purpose of identifying these traces and signals and everyday social relations as situated within and productive of militarism is not to thereby declare these gestures (and indeed ourselves as subjects) as *bad*, but to recognise the scale and scope of political work that is needed. Reflecting on the nature of ethical judgement, Foucault makes a similar point when he says:

> my point is not that everything is bad, but that everything is dangerous, which is not exactly the same as bad. If everything is dangerous, then we always have something to do. So my position leads not to apathy but to a hyper- and pessimistic activism. (Foucault 1997: 253)

While the route into this discussion has been personal, the work of negotiating these dynamics need not be individualised. A major argument of the next chapter is that many anti-militarist practices and spaces are constituted precisely in order to facilitate these processes. For now, one illustrative example of the collective negotiation of militarised desire comes from VfP, several of whom in 2015 gathered outside Downing Street and publicly threw away their service medals. Part of their aim in doing so was public – to protest against ongoing wars and to challenge established discourses about the heroic status of soldiers. But just as significant was a more private aim. As one member explained during a public talk, whilst in many ways he had rejected and turned against the wars in which he had fought, he also recognised that deeply ingrained military values concerning heroism, masculinity and violence remained part of who he is, and that symbols such as medals play an important role in validating and preserving those values. Their public discarding constitutes one part of contending with this militarised desire.[8]

*

This chapter has introduced a series of anti-militarist practices which call forth the imagination and prefiguration of subjects against-and-beyond the terms of militarism. They have been introduced not as alternatives in any concrete or absolute sense, but as experiences and experiments which might, in margins and interstitial spaces, gesture towards the possibility of alternative ways of being, relating and contesting. They signify refusals of the roles (as students, shoppers, soldiers, or simply as subjects of particular systems of rationality) imposed upon us and (re)performed by us as subjects of militarism, and as a series of affirmations that things could be otherwise (even though those resisting might not exactly be sure how). We see this both in the content of anti-militarist discourse and in the particular tactics through which they assert themselves. However, such practices cannot be treated in isolation, as abstracted and individualised whispers of possibility. They are made possible and produced within the broader environment of anti-militarist organising, the ongoing series of debates, tensions and sensibilities through which anti-militarist communities are constituted. These processes, and their relation to prefiguration and militarised forms of subjectivity, are the subject of the next chapter.

Notes

1. Heckler & Koch are a German small arms manufacturer.
2. A personal favourite, from a chemistry-themed protest outside the Science Museum while the Museum hosted a reception for arms dealers: 'We'll be here until the arms dealers argon.'
3. The BAE Systems AGM is regularly reduced to pantomime. In previous years activists have dressed as cheerleaders and danced on chairs, sung specially amended songs ('What Shall We Do with BAE Systems Early in the Morning?!'), whistled, jeered, and played bingo during the chairman's speech (interjecting with 'PHWOOOAAARRR' each time he mentioned the company's most recent buzzword, 'Total Performance'). At the 2014 meeting, when the chairman angrily chastised the audience by complaining that 'this pantomime act isn't very funny', they naturally replied, 'Oh yes it is!'
4. The campaign was developed by the artist Darren Cullen.
5. The campaign is drawing on a report by ForcesWatch (Gee and Goodman 2013).
6. Read in this way, the logic (and attendant critique) here is not dissimilar to the infamous anti-Vietnam war, anti-draft poster of 1968, which featured Joan Baez alongside two of her sisters, and read 'GIRLS SAY YES to boys who say NO'.

7. In 2009 some friends and I bought eight plastic AK-47 machine guns to use as props on actions, the idea being that they would be a good visual cue. We had to stop using them after we proved incapable of not descending into ridiculous war games whenever we used them (spurred on by the satisfying ra-ta-ta-ta-ta sound they made when the trigger was pulled), ruining whatever tableau we were trying to create.
8. On the practice of self-demilitarisation by US veterans, see Schrader (2017).

CHAPTER 7

Diversity

The work of contesting militarised social relations and subject positions, and of prefiguring alternative modes of relation, contestation and subjectivity, does not only take place in the more public spaces explored in the previous chapter. It can be found throughout anti-militarist organising. This chapter uses a prefigurative lens to consider the organisational principles of British anti-militarism, demonstrating how the politics of resistance, militarism and militarised subjectivity are negotiated in less visible ways by anti-militarists.

Prefiguration is most frequently articulated in terms of the democratic, non-hierarchical and consensus-based qualities and aspirations of movements. While those features are undoubtedly important, they have also received substantial attention both with respect to anti-militarist movements and more widely, such that prefiguration is often conceptualised almost exclusively with reference to those features. My focus therefore lies elsewhere. In this chapter I look at how anti-militarists negotiate questions of strategy and politics, exploring tensions and debates concerning appropriate tactics, (non)violence, and the role of whiteness. I argue that attention to prefiguration alerts us to how the movement subverts militarised forms of organisation, helpfully situates debates amongst anti-militarists about the nature of militarism and resistance, and provides avenues to think critically about the limits of anti-militarist practice. Through these arguments we see prefiguration not as the straightforward manifestation of a utopic future, but as the work of building movements and social relations which are particular to and sensitive to their context even as they imagine and call for new pathways.

The first part of the chapter explores the concept of 'diversity of tactics'. The idea that social movements should embrace a diversity of tactics – that they should avoid establishing particular tactics and strategies as axiomatically superior and should seek to work with those using different tactics – has become integral to the constitution of many radical movements in the post-Seattle era, including much of British anti-militarism. While the reasons for this are largely pragmatic, insofar as the principle permits the growth of large and diverse coalitions, it also has important prefigurative dimensions, deferring centralised and hierarchical forms of organising and challenging the notion that effective movements should be gathered and disciplined in accordance with the general strategic imperative. On such terms, I suggest that diversity of tactics can be understood as subverting militarised forms of organisation. I establish the role that diversity of tactics plays in the contemporary movement and show how the principle does not simply involve a disinterested permissiveness, instead entailing active and continual work on the part of activists to cultivate a certain ethos, to avoid establishing particular standards of legitimacy, and to negotiate the inevitable limits and contradictions which arise. These negotiations draw activists to confront central questions about both the ethics and politics of resistance and the nature of militarism itself.

Nowhere are these negotiations more contested than around questions of violence, nonviolence and the status of pacifism within the movement. It is here that the principle of diversity of tactics most often meets its limits, and where we see some of the most important debates amongst anti-militarists. For some, pacifism and nonviolence should be the guiding principles of anti-militarism, such that their relationship is almost tautological, whereas for others pacifism and the insistence on nonviolence can themselves function as disciplining and even militarising forces. The second part of the chapter looks at how anti-militarists navigate these tensions. I argue that the different positions with respect to pacifism and nonviolence reveal contrasting understandings of both militarism and prefiguration within the movement, and show how the diversity of tactics principle makes living with these contrasts possible (while perhaps also closing down debate). I also argue that, while anti-militarist politics are most commonly associated with pacifism and nonviolence, it is important to make space for a conception of prefigurative anti-militarism that remains critical of these principles.

The first two sections show how the movement operates in an inclusive manner while thinking critically about its boundaries. However, it is also imperative to think about the boundary-producing performances that circumscribe this diversity. In the last part of the chapter I therefore look at how racialised processes of exclusion operate within the movement. The groups studied in this book are largely composed of white activists, and I suggest two ways of reading this whiteness. The first is to recognise how the kinds of activism and solidarity practised in the movement are dependent upon (and reproduce) white privilege. The second is to highlight the normative whiteness shaping how militarism (and anti-militarism) are conceptualised within the movement. I argue that these issues mean that the movement struggles to account for the entanglement of racism and militarism, and point towards some attempts to negotiate these dynamics.

Diversity of Tactics

'Diversity of tactics' has become a key organising principle for many radical groups over the past twenty years. Its central feature is 'an ethic of respect for, an acceptance of, the tactical choices of other activists' (Conway 2003: 511). Whilst the ethos has historical precedent, contemporary articulations developed through the large alter-globalisation mobilisations at the beginning of the twenty-first century. As Gordon shows, it was infighting over the issue of violence in the 'movement of movements' which led to calls for a diversity of tactics:

> many NGO figureheads and communist spokespeople chimed in, complaining that the anarchists were 'distorting the message of the protests'. As a result, a breach of solidarity was perceived in many grassroots and direct-action groups. Especially after Genoa, many activists who would

not normally condone violence saw the stock denunciations of the anarchists as an expression of gross insensitivity and lack of solidarity with hundreds of traumatised and imprisoned activists, playing along with the G8 leaders' and corporate media's obvious divide-and-conquer strategy of separating 'good protesters' from 'bad protesters'. As a result, many grassroots activists now began refusing to denounce anarchist violence, eroding the position of the ethos of non-violence in their discourses. This was replaced by the call for diversity of tactics – a measure taken in order to move beyond seemingly irreconcilable debates and towards cohesion and solidarity in the horizontally organised, direct-action end of the alternative globalisation movement, which now felt abandoned and isolated. (Gordon 2007: 84)

Graeber notes that, following the 1999 protests against the World Trade Organization in Seattle, some activists boasted at having pointed out Black Bloc activists to the police for arrest, and others 'accused the Black Bloc of violating solidarity by refusing to take part in meetings or abide by the agreed-on code of conduct' (a code of conduct which Black Bloc activists themselves had not agreed upon) (2009: 293). In this tense and divisive context, diversity of tactics stood as the condition of possibility of a 'movement' (however ambiguous) which did not either turn against itself or enforce totalising standards on action.

The diversity of tactics principle seeks to establish terms by which individuals and groups can take action in accordance with their own needs, desires and limitations while remaining in solidarity with those who favour other approaches. While neither uncontroversial nor unproblematic, it is an important example of prefigurative politics, demonstrating a commitment to forms of political organisation which do not impose totalising or hegemonic standards of legitimacy, and which do not enforce conformity in the name of 'The Cause' (Maeckelbergh 2011: 11–13). It is emblematic of the anti-strategic ethos of direct action outlined in Chapter 1, maintaining a tension between the need for collective plans and the refusal to determine a general strategic imperative. I would cautiously suggest that diversity of tactics can be read as a form of *anti-militarist* prefiguration, insofar as it displaces certain principles – centralisation, hierarchy, the dominance of strategy – through which movements become militarised. It is through such a lens that Hardt and Negri read the subversive nature of the postmodern multitude: 'The party, the people's army, the modern guerrilla force all appear bankrupt from their perspective because of the tendency of these structures to impose unity, to deny their differences and subordinate them to the interests of others' (2004: 86).

The work of affirming the place for a diversity of tactics involves building movements where participants retain autonomy within the collective space. This sensibility forms part of a broader trend in contemporary social movements towards a pluralist orientation 'which disemphasises unity of analysis and vision in favour of multiplicity and experimentation' (Gordon 2007: 42). This refusal to set prior determinations on what subjects in-and-of resistance must 'be' is, clearly, a limited affair: resistance consists precisely in the critique of particular subjectivities and practices, and a prefigurative imaginary insists that such critique is directed inwards. Furthermore, setting the boundaries of resistance and solidarity, determining who is 'in' and who is 'out', is itself an indefinite project which should be subject to ongoing processes of critique. It is in this tension, between the affirmations of diversity and the importance of ongoing critique, that a second prefigurative dimension of a diversity of tactics emerges; a conception of radical subjectivity which remains mobile, multiple and critical, but which nonetheless continues to form chains of solidarity and affinity, to explore and experiment with political connections. This second point will be discussed more extensively in the book's Conclusion. Here, I focus on drawing out the ambiguous attempts to affirm diversity of tactics amongst anti-militarists.

There are obviously challenging elements involved in affirming a diversity of tactics. Many feel uncomfortable at the prospect of enacting solidarities with those employing tactics with which they disagree (whether strategically, tactically, or ethically), and while friendly critique is not necessarily shut down, silent complicities can emerge. Similarly, few would accept the logic that *any* action undertaken against a common opponent is to be affirmed. In this sense, there is always a limit to solidarity and diversity, a negotiation at the margins, and a struggle to take account of the inside(s). The discussions below show some of the processes through which this is worked out amongst anti-militarists. While the examples are sometimes awkward and fractious, this is not so much a sign of failure than a taking seriously the contradictory but crucial imperatives at play.

This book has already examined a wide variety of anti-militarist tactics, which range from more to less disruptive, legal and spectacular. Amongst anti-militarists significant attempts are made to generate common narratives while making space for that variety, without overly privileging particular approaches. Throughout its campaign Smash EDO emphasised the importance of a 'toolbox of tactics', which included those examples already discussed alongside weekly noise demonstrations outside the factory, street theatre, readings of the names of the dead, and phone blockades (*On the Verge* 2008). The diversity of tactics ethos could also be found in the principles of the Anti-Militarist Network (AMN), an association which was active between 2008 and 2012 and included Target Brimar, Disarm DSEI, Smash EDO, and Shut Down Heckler & Koch. The AMN was based around four principles:

- The network organises along the principles of autonomy and non-hierarchy
- We embrace a diversity of tactics
- We will not publicly condemn other people's actions
- We have a respect for life. (Anti-Militarist Network 2008)[1]

Particularly significant in these principles was the agreement to refrain from publicly condemning one another's actions, and the absence of a commitment to nonviolence. The network, comprised of groups who 'believe in the necessity of direct action' in the terms of one interviewee, did not itself organise actions (thereby avoiding the need to decide on particular tactics), instead serving to provide a basis for mutual solidarity and support amongst its constituent parts (Interview F).

The most significant contemporary example of diversity of tactics can be found in the STAF coalition. The coalition includes CAAT, Disarm DSEI, War on Want, London Catholic Worker, Trident Ploughshares, East London Against Arms Fairs, the Student Christian Network and more, alongside individual members, all of whom have committed to working together along the principles of diversity of tactics. In the coalition, CAAT are undoubtedly the dominant group in terms of resource commitment; this is significant, as CAAT's facilitation of a diverse range of resistances is a central part of its action and ethos. Indeed, the theme of its 2010 National Gathering was 'Diversity of Action to End the Arms Trade'.

The STAF coalition was established in 2011 to try to bring together what was then a highly polarised movement, with little trust or communication between groups like Smash EDO and Disarm DSEI, and more pacifist, faith-based and anti-nuclear groups. One organiser recounted the opening steps of the coalition:

> From the beginning we agreed to disagree on tactics. And that's because people knew enough about each other and themselves to know that they were never going to convince [each] other . . . you know, the pacifists are not going to stop being pacifists and the people who believe that all tactics are valid, including violence, weren't going to change . . . So we agree to not have a movement spokesperson: it was very much 'we're working together with a specific aim of stopping this arms fair and that's our base agreement' . . . We'd never planned for it to be a long-term coalition or campaign . . . [but] I think people felt benefits from it straight away, we felt stronger. (Interview K)

As I explore further below, the STAF coalition's commitment to diversity of tactics was not without its difficulties. However, the coalition has also been remarkably effective. It has created a space through which groups using a range of different tactics can work together, and its successes are reflected in the fact that the scale of action opposing the arms fair increased dramatically from 2009 to 2017, as did the number of groups who became involved. While some have cautioned that diversity of tactics risks depressing genuine diversity and the space for coalitional politics (Conway 2003), STAF has provided a powerful example to the contrary.

The emergence of the ethos of diversity in the STAF coalition can perhaps be best demonstrated with reference to a particular moment, at a STAF gathering in June 2011. It was the first major event for the coalition, organised to provide spaces for activists to meet and prepare for DSEI 2011. The introduction to the one-day event was familiar in its affirmation of difference and diversity; participants were encouraged to be mindful of their privilege and reminded not to assume the gender identity of other attendees, and spaces were made available for activists to run their own sessions. It was in this context that the first event of the day was introduced, a 'spectrum line' exercise designed to allow people to meet other like-minded activists (with whom they might then plan actions). Spectrum lines are a common feature of activist workshops, helping to generate conversations about particular issues. In response to a question or statement, participants are invited to position themselves on an imaginary line (or grid) on the floor, and to explain their stance. For example, at the Peace News Summer Gathering in 2011, a spectrum exercise asked us to stand between two points depending on whether participants had a positive or negative reaction to the term 'hero'. Rarely do people stand at either extreme, and people tend to move around as they hear others speak. It is, at its best, an exercise in fluidity, listening, and appreciating the range of viewpoints held by those bound more or less tightly by a sense of common purpose.

The particular spectrum line under discussion here focused on the tactical preferences of participants. Those running the session first asked whether or not activists would or would not be prepared to lock themselves to a bus full of arms dealers (to stop them reaching the arms fair, an action which took place during DSEI 2007). We began to move around the room, with a sizeable portion of the group moving towards the 'yes' end. However, before anyone began discussing the relative merits of different positions, a number of people began to voice discomfort. To the agreement of most if not all of those present, it was argued that the exercise was unnecessarily divisive, and that it risked establishing a hierarchy of action and a culture of machismo as participants felt compelled to affirm the most dramatic and spectacular tactics. People were keen to avoid beginning the day with the assertion that some activists are more valuable or impressive than others. One argued that those people holding a banner, talking to members of the public, taking pictures and handing out leaflets would be just as fundamental to the overall coherence of the action as those lying under the bus, and that to divide those involved misses what is valuable about a diverse approach to political action. This particular intervention drew almost unanimous support, challenging what one interviewee referred to as 'front-line fetishism' (Interview B). It is perhaps significant that the calls to abandon this exercise on these grounds came largely from those who had gravitated towards the 'yes' end of the room.

We cautiously agreed to try one more question. This time, we were asked to position ourselves in relation to our opinions about the value of lobbying politicians. Most clustered towards the 'negative' end of the room, while around a third dispersed along the line, with only a few standing at the extreme 'positive' end. However, when asked why they were so sceptical, all those standing at the negative end refused to give specific answers beyond the fact that it wasn't 'for them', insisting that their position did not mean that they disrespected the choices of those who do find value in lobbying. The exercise was productively disrupted as participants insisted on affirming the space for diversity as a priority ahead of particular tactical choices and debates. This does not mean that debates about the usefulness of differing tactics did not take place during the day, but rather, that they occurred within a context which had been shaped through the principles of diversity.

This openness was not performed or affirmed easily. Discussing the spectrum exercise with a group of participants after the event, most acknowledged struggling with, on the one hand, resisting the public valorisation of particular forms of action and, on the other, holding strong opinions about different tactics. In that same conversation, participants referred to attempts to 'raise' their own consciousness, before quickly taking back their words and looking for ways of expressing their political journeys which did not place them in a hierarchy above others (Interview D). This tension, between seeking change, of the self and beyond, and seeking to guard against the exclusions, hierarchies and suspension of self-critique which can result from secure conceptions of the progressive subject, is a common one. It might be seen as creative experience, where resistance is situated within a contested but sincere desire to create non-hierarchical and non-hegemonic relationships. That one of the first acts of a gathering organised to coordinate resistance was to deconstruct its own space and the possible exclusionary dynamics contained therein showcases the prefigurative nature of diversity of tactics.

Part of the tensions which define the space within which a diversity of tactics is negotiated concerns debates about what, for activists, constitutes 'the political'. I have already shown that activists work with conceptions of politics which encompass a wide and unlikely array of practices and spaces. However, within this broadness there is a tendency to reproduce a public/private distinction which might be subject to critique. Eleanor Wilkinson's reflections on the place of queer politics within activist groups help to develop this point. She notes how activist approaches to queer politics often reflect liberal discourses of tolerance; 'these groups felt that they were being inclusive, and therefore there was no need to take the discussions of these issues any further' (2009: 39). She cites one interviewee describing their experience of a group conversation about radical sex:

> when discussing queer politics the issue of radical celibacy came up. One person was like 'I don't get [celibacy,] I mean if not having sex was going to free Tibet then I'd stop having sex, but it's not, so I don't see the point.' Pretty much everyone in the group agreed with him ... The dominant line is like, why does it matter who you fuck, or who you're sleeping with ... and yeah, I get this, and I even support this view ... but at the same time, maybe I actually think it does matter y'know? (Wilkinson 2009: 39)

We might take this beyond questions of queer politics specifically and interpret Wilkinson as identifying a private/public distinction made by activists whereby 'private' political performances are subordinated to 'public' ones.

An argument which developed during the group interview referenced above demonstrates how these logics are manifested (and resisted). One participant was expressing his admiration for Catholic Worker activists in the US who routinely make the 'sacrifice' of spending large stretches of time – up to twenty years – in jail for anti-militarist activities (primarily property damage). Another expressed discomfort at the tendency to pedestalise such activities, not because they are not important, but because the valorisation (and even mythologisation) of those sacrifices can tend to marginalise subtler and more everyday political practices, while privileging particular aggregations of arrest counts, bruises and broken windows. Her specific concern was the ways in which the responsibilities and politics of parenthood and child-rearing are under-recognised in anti-militarist contexts, the focus on the heroic and spectacular serving to discipline anti-militarism and subordinate more private performances. The argument, which continued for some time, was resolved when those involved agreed that particular people and actions can be respected without necessarily marginalising other forms of intervention, but, crucially, with the (by then generally agreed) caveat that more domestic and feminised roles are severely under-respected in anti-militarist politics. Encounters like this demonstrate how public/private logics can operate to complicate the negotiation of a diversity of tactics, alongside the affirmative (rather than merely permissive) work involved in maintaining the principle.

Inevitably, diversity of tactics meets its limits. Whilst activists may go to great lengths to work in coalitions across lines of difference, most people have their red lines. As one activist put it,

> diversity of tactics cannot mean that all tactics are OK. You know, if I was to murder the chair of BAE Systems, that would not be OK, and 99 per cent (I hope well over 99 per cent) of the peace movement would agree that it was not OK and that diversity of tactics was not infinite. So once you establish the principle that it's not infinite and there are some things that are not morally OK, then it's a matter of marking out where the boundaries are, and that can be quite difficult. (Interview M)

Such negotiations can indeed be difficult. This is not only because finding common ground is highly challenging, but because it is through the acts of deciding where the boundaries are, and how the boundaries might be negotiated and policed, that the ethical, political and strategic contours of the movement are constituted. These boundaries often remain implicit; however, when they come to the fore, they tend to shed light on the politics of the movement and its practices. Nowhere is this more apparent than where the politics of pacifism and nonviolence are concerned.

Violence and Nonviolence

It is through difficult debates about the place (and definition) of violence that diversity of tactics has become central, but remained controversial, in contemporary anti-militarism. While the distinction is a little crude, there is something of a divide between individuals and groups for whom pacifism and/or a commitment to nonviolent activism is a defining principle of their anti-militarism, and those for whom those principles should be treated with more caution. In this section I look at how this divide is manifested, and consider the particular arguments advanced from various perspectives. Through these debates we see both the complex work involved in maintaining the diversity of tactics principle, and important differences in the understandings of militarism and prefiguration operating within the movement.

Much of anti-militarism activism, historically and contemporarily, is signified precisely and principally through its opposition to the use of violence, its defence of pacifism, and its centring of nonviolent resistance.[2] The latter of these guides large swathes of British anti-militarism. CAAT, founded on the principle of nonviolence, requires that any direct action associated with it adheres to a series of nonviolent action guidelines. The Plowshares movement is emphatic about its commitment to nonviolence, the newspaper *Peace News* has the slogan 'For Nonviolent Revolution' written on its logo, the PPU explicitly commits to 'active nonviolence' as a means for resisting war, and many other groups and individuals operate with 'nonviolence' as a non-negotiable component of their activism.

The motivations behind this commitment to nonviolence vary. Many activists, particularly those associated with religious anti-militarist organisations such as the Quakers, Catholic Workers, and Plowshares communities, centre a moral commitment to nonviolence (Christoyannopoulos 2011: 162–4). For others, nonviolence is justified on more tactical grounds, through the understanding that violent action is politically and strategically counterproductive, and that nonviolence offers more scope for building coalitions and evoking moral sentiment (Chenoweth and Stephan 2011; Ğahānbiglū 2014: 88–111; Schell 2004; Sharp 2005). Both principled and pragmatic approaches (and in reality, most find themselves working with some combination) are often articulated in terms of prefiguration.[3] If the goal is a world without violence, and if we create that world through the methods we use to fight for it, then experimenting with and learning about nonviolence is imperative (Gillan et al. 2008: 95; see also Vinthagen 2015: 285–98).

A prefigurative account of nonviolence recognises that the principle is more than mere proscription, and that its real value lies in the active and creative interpretations of nonviolence developed by activists. In response to suggestions that nonviolence might be associated with passivity (as has been the case with pacifism), supporters insist otherwise. Many activists have told me that they see themselves as mobilising '*active* nonviolence', a modification mobilised to emphasise the affirmative politics contained therein. The Feminism and Nonviolence Study Group's pamphlet develops this point further, arguing that nonviolence 'is much more than simply an absence of violence. It is both a principle and a technique, a set of ideas about how life should be lived and a strategy for social change' (1983: 28).

In refusing to respond to violence with more violence, nonviolence exhibits practices that align with the politics of vulnerability discussed in the previous chapter:

> nonviolence means a willingness to take personal risks and, at times, to bear suffering without retaliation ... Nonviolence does not say that nobody gets hurt, that violence won't be meted out to us, nor that the last vestiges of institutionalised violence are going to be given up without a fight. But it *does* say that real lasting changes can be made in this way, and that in the long term fewer people, and other forms of life, will be destroyed. (Feminism and Nonviolence Study Group 1983: 29; original emphasis)

As she discusses the history of the nonviolent conscientious objector movement War Resisters' International (WRI), Cockburn writes that '[t]o some [nonviolence] might suggest passivity, but this was far from WRI's meaning. From the start they interpreted nonviolence as an energetic, risk-taking and creative process: *direct action for change*' (2012: 48; original emphasis). For WRI, nonviolence was and is not so much a constraint as a limit-condition through which they explore political possibilities beyond the terms of militarism. Importantly, this is enacted without collapsing into simplistic or dogmatic conceptions of nonviolence, or refusing to form connections with those who do not share the same position (2012: 63–5). Nonviolence can therefore be understood as a creative and prefigurative principle, as an affirmation of the desire to recognise the proximity and even potentially the utility of violence to resistance, but nonetheless to focus on alternative practices of contestation.

While many anti-militarists centre nonviolence, others are considerably more sceptical. Groups including Smash EDO and Disarm DSEI, and coalitions like the AMN and STAF, have conspicuously avoided making commitments to nonviolence. The reasons that underpin this scepticism have less to do with any particular commitment *to* the use of violence than with concerns about the hegemonising implications which often accompany declarations of nonviolence. In a workshop on direct action skills, one member of Disarm DSEI explained that the group refuses to affirm a principle of nonviolence not because they believe in the necessity of violence, but 'because it's up to individuals to decide what is appropriate' in given circumstances. There is a sense that establishing clear boundaries between legitimate and illegitimate, violent and nonviolent protest are in danger of disciplining movements in uncomfortable ways, facilitating the division and subsequent repression of activists.

This critique is often expressed through the fear that an absolute insistence on nonviolence can serve to inhibit the building of relationships of solidarity, in ways which are inattentive to the relatively privileged position in which many British anti-militarists find themselves. As one activist stated, 'who am I to sit in London saying I'm a pacifist and you should never take up arms? Because I've never been in a situation where I might need to, and so I'm not going to judge people who take up arms' (Interview K). Activists often point out that making sweeping statements about what kinds of resistance are to be considered legitimate and illegitimate is unlikely to affect what kinds of action people take, but will have a major effect on the kinds of networks, communities and solidarities which can be formed. To give one small example of the gestures they are concerned about, at a meeting to discuss how to respond to the 2011 uprisings in the Middle East and North Africa, and in particular how to build solidarity with Bahraini communities resisting their British-armed government, one activist urged caution because 'many of these [Bahraini] groups haven't committed to nonviolence'. Closer to home, a number of interviewees cited examples of pacifist organisations collaborating with the police to identify activists who had engaged in what they saw to be violent action. In both of these cases, the principle of nonviolence has been interpreted in ways which shape the kinds of solidarities and coalitions that can be built.

These debates are further complicated by the differences between what various activists recognise as violence. For some anti-militarists, damage to property falls within the rubric of violence – a conception which Anna Stavrianakis notes is especially common amongst NGOs, and which she criticises for reproducing capitalist social relations (2010: 175–6; see also Cockburn 2012: 248–9). However, for most anti-militarists who engage in some form of direct action, damage to property is not recognised as a form of violence.[4] A more common point of tension concerns conduct during encounters with the police and security guards. Whilst some who centre nonviolence insist that all measures should be taken to avoid physical confrontation, others are happy to stand their ground, link arms with other activists and all but wrestle with the police, with the caveat that they would not actively strike out and kick or hit back.

Beyond those more corporeal issues are questions of structural violence (Farmer 1996; Galtung 1969; Tilly 2010). One of the arguments raised by those who are critical of centring nonviolence is that doing so tends to prioritise physical over systemic violence, focusing attention on relatively inconsequential issues such as whether someone kicks back when facing police aggression, and overlooking or normalising less visible forms of violence. It was on those terms that Frantz Fanon critiqued the idea of nonviolence, as a position that obscured the violence inherent to the colonial condition (2004: 23–4). As one activist argues,

> sometimes people can be really down on different kinds of direct action, or have a very narrow definition of violence which includes shouting,

predominantly shouting at the cops, and maybe property damage, and say that if you do those things you're totally unacceptable. Whereas I've seen much more violent things happen in meetings when someone's been shut down or someone's said something really racist . . . Like, there have been tears in the movement where people have dobbed people into the cops . . . collaborating with an institution and reinscribing its power and getting activists in trouble with the state: fuck that, that is so bad. (Interview N)

The point here is that the insistence on nonviolence, rather than challenging or limiting violence, can have the effect of obscuring more subtle and systemic forms – or in the case of turning people over to the state, actively reinforcing them.

It is perhaps counter-intuitive to outline a prefigurative anti-militarist politics which refuses to centre nonviolence and which remains actively suspicious of pacifism. If, as many have argued, the idea that violence is both normal and effective is an integral component of militarism, then the formation of political communities and styles of contestation that challenge this principle is crucial for anti-militarists. However, there are good prefigurative reasons for a critical position on nonviolence. The first of these is that the articulation of universal standards for 'legitimate' resistance is likely to imply the disciplining, marginalisation and even exclusion of those who fail to fit these standards. As Peter Gelderloos argues, this hegemonising move has certain patriarchal and racist dimensions, insofar as it tacitly places a far greater burden of expectation and restraint on those for whom violence is an inescapable feature of life (Gelderloos 2007). Similar arguments were made by Wilmette Brown in her classic pamphlet on black women in the peace movement:

> As long as Black people are denied self-determination, reliable allies, and the resources to liberate ourselves, we are forced to resort to our power to destroy – as the only power we have, and as the only way to get more power. In that context our violence is always in self-defence, and white people who have more power than we do, counselling us against violence, place themselves in the indefensible position of presuming to choose our weapons for us. (Brown 1990: 22–3)[5]

These concerns are compounded when we consider the ambiguities about what is to be considered violence. As the disagreements about whether or not property damage is to be considered violence make clear, the categorisation of violence and nonviolence, and the identification of the line between the two, is a highly political question. What for some might be an experience of peacefulness may simultaneously, and very possibly even parasitically, be one of violence and dispossession for others. Claims about violence import assumptions about subjecthood, harm, power, consent and legitimacy, which are themselves always contingent and political positions. More importantly for the discussion here is how that act of distinguishing violence from nonviolence, and thus designating certain actions and actors as violent, places the latter within a discursive framework that invites particular (and potentially violent) responses. It is on these terms that the CrimethInc collective opposes the centring of nonviolence:

> The discourse of violence and nonviolence is attractive above all because it offers an easy way to claim the higher moral ground. This makes it seductive both for criticizing the state and for competing against other activists for influence. But in a hierarchical society, gaining the *higher ground* often reinforces hierarchy itself. (CrimethInc 2012; original emphasis)

They continue, arguing that:

> [l]egitimacy is one of the currencies that are unequally distributed in our society, through which its disparities are maintained. Defining people or actions as violent is a way of excluding them from legitimate discourse, of silencing and shutting out. This parallels and reinforces other forms of marginalization: a wealthy white person can act 'nonviolently' in ways that would be seen as violent were a poor person of color to do the same thing. In an unequal society, the defining of 'violence' is no more neutral than any other tool.
>
> Defining people or actions as violent also has immediate consequences: it justifies the use of force against them. This has been an essential step in practically every campaign targeting communities of color, protest movements, and others on the wrong side of capitalism. If you've attended enough mobilizations, you know that it's often possible to anticipate

exactly how much violence the police will use against a demonstration by the way the story is presented on the news the night before. In this regard, pundits and even rival organizers can participate in *policing* alongside the police, determining who is a legitimate target by the way they frame the narrative. (CrimethInc 2012; original emphasis)

Such arguments sidestep debates about the ethics or pragmatics of violence and nonviolence in order to focus on the performative effects of claims about the ethics or pragmatics of violence and nonviolence. They make a powerful case to consider the division and repression which are risked when centring and policing that distinction.

It is important to view these arguments in prefigurative terms, as critiques which are attentive both to the kinds of solidarity and community that are developed in the process of radical action, and to how these modes of being and relating are produced within, and are potentially both constitutive and disruptive of, militarised social relations. While those who centre nonviolence are perhaps proceeding with a more straightforward understanding of prefiguration, insofar as they work to generate and explore forms of subjectivity and rationality which (seek to) set themselves apart from violence, these more sceptical positions also have a strong claim. They are still looking to engender and experiment with forms of organisation that subvert violent social relations, but they are doing so in a manner which recognises that the particular nature and relations of violence cannot be determined prior to the specific social and political context.

Furthermore, these positions recognise that militarism operates not only through the legitimisation and celebration of violence, but also through particular designations of the boundary between and nature of violence and nonviolence. The capacity to represent crippling sanctions, exploitative trade conditions, permanent military bases, and militarised police forces as sources of peace or conditions of not-violence, while determining a host of racialised and resistant Others as always already violent (and so subject to 'nonviolent' or legitimately violent responses), is central to the legitimacy of contemporary Western militarism (Losurdo 2010). That which is easily and intuitively recognised as violence and nonviolence is both a political and militarised phenomenon. Those who centre nonviolence insist that they are working to invert or disrupt those discourses; the argument of the critics is that dogmatic insistences on nonviolence are more likely to solidify than to subvert.

Whilst these arguments are clearly directed in opposition to certain forms of pacifism and nonviolence, they are also largely compatible with others. For instance, Kimberly Hutchings's account of feminist pacifism as an ethico-political project begins from the premise that we cannot easily disentangle ourselves from violence, and that political practices which may on the surface look nonviolent may actively contribute to the reproduction of violence and harm.[6] As such, she calls for an understanding of pacifism and nonviolence which 'does not claim the high ground of morality but rather identifies morality with the low ground of our mutual implication in a world of violence and injustice' (2018: 189). Elsewhere, with Elizabeth Frazer, Hutchings makes this point with reference to the anti-war nonviolent feminism of Sara Ruddick. Ruddick refused to call herself a pacifist, seeking to avoid general and abstract principles (whether about the utility or harm of violence), but still centred nonviolence. However, her commitment to nonviolence was neither legislative nor strategic, but regulative, an ethos which enlivened any particular analysis. Questions about what constituted violence and what responses might be legitimate cannot be decided in advance, but depend on context and judgement: 'the meaning of violence is not given simply by the infliction of pain and injury but also by the relations of power into which inflictions of pain and injury are introduced' (Frazer and Hutchings 2014a: 120). This understanding of nonviolence (and pacifism) is less susceptible to the critiques set out here, precisely because it positions violence and nonviolence as contingent and avoids making sweeping and universalising claims about legitimacy.

As might be expected, different positions on the question of (non)violence have generated tensions amongst anti-militarists. Founding discussions for the AMN were stalled because some groups, principally Trident Ploughshares, did not want to be part of a coalition which did not have nonviolence as one of its core principles, whereas others, principally Disarm DSEI, insisted against this. Eventually, the principle of 'respect for life' was adopted, a 'political fudge' in the terms of my interviewee, which allowed some passage through these issues. Nonetheless, Trident Ploughshares did not become full members of the network. More significantly, as a means by which to deal with this impasse, it was agreed that the AMN would operate as a network rather than a coalition. Practically, this meant that it would not itself organise events, but would facilitate communication, solidarity and affinities amongst the constituent groups and individuals (Interview F). The principle that constituent groups would not publicly criticise one another was also adopted, in order to avoid the forms of division seen in the alter-globalisation movement. Despite these manoeuvres, and in large part because of these foundational issues around the question of nonviolence, the AMN struggled to develop as a network.

It is also possible to find less compromising examples of these tensions. Kate Hudson, chair of CND, publicly denounced Black Bloc activists following a demonstration in Strasbourg, stating that '[t]hese people are no part of our movement. They are an obstacle to effective resistance and must be isolated and recognized for what they are: wreckers whose actions turned the mass of people against our campaigns' (cited in Cockburn 2012: 147). Cockburn herself suggests that anti-pacifist activists should not even be considered to be part of the anti-militarist movement, referring to them as 'supposed allies' and positing (without evidence) that Black Bloc activists 'that join mobilizations of anti-war, anti-militarist and peace movements do not have a particular loyalty or commitment to them' (2012: 259, 249). Such frustrations are common on a more everyday level. One activist within STAF referred to another as a 'terrorist' for suggesting a strategy for resisting DSEI which prioritised mounting a 'credible threat of disruption', while others privately bemoan 'holier than thou' pacifist tendencies which they see as derailing plans, coalitions and solidarities. The question of nonviolence thus stands as a significant fault-line within anti-militarist activism.

However, that nonviolence is a fault-line does not entail the constant opening up of cracks or the impossibility of functioning coalitions. While it has at times taken some care and negotiation, and whilst some members would prefer that a commitment to nonviolence formed part of its principles, the STAF coalition has flourished. There are several reasons for this. The first is that people's individual positions are rarely as straightforward or absolute as they might appear. One question I often asked during interviews was 'Are you a pacifist?', and while interviewees generally responded with arguments (of the sort explored here) either championing pacifism and nonviolence or explaining their misgivings, it was not uncommon for people to go through a small existential crisis prior to their more developed answer:

> Um, I have no idea. I don't feel like I'm in a position to make a judgement on that. Um, I think I grew up assuming I was because that's what my family probably are. I don't know actually, I should probably ask them, but I think definitely my dad would call himself a pacifist. Um, I don't really like it as a label. (Interview K)

This is hardly surprising. The question packages together issues of personal and political identity, conceptions of violence, militarism and peace, and theories of political change, not to mention ethical frameworks. While there is no shortage of statements implying certainty on these topics, it would be mistaken to overlook the fact that many activists – as with most people – experience considerable uncertainty around these topics.

While I have drawn on some uncompromising quotations, many who centre nonviolence make clear both that they are not in a position to make universal judgements and that nonviolence should not be the (sole) factor which determines with whom solidarity relationships might be formed:

> if your village is attacked by ISIS in Iraq and you gang up and get the few guns you've got together and fight them as they come, I'm not saying that I condone that but I don't think I'm in any position to condemn that. (Interview M)

> the classical peace movement completely shoots itself in the foot with an insistence on essentially ignoring a diversity of tactics approach ... I'm a pacifist, I think as a pacifist you can work with people not in your position, otherwise you're going to find yourself in a very lonely place and you're going to get somewhere between 'not a lot' to 'fuck all' done. (Interview P)

And for their part, critics of pacifism and nonviolence are keen to emphasise that their scepticism is not necessarily directed towards all variants of pacifism, nor all pacifists, but rather to articulations which universalise, limit solidarity, or imply the possibility of innocence in a fundamentally violent world:

> I don't think nonviolence in a violent world exists, like, it's more about how and when we think we would engage in particular things . . . I know some really sensible pacifists and also some really not sensible pacifists, so it depends on what kind of pacifist you are. I wouldn't describe myself as a pacifist, I would describe myself as anti-violence, but that's not the same thing. (Interview N)

> I'm not a pacifist myself, but I will work with many pacifists, but the ones that share a similar politics in other forms, who have similar theories of change . . . But I would never describe myself as a pacifist in a world where that could very easily be interpreted to mean engaging in nothing that could be deemed by anyone 'violence', including people whose opinions I really tend not to trust about what is legitimate violence, like the state. (Interview L)

These concessions help to create the spaces in which coalitional politics can take place. Part of the function of diversity of tactics is that activists work to avoid overly exposing and amplifying their differences, instead focusing on common goals while organising most intensively with others with whom there are shared affinities for specific tactics. This can have the effect of meaning that important debates are sidestepped, but it also makes collaborations possible that would not otherwise be so.

And yet, despite these conciliations, there remains a marked difference in tone across the positions. While most (though not all) activists express support for the diversity of tactics principle, those who centre nonviolence are far more likely to identify misgivings, or to caution about the dangers of diversity of tactics 'going too far'. An apt example comes from comparing comments from two different interviewees. One, a pacifist and firm advocate of nonviolence, qualified his support for diversity of tactics by suggesting that he would nonetheless like to see CAAT's nonviolence guidelines 'quoted a bit more firmly' (Interview M). The other, a critic, expressed her approval of the fact that those guidelines have largely fallen out of everyday use (Interview N). There remains, then, a certain degree of background tension.

In one sense, the violence/nonviolence debate is ironic. Very rarely is a punch thrown, and the question of physical violence remains largely abstract. However, that does not make the debate unimportant. As the arguments above make clear, the varied positions regarding violence, nonviolence and pacifism represent contrasting accounts of the ethics and politics of resistance, the nature of militarism, and the relationship between the two. This is, then, a question of how the movement, and anti-militarism more generally, is constituted. The refusal to institutionalise a principle of nonviolence within one of the most active anti-militarist coalitions in the UK indicates a shift from more traditional peace movement orthodoxies. Nonetheless, it is worth noting that, while 'diversity' rather than 'nonviolence' is the guiding principle of STAF, it is not altogether clear that the coalition would hold if people did start fighting.

To close this section I want to highlight what, theoretically, is valuable in making space for a non-pacifist anti-militarism. For many this may seem counter-intuitive, and for some even contradictory, but others have raised the possibility (Eastwood 2018). The arguments outlined above give good reasons to think critically about how the imperatives of nonviolence and pacifism can actually function to reproduce certain forms of violence. On such terms, the refusal to make these the guiding principles of anti-militarism holds certain virtues, and proceeding with a non-pacifist anti-militarism potentially leads to more nuanced accounts of both prefiguration and militarism. To make this argument, we have to conceptualise prefiguration not in terms of the idealised embodiment of a future-to-come, but as the labour of producing subjectivities that are specific to and determined by context even as they imagine and generate new pathways. In terms of militarism, a non-pacifist anti-militarism pushes us to recognise how the production and legitimisation of violence is always contingent, always determined by context, such that more general imperatives are both limited and limiting. Read in this way, a non-pacifist anti-militarism remains concerned with a critique of violence and the prefiguration of subjects and social relations which subvert violence; however, the particular meaning and negotiation of violence is not determined prior to context. This is emphatically not to claim that some pacifist approaches to anti-militarism cannot accommodate these perspectives. Instead, it is to suggest that non-pacifist anti-militarism makes the lines here clear.

The (White) Limits to Diversity

Contestations over the meaning and role of (non)violence within the movement demonstrate an explicit attempt to negotiate the nature of militarism. They also allow us to recognise the work undertaken to make space for diversity in resistance. However, while recognising the virtues of these commitments, it is also important to look at the limits and boundary-producing performances at play within the movement, and to account for how these reproduce particular social hierarchies and exclusions. Others have paid attention to the heavily middle-class nature of the movement (Cole 2017; Mattausch 1989; Parkin 1968); in the last part of this chapter I look at the role and dominance of whiteness in British anti-militarism.

The whiteness of British anti-militarism is a long-recognised feature of the movement (Brown 1990; Roseneil 1995: 95–6). In both organising spaces and on public demonstrations one can reliably expect that a large majority of participants will be white; this is particularly the case for the communities which surround CAAT, STAF, Plowshares and *Peace News*. This whiteness runs alongside a certain racial aphasia, an unwillingness or inability to contend with the causes and consequences of this whiteness, and a related lack of engagement with the relationship between militarism and race. These are not new problems for anti-militarism. In 1915 W. E. B. DuBois recounted his experience in exhorting a meeting of peace societies to discuss racial prejudice as a cause of war: 'The secretary was sorry but was unwilling to introduce controversial matters!' (1915: 713). On similar terms bell hooks criticised the feminist movement's failure to recognise the central place of race and imperialism within militarism (1995). In Chapter 9 I will show how this lack of attention can lead to the deployment of racialised (and militarised) discourse within the movement. Here, I show how anti-militarists attempt to contend with the movement's whiteness as they negotiate solidarity practices and privilege.

Historically, the British anti-militarist movement has struggled with a problem that is endemic to Western social movements, insofar as it has engaged in solidarity practices which presume to speak 'on behalf of' vulnerable, marginalised and distanced others, assuming their interests and political will. Those who are identified as the victims of British militarism are often visible only as images, faint representations, sources of outrage who legitimise campaigns. They are rarely involved in directly shaping anti-militarist politics, instead existing largely in two-dimensional form – or, perhaps, in the three-dimensional pathos of the die-in. Such representations tend to drain the specificities from particular issues, framing them instead in the language of abstract humanism, evil perpetrators and noble victims, the 'simplification of a political story into a morality play' (Muppidi 2012: 119). One interviewee expressed her frustrations with those narratives:

> if I see one more fucking banner with 'DRONES KILL BABIES' or something on it ... [the implication is] that we can't give a shit about the arms trade unless the person that's been harmed by the arms trade is this perfect, passive, unempowered, innocent with no agency. (Interview N)

These conventions of solidarity are deeply problematic. In presuming the needs and desires of those who suffer most acutely from militarised violence, rather than building relationships and campaigns which allow them to determine the nature of anti-militarist politics themselves, stark inequalities of power are reproduced (Mohanty 1984). And in representing those who suffer in abstracted, universalised and passive form, their capacity for agency is further diminished (Kapoor 2004; Spivak 1988). These narratives also provide ample space for the activist to reproduce themselves as noble and heroic, without necessarily interrogating how their subjecthood is bound up in the rationalities that make possible such violence (Razack 2007).

In no small part due to the critiques made by activists and

scholars from the Global South about the problems with these solidarity practices, the past ten years have witnessed a systematic effort towards a more inclusive politics of solidarity within British anti-militarism. Particularly visible have been the moves to centre marginalised voices both within organising spaces and in campaign communications. STAF has made this work central to its ethos. The coalition formed soon after the 2011 uprisings in the Middle East and North Africa, and so in a context of increased focus on Britain's arms trading relationships with regimes including Saudi Arabia, Bahrain and Egypt. Organisers quickly made links with Bahraini activists in London, deciding that any campaign should be shaped by those who are most acutely affected. Similar relationships have been built with Kurdish, Palestinian, Yemeni and Saudi Arabian activists (though much less with respect to the latter two). In 2013 the Peace News Summer Camp was designed explicitly in order to contend with some of these issues. The week's theme was 'Taking a Lead from the Global South', and the organising committee were all people of colour. The programme was largely comprised of workshops focusing on racism, colonialism, and Global South politics (Rai 2013a, 2013b). The edition of *Peace News* which came out at around the same time was also entirely written by people of colour. The Sisters Against the Arms Trade action introduced in Chapter 2 provides another example of such solidarity organising: the activists worked closely with Syrian women to develop the plans and the messaging for their action. Whilst, as I discuss further below, these moves have not been wholly successful, they represent important attempts to resituate basic solidarity practices.

Despite these shifts, it remains that much of the visible politics of anti-militarism, particularly when it involves illegal direct action, is dominated by white activists. One often-cited reason for this is that direct action politics are simply more dangerous for non-white activists; illegal action and conflict with the police carries fewer risks when the police do not read your body as inherently threatening, or when you have settled residency status. Indeed, as I argued in Chapter 4, many direct action tactics rely precisely on the expectation that the police will recognise you as unthreatening. Many activists are cognisant of the role of privilege here:

it's like with the Black Lives Matter action at City Airport, like what would happen if lots of black people ran out on the runway? They might get shot. Like, what happens when loads of Arabs take part in a shutdown of an arms factory? Fucking hell, you know, it's got completely different dynamics ... I think this needs to be named ... that when people are acting in this sort of direct action way, that – and I don't think we've done it enough and I don't think I've done it enough – that they [acknowledge] that they're able to engage in this tactic because of their white, middle-class status. (Interview O)

Naming this privilege may go some way towards revealing the limits to the accessibility of direct action as a tactic, but still leaves us with a familiar dilemma, wherein the political deployment of (white) privilege may be effective in a given situation, but at some level also serves to reproduce the conditions which underpin that privilege (Mahrouse 2014).[7] One white activist told me about an occasion in which he attempted a citizen's arrest on a Saudi Arabian general, at the behest of some Bahraini friends. They could not do this themselves due to the likely reprisals that their families in Bahrain would face, and so they asked my interviewee to act in their place. The stunt worked, insofar as it gained media coverage and caused a minor diplomatic incident. However, it also centred the heroic actions of a daring young white man – his pictures were soon all over the papers. My interviewee reflected on the action: 'I really didn't want to do it, I really don't like the attention. Well, I quite like the attention; I'm aware that it's not a good thing' (Interview P).

The whiteness of British anti-militarism can also be seen in the particular accounts of militarism in operation within the movement – or more precisely, in what is left out of these accounts. The axiomatic issues or targets of anti-militarism tend to include military establishments, the arms industry, nuclear weapons and public ritual. Striking by their omission are those issues around which people of colour in the UK are most likely to experience violence, notably with respect to policing, counter-terrorist and border agencies. Despite abundant accounts of how these should be understood through the frame of militarism, they remain marginal issues within the movement (Akkerman 2018; McCulloch and Sentas

2006). CAAT has had a long-running internal discussion about the extent to which the arming of police forces should be considered an arms trade issue, a debate over definitions and organisational scope overshadowed by the fact that this is terrain through which the organisation's striking whiteness might be unsettled. My point is not that those more traditional issues are not themselves racialised (even if this is inadequately dealt with in the movement), but to suggest that an account of militarism which largely overlooks the violent governance of racialised subjects in the UK is highly partial. This is far more than a definitional issue. If militarism concerns the social relations and organisation of political violence, then what is most implicitly and comfortably understood as militarism signals what kinds of violence are understood as noteworthy. On prefigurative terms, we have to read the movement as reproducing social imaginaries which ignore or downplay racialised forms of violence.

It is perhaps appropriate here to acknowledge this book's complicity in these narratives. In privileging anti-militarist action that focuses on those more conventional issues, and paying considerably less attention to those resisting police and border violence, the book risks reproducing the whiteness of the movement and its conception of militarism. In claiming that the British anti-militarist movement is an overwhelmingly white environment, the implication should not be that groups who resist British police and border violence (who tend to include far more people of colour) are not resisting militarism. Such a formulation risks severely delimiting the scope and political purchase of anti-militarist concepts and politics. It also reproduces a normative whiteness which goes at least some way to explaining the whiteness of the movement, and ill equips the movement to account for the relationship between racism and militarism. Indeed, as I argue in Chapter 9, it opens spaces for the deployment of racialised discourse within anti-militarism. My argument, then, is that what is most conventionally regarded as anti-militarism is far too narrow in its account of militarised violence and anti-militarist action.

There have been a number of attempts within the movement to work with more expansive accounts of militarism, although they are not without their shortcomings. The organisation of the 2013 Peace News Summer Camp was indeed turned over to activists of colour, and run with a focus on the racialised politics of militarism. However, the basic camp structure was decided in advance; this meant that the guest organisers' capacity to attract new faces was stymied by the need to attract people to a distant field in Norfolk and to an environment that – to put it bluntly – retained much of the aesthetics of the white peace movement. In 2015, in response to intensified public focus on the humanitarian crisis faced by migrants crossing Europe's borders, there was a last-minute migrant solidarity action at DSEI. Activists made a large banner reading 'REFUGEES WELCOME, NOT ARMS DEALERS', the road into the arms fair was blockaded by activists wearing 'alternative border force' T-shirts, and speakers from migrant solidarity organisations were hastily arranged. The messaging linked the arms trade to the refugee crisis, implying that those fleeing conflicts in the Middle East and North Africa are responding in part to devastation wreaked by British-sold weapons. While this is a relatively effective framing (and was very popular on social media), the last-minute nature of the protest is telling; the relationship between migration and militarism had not been conceived as one of the key messages prior to the emergence of a 'crisis'.[8] Moreover, the focus was kept almost exclusively on how weapons sold abroad lead to people becoming refugees, overlooking the fact that products used in the violent and coercive governance of migrants within the UK were also being sold at DSEI. And while CAAT does not tend to recognise British police militarisation as an arms trade issue, it has also criticised and organised direct action in response to the yearly Security and Policing event, organised by the British Home Office. While CAAT's own focus lies on the sale of policing equipment to repressive regimes such as Saudi Arabia and Bahrain, it has also posted articles and literature highlighting the problems with racist policing in the UK, the US and elsewhere (CAAT 2015c, 2016a, 2016b). In a movement environment where the general account of militarism struggles to contend with its racialised dimensions, we can therefore discern attempts to shift the terms.

There is clearly a need to expand accounts of militarism so that they are better able to contend with the racialised character of political violence. This process is likely to work better when not based on the expectation that substantive anti-militarism happens within a particular movement, which people should be encouraged to join if they can link it to their issue. Instead, the impetus should be towards a more generalised account of both militarism and anti-militarism, open to connections and recognitions of common struggle without attempting to impose a general framework for action. Brown makes a similar argument when considering the role of black women in peace activism. She argues that the lack of visibility of black women within the movement does not mean that they have not been fighting for peace, but that pressures of time and money, attention to different political issues, alongside the disproportionate risk from police violence faced by people of colour, mean that their peace work has manifested differently (1990). As an example of how a wider account of peace organising might work, she recounts a series of events from the time of Greenham Common, when sex workers (of whom about half were black) occupied a church in Kings Cross in London. They sent a message to the women at Greenham saying, 'if prostitutes had the military budget we wouldn't go into prostitution'; in response, a group of women from Greenham went to stay at the occupation. The occupation 'turned the church into a peace camp', the two groups joined by a 'focus on the State's enforcement of women's vulnerability' (1990: 39–40).

For Brown, the principle challenge is to organise in a manner that broadens our conception of peace work, to figure out

> how to connect issues; how to connect situations and struggles; how different sectors of women, children and men can most usefully connect our different levels of power in a movement to which each of us is contributing, and acknowledged to be contributing, our own experience, issues and priorities, without undermining the least powerful. (Brown 1990: 43)

We see some moves towards such an approach in the examples collected above. They were extended during DSEI 2017, when a Solidarity Without Borders day focused on how migrants and people of colour are rendered particularly vulnerable by militarism. The day was predominantly organised by queer activists and activists of colour, and involved groups who would not normally take part in these events such as the All Africa Women's Group,

Diversity / 203

who performed a play about the British asylum process. This linking of issues broadens the conception of militarism at play within the movement, unsettling the whiteness of anti-militarism and building relationships which challenge multiple forms of violence. Where this takes place, there are clearly important possibilities. Their rarity demonstrates something of the limits and closures of the movement as it currently operates.

*

The question of how to form coalitions which have collective force, but which can also account for and explore their own contradictions, limits and exclusions, is a perennial subject of political and theoretical debate (Day 2005; Laclau and Mouffe 2001). Diversity of tactics can be recognised as one particular response to this debate, and as one which makes interesting moves in subverting normal rules of cohesiveness and hegemony without collapsing into division and fracture. Its role within a prefigurative imaginary is a creative and anti-hegemonic one, as seen in the work that is undertaken to generate spaces and relationships which refuse to impose a strategic imperative, which resist setting limits on how and what subjects of resistance must be, which hold space for experimentation and autonomy, and which caution against valorisations and criticisms that privilege particular (often more spectacular) forms of action.

This prefigurative account extends to encounters with the limits of this diversity, where attempts to find common purpose break down and the limits of solidarity and affinity are made manifest, as was the case with the AMN. The struggles to determine with whom solidarity might be shared, and to negotiate (and hold in contingency) the boundaries of affinity represent important moments of self-examination and political negotiation. That diversity of tactics works, but always with a certain amount of tension, should not be surprising. If diversity of tactics is contoured by the fact that resistance always involves a critique of resistance, then such tensions should be expected and embraced as political experiences which test those limits without immediate recourse to hegemony or fracture.

In the tensions and debates about the status of violence, non-violence and pacifism within the movement, we see contestation not only about what tactics should be considered legitimate, but about how militarism should be conceptualised. What counts as violence, how violence is produced, whether and how we place violence in context, and what we understand as the relationship between militarism and resistance all shape particular approaches to nonviolence. I have suggested that the relationship between militarism, pacifism and nonviolence is perhaps not as essential as some might suggest. In so doing I stopped short of exploring the wider implications of this argument, which admittedly begs two key questions: what kinds of tactics and solidarities might this position enable, and how are we to contend with the ethics and politics of such legitimisation? Those questions are beyond my scope here, but they are clearly important for any future critique of the relationship between militarism, pacifism and nonviolence.

In the final part of the chapter I argued that any recognition of how the movement celebrates diversity should also contend with how this diversity is enclosed or curtailed. My intention has not been to reify diversity as a straightforwardly positive anti-militarist aspiration. As Vron Ware has argued, the British Army has proven remarkably adept at drawing multiculturalism and diversity into the framework of military service (2013). Instead, I have sought to suggest that, at the limits of the movement, we see its (racialised) politics of exclusion. While not the whole story, the whiteness of British militarism can in part be explained by the role of white privilege in direct action activism, and a normative whiteness shaping how militarism is conceptualised. Therefore, although the movement's prefigurative aspirations may be towards generating anti-militarist forms of social relation and subjectivity, we have to read its practices as reproducing racialised forms of exclusion. This ill equips the movement to contend with the relationship between militarism and racism. I further develop this critique in Chapter 9. Before that, Chapter 8 looks at how anti-militarists negotiate the politics of obedience and disobedience.

Notes

1. Whilst the particular phrasing 'diversity of tactics' is a contemporary formulation, the wider ethos has a longer history. While discussing the Greenham

Common camp, Frazer and Hutchings note that 'participants at the camp dealt with disagreement by way of a commitment to individual responsibility and a kind of anarchist tolerance' (2014b: 154). In similar fashion to my argument here, they show that this anarchist tolerance is rarely without tension or discord. Sasha Roseneil argues that this feature of Greenham's organising made it difficult for particular factions to impose themselves absolutely (while also, of course, making it difficult to stop people trying) (1995: 95–6).

2. In the discussion here, I make my life easier by somewhat conflating pacifism and nonviolence; there are nonetheless important differences between the two. While there are many variants of pacifism, it can broadly be understood as a politics that stands in opposition to war and political violence. Meanwhile, nonviolence is better understood as a strategy or principle of resistance. It is entirely possible to hold to one and not the other. However, there is considerable overlap between the two, and the tensions I outline here can be found in applications of either and both.

3. On the distinctions, debates and common ground between principled and pragmatic nonviolence, see Hallward and Norman (2015: 19–22); Coy (2013).

4. Some of the most substantial forms of property damage carried out by anti-militarists, including the Seeds of Hope and EDO Decommissioners actions discussed in Chapters 1 and 4 respectively, were carried out by groups who made an explicit commitment to nonviolence. The question of property damage was a matter of some debate at Greenham Common, and in the early stages of the camp activists avoided cutting the fence to gain entry into the base because consensus could not be reached about whether this contravened the ethos of nonviolence. This changed in the summer of 1983 when some women cut the fence to enter the base, and over time the feeling of the camp shifted to believing that cutting the fence could be regarded as an act of creative nonviolence (Roseneil 1995: 106–7; Young 1990: 18).

5. Frazer and Hutchings point out that the writers of the feminist pamphlet *Breaching the Peace* (Onlywomen Press Collective 1983) made similar arguments, criticising Greenham for reproducing ideas about the essentially pacific nature of women. They instead committed to 'a feminist political project of fighting back against male violence' (Frazer and Hutchings 2014b: 155).

6. Chabot and Sharifi make a similar argument in their article entitled 'The Violence of Nonviolence', where they critique pragmatic accounts of nonviolent protest for their failures to account for the violent conditions of neoliberal society (2013). See also Zalewski and Sisson Runyan (2013).

7. There is also the possibility that naming this privilege functions to reproduce the whiteness of both direct action and anti-militarism, insofar as it entertains a fantasy of transcendence without substantially deconstructing the terms of this privilege (Ahmed 2004).

8. There are serious questions about whether and how the 'crisis' narrative itself reproduces particular militarised understandings of Europe and its borders (New Keywords Collective 2016).

CHAPTER 8

Dis/Obedience

The idea of disobedience plays a fundamental role in contemporary radical politics. Movements collect around signal moments of defiance, refusal, rupture, which embody and even catalyse breaks with established conduct and carve out spaces for new political formations. Apparently solid political orders are shaken by the recognition that they are predicated on a compliance and obedience that can be withdrawn, often spectacularly. Such dynamics are, of course, not new; they sit at the very heart of modernity. But the past twenty years, witnessing countless rebellions against neoliberal economics, racist and authoritarian governments, neo-colonial and patriarchal violence and military force, have demonstrated that an account of disobedience is as vital as it has ever been for understanding the relationship between power and resistance.

Despite (and because of) the somewhat heroic status it holds, the concept of disobedience has been met with a series of important critiques, which have called into question the notion that disobedience is a straightforwardly radical practice. The first of these charges that there is nothing necessarily transformative about transgression; indeed, that a simple act of disobedience remains tied to the object, destined to reflect rather than subvert power. Todd May cites Gilles Deleuze on such terms:

> Deleuze explains that the concept of transgression remains tied to the very significations against which it transgresses: 'The signifier is always the little secret which has never stopped hanging around mummy and

daddy. . . . The little secret is generally reducible to a sad narcissistic and pious masturbation: the phantasm! "Transgression", a concept too good for seminarists under the law of a Pope or a priest' (May 1994: 114, citing Deleuze and Parnet 1987: 47)

Within this schema, an act of disobedience can adopt an aesthetic of refusal without actively subverting power relations or creating something new. Foucault avoids the language of disobedience precisely because it implies a lack of creativity. As he sets out his justification for introducing the term 'counter-conduct' to conceptualise resistance to pastoral forms of governance, he explains his reasons for avoiding the language of 'disobedience' or 'dissent'. The latter is avoided for fear of the 'process of sanctification or hero worship' that can accompany the term dissident, which blinds us to the specificities and reproductions of self-professed 'dissidents' (2007a: 202). 'Disobedience' he avoids not because it is not important – 'the problem of obedience is in fact at the center of all this' – but because it is too negative; 'these movements that I have tried to pick out definitely have a productivity, forms of existence, organization, and a consistency and solidity that the purely negative word of disobedience does not capture' (2007a: 200).

Disobedience as a straightforward mirror to obedience is indeed problematic. However, the concept (and practice) holds considerably more productivity and creative potential than is acknowledged by such readings. Foucault acknowledges as much when he speaks of critique as 'the art of voluntary inservitude, that of reflected intractability' (2007b: 47), and in his wider recognition of 'our ceaseless involvement in the construction of diagrams that we dream of fleeing' (Prozorov 2007: 21). The practice of disobedience has played an important role in radical political theory, due both to the space it opens for resisting authority, and to the instinct, well expressed by Goldman, that it is 'the *struggle* for, not so much the attainment of, liberty, that develops all that is strongest, sturdiest and finest in human character' (1996: 49; see also Rossdale 2015b); that is, that disobedience to authority is itself an important site of self-creation.

To acknowledge a radical politics of disobedience is not to rest at the logic of transgression, to mirror (and, thus, fix) the object of obedience. Rather, it is to understand disobedience as part of the process of becoming otherwise, as a practice through which anti-hegemonic and anti-authoritarian politics might be explored. It is to cultivate, in Newman's terms, a *'discipline of indiscipline'* (2010b: 46; original emphasis) which weakens hegemonies of their totalising force and refuses their governmentality (Foucault 2007a: 46–7). Whilst there is no positive programme attached to the concept of disobedience *per se*, we can recognise disobedience as a practice that opens spaces for creativity. In the 'insurrection of the self against the identities and roles imposed on us' which is involved in these processes of disobedience and desubjectification (Newman 2010a: 118–19), more particular relations are developed, explored and prefigured.

A second critique often addressed towards apparently radical acts and theories of disobedience is that they are, upon closer inspection, better understood as examples of obedience to the second degree, obedience to a higher order (whether political, revolutionary, moral, theological). Such is the status of much of the political theory on disobedience, which seeks to establish the higher terms by which disobedience might be justified (Laudani 2013; Sitze 2013). Political and activist discourses on civil disobedience also adopt such a position, situating particular acts of disobedience within a more general posture of obedience to the law and institutions (which are, through that disobedience, revitalised) (Loizidou 2013; Zinn 2002). In these accounts, disobedience is always subordinated, the derivative component of a hierarchical opposition.

There are, however, understandings of disobedience which position it not as a regrettable and temporary departure from obedience, but as a prior political energy. Writing about the Occupy movement, Bernard Harcourt argues that contemporary disobedience has moved from civil disobedience to political disobedience, away from the resistance to particular laws towards a more fundamental resistance to how politics is organised (2012). Lucy Finchett-Maddock emphasises the productive potential of *naughtiness*, as a subjective politics of disobedience that laughs and plays with the aesthetic experience of rebellion (2013). And Raffaele Laudani reads in the perpetual gaps in attempts to systematise and taxonomise the formal politics of disobedience a more general expression of what he terms 'destituent power', which tends towards the dissolution and abolition of law (2013: 3-4). Such accounts are vitally important, not because they posit practices which exceed any relationship with obedience, but because they trouble the idea that obedience is the fundamental political experience and horizon. At their core is the understanding that disobedience should not only be thought in terms of particular acts, but as a subjective and subjectifying political labour (Loizidou 2013).

In this chapter I look at how anti-militarists navigate the politics of obedience and disobedience, arguing that the tensions briefly outlined here are alive within the movement. I begin by considering the intentional work that activists undertake, through direct action, training workshops and the maintenance of anti-police positions, to cultivate themselves and their practices as disobedient. I then reflect on how these processes risk heroisation, suggesting that such concerns might draw us to a subtler, less spectacular account of how disobedience is cultivated within movement spaces. In the second part of the chapter I turn to look at how, despite the centrality of disobedience to anti-militarist politics, anti-militarist politics is also structured through relations of obedience. My particular focus is on how activists negotiate their status as legal subjects. I examine the common tactic by which activists allow themselves to be arrested as part of direct action, a practice I term 'voluntary submission'. The differing attitudes activists hold towards arrest and prosecution (especially with respect to the idea of accountability) represent contrasting understandings of obedience and disobedience within the movement, with some of these reproducing surprisingly conservative political imaginaries. Nonetheless, I argue that all tactics which incorporate arrest involve some kind of encounter with obedience, and risk reproducing a hierarchy of obedience over disobedience. In the third part of the chapter I show how, even in practices of compliance with the police and legal system, activists develop important spaces for some form of disobedience. In the chapter's conclusion I argue that, while much of anti-militarist disobedience tends towards an obedience/disobedience hierarchy, there is an element which exceeds this and which cannot be captured by a rational framing. That excess is an invaluable space for the constitution of radical political subjects.

In previous chapters I have argued that uncritical respect for authority, beliefs about the importance of discipline and hierarchy, and practices of obedience can all be seen as social relations through which militarised social relations are constituted and legitimised. This analytic has led to a cautious attitude towards forms of resistance which replicate these dynamics. This is not to suggest that any particular instance of obedience (for example) *is* militaristic in some ontological sense, but rather to call attention to the micropolitics of militarism and the subversive role of prefiguration. In such a context, the practice of disobedience can be understood as not only central to the constitution of anti-hegemonic or anti-authoritarian movements, but as specifically disruptive of militarised social relations. Insofar as acts of disobedience bring activists into critical encounters with authority, obedience and discipline, we might read them as attempts to effect distance between the subject and militarism.

Disobedient Subjects

Most of the examples explored throughout this book refer explicitly to forms of disobedience practised by anti-militarists, whether to laws, the police, or indeed to other activists. However, perhaps more important than any particular act or statement of disobedience are the efforts made by anti-militarists to nurture a general ethos of disobedience. In Chapter 5 I argued that large-scale acts of disobedience are made possible by the far quieter work of supporting those involved. This work can involve serving food or acting as a legal observer on demonstrations, running training sessions, collecting witness statements, fundraising for legal defence funds, or providing childcare. It is considerably easier to disobey the law when you know that others will be waiting for you when you are released from the police station at 3 a.m., and that they will support you in your court case. Alongside these more practical efforts, we might look at the considerable work anti-militarists undertake to confront their own instinctive obedience and respect for authority, and to cultivate a spirit of indiscipline and disobedience.

The idea of recognising and 'unlearning' one's respect for, deference to, and deployment of authority is a common topic of discussion amongst anti-militarists, as a feature of resistance which demands conscious and sustained effort. Direct action which brings activists into confrontation with more formal sources of authority, such as the police or security guards, is conceptualised explicitly as a practice through which activists come to terms with (and refuse) themselves. While for some, refusing to follow the instructions of police is a straightforward act, for others it is an ordeal. Behind confident expressions lie shaking hands and sweaty foreheads. One interviewee's reflections on his arrest for blockading an arms trade facility are pertinent:

> It was a big thing for me, it was something that I worked up to over years. I'm not . . . I've never been that good with confrontation, especially not with authority figures, possibly because I was brought up in a very authoritarian family . . . it really goes against my grain to stand up to a big scary policeman and say, 'No I'm not going to move.' It's something that, at demonstrations over the years I've pushed myself a bit further and a bit further, because I think it's important for my personal development as much as anything else, to be able, when I think something is wrong, to stand up for it.
>
> Obviously these are very personal reasons, and each one on that action would have had their own reasons. The fear of arrest had stopped me, had held me back on previous demonstrations, and I felt that . . . I've got to pop my cherry really . . . I've got to . . . I can't have this fear of what the system will do to me hanging over me. It's about time . . . I came to believe in the necessity of direct action, and that means sacrifice, and people have to be punished by the state . . . be prepared to be punished by the state, otherwise we're not going to get anywhere, and I think there's only a few thousand people at most in this country who a) appreciate that and b) are prepared to do that, and I think that's very precious and the more people who are prepared to break the law in a principled way the better, and I think once I realised that, I thought, 'I've got to step up and do that'. (Interview F)

Set within this context, the particular action to which the interviewee is referring is not an isolated incident, but part of a longer-term project. As Elena Loizidou argues, this break with habit and overcoming of fear is a labour-intensive process, which 'requires one to disobey oneself or otherwise to act despite oneself' (2013: 121). This line of thought often emerges in conversation with activists. It also forms a significant theme within activist training events.

Training is an important activist practice, and several collectives (including Seeds for Change and Rhizome) exist purely to run training workshops and sessions. These cover topics including consensus decision-making practice (and facilitation), recognising and confronting privilege, DIY lessons for building blockading equipment, and the art of 'de-arresting'. It is not uncommon for spaces like peace camps to involve training sessions, and groups will often organise training events prior to carrying out direct action (whether as a means by which to get to know other participants, to practise different tactics, or to make plans). Anna-Linnea Rundberg stresses that it is important not to see training as being merely (or even mainly) about a hierarchical process of knowledge transfer. It is as much 'about exploring your personal hopes, fears and responses in the context of taking direct action', as well as forming relationships with your fellow activists (2008: 110–11).

Training sessions can operate as spaces through which activists undertake the labour of becoming disobedient. One particular simulation exercise, sometimes called a 'hassle line', is exemplary here. Usually seen in more practically oriented sessions, the hassle line focuses on preparing activists for encounters with the police or security guards. Participants pair up and role play situations wherein one plays the authority figure and the other, themselves. Usually the activist playing the police officer will begin with polite (even pleasant, or 'supportive') requests for the activists to cease their hypothetical action. They then progress to more assertive and even aggressive instruction. Activists experiment with their responses. There is no model form of conduct in the situation: while some will attempt to remain calm whilst refusing to comply, others might be sarcastic; some remain silent, others try to reason with the officers, or explain themselves. Many simply stare blankly into the middle distance. Each activist thus spends this time and attention cultivating their own practice of disobedience.

This labour runs alongside more general work to institutionalise disobedience to the police within the movement. Many groups, including Smash EDO and Disarm DSEI, have explicit policies not to negotiate with the police (Stavrianakis 2010: 176), and an ongoing effort by GBC to teach activists that there is 'no such thing as an innocent chat with the police' means that police liaison officers often have a hard time gathering evidence on demonstrations. This aversion is not total, and there are some voices calling for a less hostile relationship. In one workshop, after a facilitator made a disparaging remark about the police, a middle-aged white woman interjected to suggest that we should act with good faith towards the police, should avoid confrontation, and should instead be trying to convince them of the moral force of our position. Another woman in the same demographic responded by noting the intensely privileged position from which such a statement can be made, and arguing that the structural position of the police means that they will only ever work to undermine anti-militarist politics. That opinion, met with furiously nodding heads in the room, is the dominant opinion within the movement. Such is the level of antipathy that, when several police officers approached activists and suggested a game of football at a quiet period during the week of action against DSEI 2015, they were quickly rebuffed.

This cultivation of disobedient practices is not simply about straightforward acts of transgression; it is closely tied to the prefigurative quality of the movement, and cannot be extricated from the social relations which are produced (and which have been discussed throughout this book). Disobedience is a rupture, a practice of ungovernability through which alternative forms of political intervention, community and subjectivity can be produced. This becomes more apparent when we recognise that the object of disobedience is not simply the police officer giving an instruction. It is a cluster of imperatives shaping space and conduct in particular ways. When anti-militarists drive a tank through the city streets, hold a Palestinian dance workshop in front of an arms fair, or break into an aircraft hangar with hammers, they are disobedient with respect not only to particular sources of authority, but to established conventions of how politics is supposed to be done, to how subjects are supposed to act, and to how spaces are supposed to function. While disobedience is perhaps most visible in explicitly confrontational situations, it is when that disobedience extends to a wider set of social relations that it is most subversive.

While identifying the disruptive potential of disobedience, it is also important to acknowledge that the cultivation and celebration of disobedience can quickly become a site of valorisation and heroisation. This is problematic for a number of reasons. Hero narratives tend towards privileging individual moments of daring and sacrifice over more collective projects (Cockburn 2012: 92), and they mask the social work that underpins and makes possible dramatic moments of disobedience. Moreover, they obscure the power relations which shape who is and is not able to engage in such actions, concealing (white, middle-class, able-bodied) privilege while elevating understandings of disobedience which retain a certain machismo (Cockburn 2012: 57). Hero narratives also risk valorising success in ways which hide the messy, ambiguous, or even downright counterproductive politics at play in activist environments, potentially closing down the space through which those politics might be investigated (Gardner 2005: 65–6). And through these dynamics, heroic narratives (and experiences) of disobedience reproduce somewhat militarised anti-militarist subjects; white saviours and masculine protectors and A-Team aficionados.

Activists are, to an extent, aware of and attentive to this problem. As I discussed in the previous chapter, some of the work which goes into maintaining the diversity of tactics principle involves trying to displace hierarchies which pedestalise spectacular acts of disobedience. During an interview with an activist who took part in a rooftop occupation of an Israeli arms factory, she detailed the attempts her group made to avoid individuals being represented as heroes. These included not naming the individuals involved in the action, having spokespeople (in this case specifically Palestinian spokespeople) talking to the media instead of those on the rooftop, and rotating roles as much as possible amongst the group to avoid any 'internal hero dynamic'. Nevertheless, attention was hard to avoid and, insofar as those involved were seeking to bring public focus onto the UK's arms trading relationship with Israel, not unwelcome (Interview O). This is a similar dilemma to that encountered by the activist who attempted the citizen's arrest on the Saudi Arabian general in the last chapter, signalling the ease and swiftness with which hero narratives can be applied. As such, and despite the widespread acknowledgement of the problems with hero narratives, they abound. Signal moments of disobedience and daring play a central role in the movement's self-image (and this book is clearly not innocent on that front), and a certain activist celebrity culture persists.

In the light of these concerns it is valuable to think about less immediately apparent forms of disobedience, in pursuit of an account that is less likely to reify spectacular moments or actions. The risk otherwise is that disobedience becomes an imperative which reflects and reproduces particular ideas of what resistance should look like, the problem here not only being the compliance that such ideas ironically demand, but the ways that they also blind us to central processes of political transformation. As James C. Scott cautions, when we focus our attention on visible and dramatic processes of disobedience, we fail to account for the myriad moments of refusal which remain largely invisible but which play a substantial role in restricting and subverting systems of power (2000). Doing so both limits our analysis of radical political processes and does so in a manner which elides the agency and capacity of those whose disobedience must necessarily remain concealed (that is, those who are most marginalised).

Rather than turn disobedience into an abstract and hegemonic imperative, we might think about disobedience in ways which recognise the complex, plural and particular relations of authority, obligation and possibility within which subjects find themselves. Ewa Jasiewicz, herself an activist within the movement, steers into this territory when considering the complex question of what level of political action might be considered 'enough' when confronting the seemingly endless brutality of state violence:

> I think a tentative definition of enough could be, to transgress, to cross our own lines of possibility. Our own lines of what we believe we can and cannot do have been authored by others and adopted by ourselves. Lines drawn by authorities, re-inscribed with violence and drawn thick with the threat of detention ... we will never get close enough to where we need to be as a critical mass to effect change unless we cross our own lines of fear. (Jasiewicz 2009: 15)

Disobedience here becomes a process of making possible, of expanding the space for action. This process is always context specific, often invisible, but it can be found everywhere; not only ignoring police officers, but reshaping how to understand and move through spaces, how to hold a 'serious' protest, how to 'be' a proper activist. During the Sisters Against the Arms Trade action recounted in Chapter 3, the participants wore red lipstick, not only because red is the colour of the Syrian resistance, but as a conscious rejoinder to the idea that radical women should not. During the STAF spectrum line exercise described in Chapter 7 we refused to follow the instructions of the facilitators, preferring instead to challenge the terms of their exercise. Such acts of disobedience fold less straightforwardly into hero narratives, but nonetheless serve to redraw lines of possibility – albeit in ways which might not be wholly visible. Disobedience in this respect involves the continual becoming of the subject, the never-ending struggle with and between and against multiple lines of obligation.

Obedient Subjects

Accounting for the role of disobedience within British anti-militarism is a relatively straightforward exercise, and accords neatly with the movement's self-image. It is perhaps less intuitive to set out the processes by which the movement also reproduces relations of obligation and obedience. In what follows I argue that, even as they engage in illegal acts of disobedience, activists remain obedient subjects. I look at a particular set of practices, acts of 'voluntary submission', in order to unpack how activists navigate their status as disobedient and (il)legal subjects. Voluntary submission refers to tactics which involve the certainty (or extreme likelihood) of arrest, that arrest being accepted as an inevitable or necessary feature of the action itself. Many of the actions engaged throughout this book, including the Seeds of Hope actions and Block the Factory, have involved voluntary submission.

Tactics incorporating voluntary submission are common, but the arrest process itself is understood, valued and pursued in quite different ways. For some, arrest is viewed in highly instrumental terms, as the unavoidable but tolerable consequence of carrying out a particular action, while for others, arrest, prosecution and even prison are integral to the nature and success of certain actions. Below I provide examples of these different attitudes in operation, showing that they represent contrasting accounts of the politics of obedience and disobedience. My argument is that that those approaches which positively welcome encounters with state apparatuses are more vulnerable to critique, but that even those with a more instrumentalist approach struggle to avoid their entanglement in relations of obedience. Both approaches tend to reproduce a hierarchy of obedience over disobedience, tempering the subversive qualities of disobedience outlined above.

The Plowshares movement exemplifies attitudes towards voluntary submission which welcome arrest and prosecution. The movement began in the US in 1980 when the Plowshares Eight entered the General Electric plant in Pennsylvania where the nose cones for the Mark 12-A nuclear warheads were manufactured: 'With hammers and blood they enacted the biblical prophecies of Isaiah (2:4) and Micah (4:3) to *"beat swords into plowshares"* by hammering on two of the nose cones and pouring blood on documents' (Laffin 2003: 1; original emphasis). Since then, there have been over seventy-five Plowshares actions in a number of countries, all of which aim 'to empower ordinary citizens to peacefully tear down the machinery of violence and to build up respect for fundamental human rights' (Zelter 2009: 21). Most have focused on doing damage to military equipment, and this has ranged from symbolic actions to those designed to cause the maximum possible damage, a tendency introduced after the Harriet Tubman-Sarah Connor Brigade Disarmament Action caused $2.75 million worth of damage to a NAVSTAR military satellite, 'thereby challenging plowshares and the wider disarmament movement to go beyond symbolic witness in addressing the war machines' key technologies' (Laffin 2003: 49).

A core principle of the Plowshares movement is that arrest and prosecution should be accepted as a central component of direct action. Plowshares activists, refusing to 'conceal the truth of what happened', remain at the site of their action so that they can publicly explain their witness (Laffin 2003: 6). The example of the Griffiss Plowshares action from 1983 shows the lengths to which some Plowshares activists have gone in complying with established routes of responsibility. Seven activists entered Griffiss Air Force Base in New York and hammered and poured blood on a B-52 bomber and on B-52 engines. After remaining unnoticed on the base for several hours, they approached security guards and turned themselves in, eventually receiving prison sentences ranging from two to three years (Laffin 2003: 18–19). In 1985 Plowshares activist Tom Hastings sawed down a US Navy transmitter antenna in an isolated part of Michigan's Upper Peninsula; the next day, he also turned himself in to the local sheriff, eventually receiving a prison sentence. In 2003 the Pit Stop Plowshares group, who damaged parts of the runway of Shannon Airport in Ireland after learning that the US military was using the base to support the invasion of Iraq, knelt praying whilst waiting to be arrested. And the Seeds of Hope women whose action was recounted in Chapter 1 remained undetected for some time after hammering the Hawk jet and, rather than attempt a perfectly feasible escape, waited patiently to be arrested.

Once arrested, Plowshares activists adopt varying levels of cooperation, though most refuse to accept bail conditions prohibiting further actions and refuse to pay fines, preferring to bear witness in jail. On the court cases which result, Angie Zelter (one of the Seeds of Hope activists) argues that

> [e]very trial is important because each one confronts the state and the legal system where they are most vulnerable – on a major law and order issue. We have won many of our cases and we have found that the more we rely upon ethical and legal arguments and the more 'effective' (capable of actually stopping the illegality – i.e., damaging the weapons themselves) the action is the more likely we are to persuade juries to acquit us . . . Traditionally the law has been used against the 'people' rather than the 'state' – predominantly against the poor and disadvantaged. Yet now, the people have turned this around and have openly challenged the whole legal basis, and thus legitimacy, of the Armed Forces – one of the pillars of the State. (Zelter 2009: 21)

Trials, and the performances which they enable, are central to the political strategy of the Plowshares movement (Tobey 2017). In going to such lengths to incorporate arrest as part of the process of direct action, Plowshares activism is an extreme example (one group of interviewees gasped when I told them about the Griffiss Plowshares activists turning themselves over to the police). For many other activists, the possibility of arrest is better conceptualised as an occupational hazard, to be avoided if at all possible but sometimes necessary to carry out an effective direct action.

There have been numerous examples in this book of activists carrying out illegal action while attempting to avoid arrest. The Hammertime demonstration and the Spies for Peace infiltration are two exemplary cases here. Small, anonymous, 'pixie' actions, including acts of vandalism and illegal subvertising, are common. More importantly for the argument being developed here, however, are those actions where arrest is accepted as nearly inevitable but which operate under a more instrumental logic, as summarised by one activist:

> the times I've been arrested (where I was sort of expecting that I could be arrested) were all the times where I weighed up basically the effectiveness of what I was doing and the only way of not getting arrested was probably ... legging it halfway through a thing I was trying to do, [which] probably wasn't the best plan. (Interview L)

An example of this attitude comes from an action that I took part in during DSEI 2013, when a small group of us decided to shut down Lockheed Martin's Regent Street office for the day. After surveying the building, we reasoned that the most effective method of preventing entry would be for people to be attached to the front and back doors. Three activists, all of whom considered themselves 'arrestable', volunteered to be superglued by the hands to the glass doors. The tactic worked; while police arrived on the scene quickly, it took them over four hours to safely prise the hands from the doors. The three activists were arrested, and subsequently charged with criminal damage and aggravated trespass. This, then, is a straightforward example of voluntary submission. However, in an important distinction from Plowshares actions, those arrested placed no particular value on the arrest process or subsequent legal proceedings (during which they all pleaded guilty and were given conditional discharges). These were understood as the cost of an effective action, and had the opportunity arisen to conduct the action without being arrested, the activists would have taken it. It is notable that part of the action involved a large chain being locked around some delivery gates at the back of the building, for which no one claimed responsibility.

We can, then, identify two contrasting attitudes towards arrest within the context of voluntary submission. In one, the encounters with the police and legal system are themselves an integral part of the action (and wider campaign), while in the other arrest and prosecution are conceptualised as a risk worth taking and/or a price worth paying. While it is useful to identify this distinction, it is also important to acknowledge that these rationalities often cannot coherently be separated in any particular example. Both framings are usually present to some degree. It is not uncommon for activists to proceed on broadly instrumental terms but to recognise that arrests will increase the media exposure of an action, or, when faced with prosecution, to decide that the legal battle can be an effective campaigning tool. Nevertheless, the different attitudes are discernible, and at times lead to disagreements. A key point of contention here concerns the politics of 'accountability'.

Activists who tend more towards accepting arrest and prosecution as part of direct action often explain that position with reference to the need for 'accountability'. Andrea Needham, one of the Seeds of Hope women, is representative here:

> Perhaps the most striking aspect of Ploughshares for those unfamiliar with the movement is that of accountability. Despite the apparently high security of military bases and factories, many activists have shared our experience of being undetected for several hours, giving ample opportunity to escape. Why not run away, and live to disarm another weapon?
>
> I didn't want to escape after our action because I was clear in my own mind that – whatever the criminal justice system might think – we hadn't committed a crime. In addition, I believe that one of the main problems in our political system is lack of accountability. The government had granted licences to sell weapons to a military dictatorship, British Aerospace could make and sell the weapons, and yet nobody would be answerable for the deaths those weapons would cause. Ploughshares sets

an example and says that we should all be accountable for our actions. We are willing to face the consequences of what we have done, and we expect nothing less of governments and corporations. (Needham 2016: 39)

Sam Walton from the Seeds of Hope 2 action gives a similar account:

> Well Gandhi talks a lot about . . . nonviolence of the weak and nonviolence of the strong. And I think most direct action in the UK I would class as nonviolence of the weak, where direct action is done and then we run away and try and get away with it. We don't own up to the consequences. And there's something very special about, you know, if [we had] tried to get away from the aircraft hangar or something it would have looked shit. We were both offered cautions, we could have taken those cautions and it would have looked shit. We are definitely going to go through more shit than a caution is worth, even if we get off, 100 per cent. But it makes the action so much stronger when you're willing to say, 'Yeah you're fucking wrong and your system's wrong and if you say we're guilty then you look like a prat.' (Interview P)

The second of these quotations argues the case for accountability in largely strategic terms; that is, that the action will be better regarded by others if it is conducted accountably. Any trial process and legal defence is likely to proceed more smoothly if activists have behaved in this way. But both of these quotes also contain *prefigurative* arguments for accountability. Needham's desire to embody the accountability that is lacking from our political systems, and Sam's call for a Gandhian 'nonviolence of the strong' (which, for Gandhi, concerned the cultivation and moral force of self-suffering as an essential component of *satyagraha*), both position the process of arrest and prosecution as a personally and politically transformative experience.[1]

It is notable that more forthright defences of accountability often come from Christian and Quaker anti-militarists. Christian pacifism has been an influential current within British anti-militarism, running through organisations including the Plowshares movement, the Quaker church, the Catholic Worker movement, and the Fellowship of Reconciliation (Meaden 1999; Nepstad 2008;

Ormrod 1987). Christian and Quaker activists are often amongst the most willing to engage in illegal direct action, to risk arrest, and to face punishment for their actions. An important element to their direct action is the idea of bearing witness, of marking injustice and proclaiming a different truth (Nepstad 2008: 181–202). One interviewee reflected on his experience blockading the entrance to DSEI by supergluing himself to other Christian anti-militarists:

> Jesus said to his followers, 'The gates of hell will not prevail against you,' and the door to the ExCeL centre in that context was the gate of hell and we were saying it will not prevail against us, we are witness to a different power. (Interview M)

The practice of witness is often tied into an acceptance of accountability, such that time spent in jail can itself be regarded as a spiritual experience, as a kind of prayer (Douglass 2013). As Philip Berrigan, one of the founders of the Plowshares movement, writes, '[b]eing imprisoned for one's convictions is a Christian phenomenon above all' (1970: 185). This follows a long tradition of open defiance of unjust laws within Christian pacifism:

> to quote the New Testament, 'always be prepared to give an account of the hope that is within you' and I'd want to do that in the context of pacifist activism. And I'm not necessarily saying it's wrong not to do that, and obviously I'd probably feel very differently if I lived under the sort of regime where I'd be shot for doing it . . . but actually, I feel I've got nothing to hide, it's the arms dealers and the militarists and the state and the corporate power who've got something to hide. And I am doing this openly. (Interview M)[2]

In framing their accountability with reference to a 'different power', Christian activists thus rationalise their disobedience and its consequences with explicit reference to an alternative, godly, morality (Nepstad 2008: 59–86).

A commitment to accountability is not, however, the sole preserve of religious anti-militarists. As Thomas Woodhead, one of the EDO Decommissioners, reflects:

I chose not to hit and run, as others have done in the past. I wanted to take full responsibility for my actions, as I believe them to be lawful. So I stayed and prayed in my own little atheist way hoping a jury would be able to understand that I was only working towards peace and justice. (Woodhead 2009: 18)

Here, legal rather than spiritual authority grounds the relationship to accountability. This recourse to ultimate legal justification is a common theme within the movement. For example, one interviewee explained her commitment to open organising in the face of police infiltration, stating that it 'comes from the conviction that we're not in the wrong, and yes [we] might be doing something illegal, but, ultimately, we are not the criminals here. Um ... so bring it on basically' (Interview K). Activists regularly make claims about the illegal conduct and nature of nuclear weapons, the arms trade, or military intervention in general, and slogans such as 'War Stoppers Are The Real Crime Stoppers' are commonplace. In these contexts, welcoming accountability becomes a means of invoking legal truths not reflected in political arrangements.

Notwithstanding the important strategic reasons why people decide to take action 'accountably', nor the bravery and sacrifice often involved in doing so, there is a certain conservatism to this approach. In previous chapters I have argued that obstructive direct actions of the kinds usually associated with voluntary submission hold radical possibilities, insofar as they subvert hegemonic and statist political imaginaries, reshape the politics of security, and even entail the exploration of anti-militarist forms of subjectivity. However, the expectation and practice of accountability can also serve to reinforce hegemonic and statist political imaginaries. While the legitimacy of state *actions* is being challenged, the role of the state and its legal apparatus as the arbiter of responsibility and legitimacy is reproduced. Direct action's potential as a reshaping of political agency is curtailed insofar as the state and judiciary reappear as the locus of accountability. In this context, prefigurative arguments in favour of accountability appear as ethical rather than political, seeking to embody the image of the future without fully engaging with the situated, productive and potentially counter-intuitive implications of particular figurations of subjectivity or accountability (Gordon 2018).

This critique is similar to those which have called attention to the relatively conservative nature of civil disobedience. Most understandings of civil disobedience, understood as targeted disobedience as a strategy of opposition to unjust laws, have tended to stress that the practice of disobedience should involve submission to the judicial apparatus of the state and acceptance of punishment.[3] Martin Luther King, Jr. wrote in 'Letter from Birmingham City Jail':

> In no sense do I advocate evading or defying the law, as the rabid segregationist would do. That would lead to anarchy. One who breaks an unjust law must do so *openly, lovingly* . . . and with a willingness to accept the penalty. I submit that an individual who breaks a law that conscience tells him is unjust, and willingly accepts the penalty by staying in jail to arouse the conscience of the community over its injustice, is in reality expressing the highest respect for law. (Luther King, Jr. 1991: 74; original emphasis)

Civil disobedience thus challenges particular laws while fixing in place law-making institutions and the wider structure of governance (Harcourt 2012: 33–4). In critiquing Hannah Arendt's account of civil disobedience on precisely these terms, Loizidou argues that such a position makes the mistake of viewing formal law as a neutral and even democratic apparatus, rather than as 'steeped in a bourgeois tradition' (2013: 120). The problem here is not only that civil disobedience-type formulations leave wider systems of power unchallenged, but that they reproduce a political imaginary which fails to account for the intimacy of the relationship between law and politics. In the specific context of anti-militarist mobilisations of accountability, we see the re-centring of political institutions (the state, the judiciary, and both domestic and international law) which are deeply bound up in war-producing rationalities (Anghie 2005; Jochnick and Normand 1994; Owens 2007: 72–90). Not only are these institutions unlikely to recognise the (substantive) claims of anti-militarists, but positioning them as arbiters risks depoliticising their role within militarism.

Framing voluntary submission through the lens of accountability also risks limiting the radical potential of disobedience set out in the first part of this chapter. While disobedience is being practised, that practice is grounded through a performance of societal obedience. This is also a charge that has been directed towards theories of civil disobedience, which are largely concerned with determining the acceptable limits, levels and justifications of disobedience within a wider framework of obedience to the law and the body politic (Finchett-Maddock 2013: 90).[4] Posing civil disobedience as a problem to be rationalised (rather than, say, the problem of civil *obedience*) means that the status of obedience as the assumed and necessary prior condition of politics is almost inescapable (Zinn 2002: 16–18). Similarly the emphasis on the need for moderation and restraint that runs throughout theory on civil disobedience, and the expectation that illegal action should be regarded as a tactic of last resort, signals the folding of disobedience within (rather than as a challenge to) modern political categories and structures (Laudani 2013: 5–7). Disobedience is tolerable only insofar as its more disruptive or revolutionary potentials have already been neutralised, and its subservience to obedience established.

The role of Christian thought and practice here is important. Great effort has been expended within Christian theology towards rationalising and enacting disobedience to political authority; these efforts have formed the basis for contemporary accounts and legitimisations of disobedience. However, the role of disobedience within Christianity turns on a contingent relationship with secular authority, which is legitimate only insofar as it accords with God's law. Christian *dis*obedience is therefore more properly understood as obedience to the higher law of God. Laudani conceptualises this as 'derived disobedience' or 'second-level obedience', arguing that, even when it has vindicated the lawfulness of disobedience to political authority, 'all Christian political thought . . . has claimed to be a catechesis of obedience' (2013: 22). Plowshares activist Sister Anne Montgomery makes precisely this point when she writes that 'we should speak of [principled lawbreaking] as divine obedience, rather than as civil disobedience' (2010: 1; see also Christoyannopoulos 2011: 164–5). To call attention to this is not to downplay the immense contribution of Christian radicals to the development of disobedience (in theory and in practice), but to highlight the role they have also played in establishing a hierarchy of obedience over disobedience that is to some extent reproduced both in theories of civil disobedience and in anti-militarist mobilisations of accountability.

Many anti-militarists express misgivings about the idea that direct action should be 'accountable' in the terms outlined above, fearing that this cedes too much authority to the state and its legal mechanisms, while obscuring the very real danger these institutions pose to marginalised subjects. While this contention rarely spills into open debate, it is a frequent topic of conversation amongst activists. One activist recounts her decision to risk arrest in order to blockade an arms factory:

> So I have absolutely no attachment to what is commonly known as accountable actions because I, I don't even like that phrase, like, that's fucked up . . . I don't ever feel like I want to be personally accountable to the state for an action that I have done, that's not the people I'm interested in being accountable to. But I decided that, given that I'm in a job position and a social position where I could get arrested and it wouldn't be a disaster for my life, that a useful way for us to definitely make sure that we held the space . . . was to have some people that were blockading with equipment who would stay there and be difficult to remove and if the police wanted to remove them, they were going to have to dismantle the equipment and arrest the activists . . . So I was like yeah, I feel like I can be one of those people, that's fine for me, so I went planning to get [arrested] – not like 'oh my God I really want to be arrested' because I never want to be arrested, but like 'I feel like I can take one for the team in this context.' (Interview N)

This more tactical account marks an important departure from civil disobedience-type justifications, dismissing the role of dominant political and legal institutions as legitimate arbiters. In calling forth and basing her actions on other sources of accountability – such as fellow activists and people from communities affected by the arms trade – this activist gives an account of disobedience that is more political than civil, reshaping the terms by which contestation takes place (Harcourt 2012).

However, this scepticism of accountability does not therefore mean that activists with a more instrumental attitude towards voluntary submission are not also bound up in relations of obedience. The processes of arrest and prosecution themselves tend to have the effect of compelling subjects into an obedient relationship with the state; this is their very purpose. With arrest and prosecution come court dates, legal aid applications, meetings with lawyers and other defendants, uncomfortable conversations with employers, fines, perhaps even prison. These are often exhausting, entail continual and low-level compliance with state bureaucracies, and take up a great deal of time and imagination. One's conduct is incorporated into the realm of legal contestation and, often, legalist discourse. If you want to defend yourself in court (or even to speak in mitigation), you tend to find yourself speaking the language of civil (dis)obedience – last resort, moderation, highest respect for the law – in what functions as a paradoxically dual affirmation of disobedience and obedience. This is not so much a critique as a diagnosis, of how using arrest and facing prosecution can tend to conduct activists within 'explicitly delineated political and legal spaces' (Odysseos 2012: 51). This conduction acts as a constraint on prefigurative explorations, as the opportunity to explore modes of politics, disobedience and becoming which disrupt or subvert hegemonic and militarist imaginaries is tempered, while the position and role of the state as the horizon of political possibility appears larger than ever.

Strategies of Dis/Obedience

As they face arrest and prosecution, activists are drawn into relations of obedience with the state and its legal apparatus. However, it would be limiting – indeed, dichotomising – to view their encounters with the legal system as only and straightforwardly determined by (and performative of) obedience. There are a series of ways in which anti-militarists engage with legal processes in a manner which subverts systems of power, redraws lines of accountability, and creates spaces for disobedient and prefigurative politics.

To begin with, it is important to point out that voluntary submission should in many cases be differentiated from active cooperation, and one can often see instances of refusal even in the act of submission. For example, when facing arrest activists will often 'go floppy', lying on the floor and relaxing their muscles, and thereby requiring up to four officers to carry them. This is a practice that can be both tactically useful (perhaps prolonging a blockade) and symbolically significant. Another example, more likely to be employed by those taking a more instrumental approach, occurs when activists decide before an action that, if arrested, they will collectively refuse to provide their names and addresses. Whilst to do so individually would probably prolong one's internment, mass disobedience may have the opposite effect. Refusals to adhere to bail conditions, and to pay any fines, demonstrate further the distinction between submission and more active cooperation.

Activists frequently claim that fighting one's case through the courts can provide opportunities to turn the state against itself, to reveal certain contradictions within the political and legal system, perhaps even to provoke a crisis. A central strategy here is the attempt to develop an 'affirmative' defence, whereby activists claim that they committed a crime in order to prevent an even greater crime from taking place (Tobey 2017: 120–7). There have been a number of high-profile cases where this defence has been successful and led to acquittals, including Seeds of Hope, the EDO Decommissioners, the Raytheon 9, and Seeds of Hope 2. Affirmative defences can be politically problematic for the government and companies; they involve activists seeking to establish that illegal practices were indeed taking place, and judges and/or juries ruling on whether these activists had reasonable grounds for action. As such, it is also not uncommon for charges against activists building cases based on affirmative defences to be dropped, as a preferable outcome to an embarrassing court defeat, or being compelled to reveal potentially sensitive information as evidence. This is precisely what happened to those arrested at the Block the Factory action, and indeed to others arrested while taking direct action against Elbit Systems.

It is not uncommon for judges to disallow affirmative defences, and to refuse to hear arguments relating to international law. Nonetheless, the attempt to pull in these factors is also important: it reveals their *non grata* status within the legal system, and thus its problematic political character.[5] In this sense, two options are available, and in both the activists can claim a partial victory. In one, an acquittal both challenges the legitimacy of official practice and establishes a public precedent which others might follow. In the other, the refusal to hear and/or accept an affirmative defence reveals the political terms of the legal system.

Many feel an aversion to arguments of this sort. As a Target Brimar leaflet states, **'That Brimar's business is legal does not make it moral'** (Target Brimar undated; original emphasis). There is a sense that challenging legality leaves too much intact, producing discourses which cede the terms of legitimacy too easily. An instructive case here is the focus on illegal weaponry (like cluster munitions and torture equipment) at DSEI. While this equipment has comprised a tiny proportion of the equipment displayed and marketed at the event, it has attracted a great deal of critical coverage, by both activists and the media (Milmo 2014; Amnesty UK 2015). This has allowed activists charged with obstructing the event to develop affirmative defences, notably resulting in the acquittal of eight defendants following DSEI 2015 (Stone 2016a).[6] While this is a smart legal strategy in the face of prosecution, such narratives also contribute to a framing which problematises the arms trade (and DSEI) with reference to particular excesses, in a manner which normalises (and renders direct action less legitimate with respect to) the vast majority of perfectly legal arms transfers.

Activists using affirmative defences are keen to stress that these approaches do not exhaust the space for legitimate action. For instance, following his acquittal for the Seeds of Hope 2 action, Sam Walton published the following tweet:

> The judge deciding we are not guilty doesn't make trying to disarm #Saudi jets bound for #Yemen any more right.
> But it is quite handy. (Walton 2017)

What emerges is a tension. Few (if any) activists really think that the problem with arms sales or nuclear weapons is that they are illegal, but they do recognise that claims to that nature can have powerful public effects, and in some ways expand the scope for direct action. Nonetheless, focusing on such claims can also have the effect of shaping or disciplining activism in ways which delimit the scope of anti-militarist critique. Those concerns are explored in more detail in the next chapter.

A third subversion that can be found in activist legal strategies involves the focus on seeking trial by jury, and the accompanying recasting of legitimacy this implies. This is generally reserved for cases where a significant amount of property damage has been caused, and activists often suggest that one is more likely to be acquitted when the case is heard by a jury (the Raytheon 9, Seeds of Hope and EDO Decommissioners cases all fall into this category), as juries are more likely to be sympathetic to affirmative defences than judges. Tactically, then, there are advantages here, to the extent that legal training sessions often reference the amount of damage one should cause in order to receive a trial by jury. However, there is also a wider, even prefigurative, politics, insofar as the desire to seek affirmation from peers rather than from a judge opens the question of agency and legitimacy beyond that of the state. At a CAAT gathering in Manchester in 2011, during a workshop led by Target Brimar about legal strategies, a number of activists expressed the desire to be held accountable by 'ordinary people' rather than magistrates. This connects into the focus on localism; discussing the matter with one of the EDO Decommissioners, he stated that the jury were 'our peers in the community', mobilising a sense of accountability more attuned to local dimensions.[7] Whilst such accounts clearly remain within a legalistic framework, and still circumscribe disobedience through a focus on accountability, that framing of accountability does not connect quite so neatly into the state form.

Legal strategies around voluntary submission can help to create spaces for direct action which might otherwise not have existed. The substantial publicity that surrounds court cases (and especially acquittals) can be highly effective in inciting further direct action, and in limiting the responses of companies and the police. In December 2010 a number of activists from Smash EDO locked themselves to the factory gates, prohibiting workers and delivery drivers from gaining access. This was not an uncommon action. What was unusual was that the police made no attempt to remove the protestors, and EDO MBM's managing director was forced to angle grind through part of the perimeter of the compound to create a new entrance (Indymedia UK 2010a, 2010b). Activists suspected that the recent acquittal of the EDO Decommissioners, and the accompanying decision by a jury that activists had reasonable grounds for thinking that EDO's sales to Israel were facilitating war crimes, had meant that EDO was resistant to going back to court to defend itself. This is an example of where pushing and expanding the limits of 'legal' action can serve as a strategy for expanding spaces in which direct action is possible.

Many activists' participation in the Faslane 365 campaign can be viewed along similar lines. This 2006–7 campaign was a year-long rolling blockade of the Faslane naval base in Scotland, the home of the UK's Trident nuclear submarines. Thousands of activists from across the UK travelled to the site and took part in daily blockades, with over 1,100 of these allowing themselves to be arrested. For a large number this was their first experience of arrest. That it was a particularly safe environment in which to get arrested was not unimportant; Strathclyde police are used to dealing with protestors at the base, a large support mechanism had been established to assist arrestees with legal and practical advice, and the vast majority of arrestees were released quickly and with no formal reprisal – fewer than a hundred were charged (Conway 2008). In this sense Faslane 365 became an advanced training session. Many of those involved had never worked with affinity groups, had never planned an action of this sort, and had never refused to obey police instructions. Through the relative predictability of the space, the police and the judicial system, a space was created to experiment with illegal direct action. The campaign served to build confidence and provide experience in a way which empowered many to carry out more actions. Several of my interviewees noted that Faslane 365 was a formative experience for them, and that much of their current activism can be traced back to it. A critical perspective on this process is important; embracing the security system built around the Faslane base is an uncomfortable contradiction. There is, however, a productive irony here, a tactical and contingent occupation of state security in order to learn new strategies of disruption.

We might also view this dynamic through a lens which attempts to demystify the experience of arrest and prosecution, and temper their disciplinary mechanisms. One interviewee, who had just spent a week in prison following arrest for a die-in and his subsequent refusal to pay the small fine imposed, suggested that fear of prison was potentially limiting, and that there may be advantages if the stigma were dispelled. Making it emphatic that his point related to the UK prison system and that he was not making light of more punitive conditions in other parts of the world, he suggested that

> there's a whole bunch of people who could quite easily go to prison, it wouldn't be a big deal for them, they wouldn't find it a horrible experience ... quite an interesting experience really ... and knowing that you have that ability or option maybe expands the tactical opportunities available. (Interview I)

He acknowledged that this would not be for everyone, nor should it be valorised above other actions, but that the self-discipline which the threat of prison and punishment effects might be deferred to some limited extent (Interview I). Berrigan, writing from his prison cell, made a similar (although clearly now quite dated) argument, suggesting that 'Americans have a phobia against jail because we have less of a tradition of resistance, and less of a tradition of jail experience influencing the national consciousness' (1970: 186).

These responses demonstrate the shortcomings of establishing straightforward distinctions between undermining and reproducing legal forms, and between obedience and disobedience. Nevertheless, the second half of this chapter has suggested that there are significant challenges that accompany voluntary submission tactics and their wider relationship with obedience and legalism. There are, of course, strategically convincing reasons why disobedience must be rationalised. As Stellan Vinthagen argues, disobedience 'must be justified with some kind of special reason or argument. Without a *rationalization for exception*, legitimisation of the breach of the rules will not convince others' (2015: 86; original emphasis). My argument is emphatically not intended to dismiss or castigate those performances which can be integral to the success of campaigns, and which have occasionally kept my friends out of prison. Instead, it is to think about the limits that are enacted by such gestures. This is perhaps less a critique than an analysis of the power relations within which activist tactics are situated, and the constraints that operate on, are reproduced by, and occasionally are subverted through their actions. One argument that has run through these reflections has been that, in voluntary submission tactics, disobedience tends to become subordinated to obedience (in more or less explicit or enthusiastic terms). In the closing discussion, I want to offer a counter-reading to that claim.

Making Mischief

The twin politics of obedience and disobedience play a paradoxical and even aporetic role in modern Western politics. Obedience to the authority of government and law is the precondition of politics. However, the very foundations on which that obedience is legitimised, principles of liberty and autonomy, create the very conditions for disobedience. Indeed, or so the story goes, it is disobedience towards pre-modern sources of authority that gives birth to modern politics and the modern subject (Laudani 2013: 1–3). Disobedience is therefore central to modern politics, though its role is often circumscribed and neutralised through processes which render it subordinated to some articulation of obedience. There is a certain tension within the concept of disobedience itself: on the one hand, disruptive of authority, while on the other, perpetually rationalised through reference to (some other) authority – whether political, religious, ethical, or revolutionary.

Some account of how disobedience is entangled with and constituted by obedience is essential. A recognition of the complex relations of obligation, duty, and consent within particular codes of reason is clearly important, while facile claims to be unburdened by authority are limited, and a diagnosis of how practices of resistance are conducted and shaped through their encounter with obligation is crucial. And yet, something important is lost if disobedience is conceptualised as only ever a practice of some higher obedience, or as always straightforwardly folded into a hegemonic project. Such accounts neutralise the aporia at the heart of obedience and disobedience, reproducing a hierarchy of one over the other and thus stabilising a central strategy by which modern politics are reproduced (Laudani 2013: 5–6).

The argument of the second half of this chapter has been that anti-militarist practices are more closely bound up in relations of obedience than might often be acknowledged. This is an important critique, but it should not be overstated to the point where all examples of disobedience are reframed as yet more obedience; doing so would only reproduce the hierarchy. Instead, and while thinking critically about the contours and co-constitutive relationships between obedience and disobedience, we might hold space for the excess, for that element of disobedience that is not so easily recaptured and framed through (second-order) obedience. This is where Loizidou takes us when she argues that only conceptualising disobedience in rational terms (as in theories of civil disobedience) empties out the subjective character of disobedience. It is precisely in the embodied labour of disobedience that discrete acts are made possible, and that the radical possibilities of disobedience are contained (Loizidou 2013).

While theories of civil disobedience are largely focused on *acts* of disobedience, a radical politics of disobedience is more concerned with the generation of disobedient forms of subjectivity. These, cultivating a certain art of disobedience, can take particular acts as their object, but it is insofar as they tend towards a more general subversion of governance and obligation that they are most valuable. There are a number of ways of conceptualising such subjectivities: 'destituent power' (Agamben 2014; Laudani 2013), 'voluntary inservitude' (Foucault 2007b: 47), 'discipline of indiscipline' (Newman 2010b: 46), or even 'anarchist calisthenics' (Scott 2012: 1–5). What draws these together is a mobilisation of disobedience which resists the straightforward subordination into a hierarchy with obedience.

One way to recognise this production and cultivation of disobedient subjects is through the aesthetic pleasure of and in disobedience. This is what Finchett-Maddock gestures towards when she exhorts disobedience not as a tragic and regretful break with obedience, but as an enjoyable encounter with *naughtiness*, which is not primarily concerned with its own legitimisation but which nonetheless serves as a potent space for the production of resisting subjectivities (2013). The delighted aesthetics of disobedience are clearly not immune to reproducing power relations (indeed, they may function precisely to mask them), nor are they innocent of their entanglement with obedience – to something, at least. But that subjective element is nonetheless important; it is here that we see disobedience as not only subordinate, but as its own political energy and presence, that can be cultivated and explored and generative of certain kinds of resistance.

The encounter with and occupation of naughtiness – of joy and comradeship and delight in disobedience – is highly visible within anti-militarism. It has been palpable in examples throughout this book. The experience of doing something that you are not supposed to, of transgressing the lines which delimit acceptable forms of conduct and agency, and discovering (again and again) that the scope of political possibility is wider than you had previously imagined, is a powerful one. Especially if you are also dressed as a dinosaur, or driving a tank, or transforming a road into a dance workshop. It is no accident that CAAT's action planning team are referred to within the organisation as the 'mischief team', nor that a quiet invitation to take part in disruptive action often begins with the tantalising question, 'Do you want to do something naughty?'

And while, in some ways, these pleasures might be more apparent amongst those who feel less attachment to taking 'accountable' actions (insofar as their action is not quite so primed to enter into a process of political obedience), this is by no means uniformly the case. To again cite Needham: 'I rather liked the codenames in the same way I liked sneaking around in the dark at Wharton; it was fun, like playing spies but with a serious purpose' (2016: 66). Those who insist on taking actions accountably are just as likely to take pleasure in transgression, naughtiness, the ridiculous and cheeky dimensions of disobedient actions, as those who do not. This is important; while the critiques that have been developed in this chapter about the role of accountability and obedience remain salient, it is notable that that rationality is to a certain extent subverted by those practices themselves, insofar as they also make space for a more aesthetic experience of disobedience.

This is not to claim that that pleasure is politically useful or defensible, nor that it cannot function to obscure the militarised, gendered, racialised dynamics which together shape what is and what can be experienced as pleasurable or desirable. The political and subversive qualities of playfulness are, as has been discussed in earlier chapters, always dependent on context. It is, instead, to suggest that there is an active, subjective politics of disobedience that exceeds the hierarchy. In considering the production of radical, disobedient subjects, that excess is a powerful political space.

Notes

1. On self-suffering and *satyagraha*, see Bondurant (1988: 26–9).
2. On open defiance in Christian pacifism, see Christoyannopoulos (2011: 162–4).
3. See Rawls (1971: 366–7); Singer (1973); Thoreau (1993: 9).
4. See Arendt (1970); Greenawalt (1987: 226–43); Hill (2013); Rawls (1971: 363–91); Singer (1973); Smith (2013).
5. On how the Plowshares movement negotiates precisely these dynamics, see Tobey (2017: 96–141).
6. This acquittal was later overturned by the High Court, but the activists were not re-tried.
7. He also firmly stated that, whilst the affirmation of the jury was important in practical terms and with respect to their wider campaign, he was prepared to go to prison, and did not feel that the legitimacy of the action truly hinged on the legal outcome.

CHAPTER 9

Regimes

7 February 2017. Central London. The Judicial Review
It's 8.30 a.m. and I'm standing outside the Royal Courts of Justice, just a few steps away from my office at the LSE. I scan the faces of passers-by and wonder whether I'm likely to be seen by any of my students, while trying not to stare directly at the bank of press photographers and television cameras pointed in my direction. Today is the first day of hearings for the judicial review that CAAT are pursuing against the British government, during which their lawyers will argue that arms sales to Saudi Arabia are unlawful. The Royal Saudi Air Force has been using British-sold weapons to bomb Yemen for nearly two years and a deal for new Eurofighter Typhoons is in the pipeline, investing the case with an urgency that is wholly unreflected in the pace of proceedings. My role today is simple: I'm holding up one side of a large banner, its stark message – STOP ARMING SAUDI – providing easy visuals for the reports that will run this evening and tomorrow morning.

*

I play a small but active part in the Stop Arming Saudi campaign. As a member of CAAT's Steering Committee, I was involved in the decision to pursue the judicial review (at significant financial cost to the organisation). I also supported Sam and Woody after their attempt to prevent the delivery of the previous order of Typhoon jets. However, as I engaged, I became increasingly aware of how the basic structure of anti-arms trade discourse – even that mobilised by avowedly more radical actors like CAAT, in important campaigns like this – might actually function to reproduce certain forms of (liberal, racialised) militarism. As activists work to generate narratives which capture public attention, and which 'make sense' within existing public discourse, they must also work to make themselves intelligible within the terms of that discourse. These processes fold anti-militarist subjects into particular rationalities and silences. While radical politics is supposed to occupy and unsettle such discourses, it is often primed to reproduce them.

This chapter begins by looking at how radical anti-arms trade activists have criticised the recently ratified UN Arms Trade Treaty. They have done so because, while it purports to restrain the arms trade, the treaty actually functions to legitimise the vast majority of arms transfers. In the rest of the chapter I argue that these activists are potentially vulnerable to the same critiques. I demonstrate how much of anti-arms trade campaigning makes use of the 'repressive regimes discourse', which implies that the arms trade is illegitimate because arms are routinely sold to repressive, authoritarian or undemocratic regimes. The repressive regimes discourse can be problematised both because it invites a focus on excesses in a manner which reproduces liberal militarism as 'non-excessive', and because it trades on implicitly racialised understandings about the kinds of subjects and forms of violence that should be regarded as dangerous.

The chapter therefore argues that problematisations of the arms trade by anti-arms trade activists can themselves be folded into and performative of militarised discourses about international politics. We see how attempts at a radical anti-militarist politics are not exempt from the legitimisation and reproduction of militarism. This has significant implications for both our understanding of resistance – which in this context is perhaps less radical than its adherents might desire – and militarism, which is structuring public discourse and anti-militarist politics in ways that might not immediately be apparent. The chapter closes by considering the implications of this argument, as well as by pointing out some directions in anti-militarist politics which are perhaps not so easily captured by this discourse and critique.

The Arms Trade Treaty

In April 2013 human rights NGOs including Amnesty International and Oxfam celebrated as the UN General Assembly adopted the landmark Arms Trade Treaty (ATT). The treaty, which came into full force in December 2014, aims to regulate the international trade in conventional arms and to prohibit the transfer of weaponry likely to be used to commit serious violations of human rights (UN 2013). The campaign to establish an arms trade treaty was led by the Control Arms coalition, which hailed the General Assembly vote as 'an incredible moment' (2013). Oxfam's Head of Arms Control claimed that

> from the streets of Latin America, to the camps in eastern Congo, to the valleys of Afghanistan, communities living in fear of attacks because of the unregulated arms trade can now hope for a safer future. The world will be a more secure place to live once the Treaty is in place. (Control Arms 2013)

The treaty was the culmination of more than ten years of concerted NGO campaigning, and is unprecedented in its attempt to institutionalise a human rights-focused standard for the international arms trade.

In contrast with the exuberant responses of the major NGOs, most of the more radical and direct action-oriented elements within British anti-militarism have remained at best suspicious, and often actively hostile, towards the ATT. CAAT has been sceptical of the idea of the treaty since its emergence, a position which has at times damaged its relationship with other NGOs. It argues that the treaty is rooted in a depoliticising distinction between 'legitimate' and 'illegitimate' arms transfers, that it is unlikely to substantially affect British arms sales (a position also taken by the British government), and that it risks legitimising and even giving humanitarian veneer to arms sales which are compliant with the regime (CAAT 2013). Writing in a personal capacity, CAAT staff member Kirk Jackson labelled the ATT a 'historic and momentous failure', highlighting the lack of transparency and enforcement mechanisms, the omission of ammunition, drones and tear gas from the treaty, and the many loopholes within the prohibition on high-risk transfers (Jackson 2013). Beyond these specific critiques, Jackson raises the concern that the treaty risks boosting the image of the arms trade at the expense of the anti-militarist movement:

> The treaty will undoubtedly be used to burnish the image of arms companies too. Already, the website of arms company BAE Systems, which supplies weapons systems to repressive regimes, talks about its support for the ATT under headings like 'meeting high ethical standards' and 'working responsibly'.
>
> The treaty's failure also comes at a cost to the movement that campaigned for it. Over the last decade, a huge amount of resources and effort was devoted to the Control Arms campaign. Over a million people signed petitions, and tens of thousands of activists were mobilised to lobby, demonstrate and publicise the campaign. Now that the UN has adopted a treaty that cannot fulfil the expectations that were created for it, grass-roots campaigners may become disillusioned with tackling the arms trade. (Jackson 2013)

The attitude of many anti-militarists towards the ATT is broadly one of hostile indifference. When asked, activists criticise the treaty both because it is unlikely to substantially reduce arms transfers and because it serves as a public relations boost for the arms industry. In practice, however, the topic rarely arises, the treaty's issues being viewed as broadly self-evident.

Stavrianakis develops these critiques of the arms trade further. She argues that not only will the ATT have little effect on arms exports from the major arms producers, but it functions to legitimise the liberal forms of militarism exercised and embodied by major Western states (Stavrianakis 2016a). The concept of liberal militarism has been developed to account for the particular form of militarism operating in and amongst certain advanced capitalist nations, including Britain. Central features include:

> [t]he capital- and technology-intensive character of the preparation for and conduct of war; a strong commitment to military production across war- and peacetime and self-understanding as a primarily 'economic, industrial and commercial power'; the distanced form of attacks on

Southern populations and simultaneous containment of social conflict at home and policing of empire abroad, often featuring supposedly 'small' massacres; a universalist ideology and conception of world order; low levels of military participation by society; and a state-capital relation that is formally separate but organically related. (Stavrianakis 2016a: 845; see also Edgerton 1991; Mabee 2016)

The legitimacy of liberal militarism and liberal violence is established by linking these to the protection of moral values, the promotion of human rights, and the sanction of and compliance with international law. The ATT functions to tie arms exports into this framework. By mandating states to weigh the risk of human rights violations against the interests of peace and security when making decisions about exports, it allows liberal states to justify potentially controversial exports in the name of the latter, while positioning the arms export regime as fundamentally humanitarian. And by placing international law at the centre of decisions about arms exports, it reinforces an international legal system that serves to naturalise the Western way of war, both by shielding practices from criticism and by criminalising low-tech violence while legitimating high-tech war. Arms exports become a site of human rights, international law, peace and security, while liberal exporting states continue to construct a 'liberal international order that is nonetheless reliant on coercion and violence' (Stavrianakis 2016a: 841).

Even if the treaty does lead to some restrictions on the transfer of arms from Western producers to non-Western customers, it is clear that it will have no impact on intra-Western transfers. Despite the fact that violations of international humanitarian law have been carried out by Western states using arms supplied by other Western nations in Iraq, Yemen and Pakistan, the refusal to transfer arms 'between Western states on human rights or humanitarian grounds are politically unthinkable' (Stavrianakis 2016a: 851). Moreover, while Amnesty, Human Rights Watch and other humanitarian NGOs have called attention to (potential) war crimes carried out by Western forces, they have stopped short of linking these to the necessity of the ATT or calling for a suspension of arms transfers. The new arms control regime thus fits alongside, rather than in opposition to, liberal militarism.

Stavrianakis's critique provides an important corrective to the claim that the ATT represents a substantial challenge to the international arms trade. Despite their lofty claims, the humanitarian NGOs that campaigned for the treaty have potentially served to legitimise those practices and institutions which any substantive challenge to the arms trade must call into question. It is this counter-productive dynamic which more radical anti-militarists have pointed out. However, even as they criticise these NGOs, those same anti-militarists often engage in very similar forms of critique, framing the arms trade in ways which call attention to particular excesses while omitting a more substantive critique of the arms trade and liberal militarism. While the political position of these anti-militarists is, in important ways, a more radical one, this is often lost in their public discourse.

Repressive Regimes

In contrast to the arms control NGOs, the anti-arms trade groups in this book have a more straightforwardly abolitionist agenda. Their *declared* focus is not on ameliorating, restraining, or regulating the arms trade, but on abolishing it completely. Such a posture puts these activists in a strong position to criticise the legitimating moves of the NGOs while articulating a more consistent anti-militarist politics. It also better places them to identify and critique the role of the arms trade in underpinning the liberal militarism and wars of Western states. However, while groups like CAAT, STAF and Disarm DSEI profess a radical critique, the specific ways in which they problematise the arms trade often place them on more conventional territory. My particular focus here is on what I term the 'repressive regimes discourse', which serves as the dominant framework through which activists criticise the arms trade. I argue that, even as the discourse operates as an effective means by which to direct critical attention towards the arms trade, it imports highly problematic tropes with respect to global North–South imaginaries, liberal militarism, and the racialised character of contemporary militarism.

Anti-arms trade activists cite a wide range of arguments in order to demonstrate the malign effects of the trade.[1] Whilst these often include concerns about international development and corruption, most prominent are critiques which focus on the sale of arms in cases where these might fuel conflict, be used to commit human rights abuses, or entrench authoritarian or repressive regimes. On its website, CAAT states the following:

> Weapons supplied by the UK have been used in Saudi Arabia's attacks on Yemen, Israel's attacks on Gaza, on democracy protesters in Hong Kong, and in the violent repression of uprisings in the Middle East and North Africa. **This is not OK.**
>
> Yet the UK still spends public money on persuading some of the world's worst human rights abusers and most unstable regimes to buy weapons. (CAAT 2017c)[2]

And on similar terms, STAF critique the DSEI arms fair: 'For one week every two years, in East London, arms companies display their weapons to buyers from around the world, including countries in conflict, authoritarian regimes and countries with serious human rights problems' (Stop the Arms Fair 2013). While a concern with arming authoritarian and 'repressive' regimes has long been an important part of this discourse, its prominence grew considerably in 2011. This followed the uprisings across the Middle East and North Africa and the use of British-sold equipment to suppress popular movements, most prominently in Egypt, Libya and Bahrain (CAAT 2012).

An important component of the repressive regimes discourse is the use of country lists. In order to call attention to the actions of a particular arms company, or to the problematic nature of an arms fair, or to the hypocritical or complicit function of a government department, activists will list the self-evidently 'bad' states involved in the relationship. Through these relationships, the violences of the arms trade are made apparent. CAAT regularly use such a framing. In a two-page spread detailing their This Is Not OK campaign against DSO (the government body which aids arms companies in conducting international sales), they state that staff '[tour] the world to recommend UK weapons at arms fairs hosting delegations from Zimbabwe, Burma, Rwanda, China' and secure '"high level" interventions to encourage authoritarian and corrupt regimes like Libya and Algeria to buy our weapons' (CAAT 2011a). Disarm DSEI, in the 'What is DSEI?' section of their website, state that '[d]elegations invited by the UK include countries involved in conflict & human rights abuses and those with desperately underfunded development needs, including Indonesia, Iraq, Angola & Colombia' (Disarm DSEI 2015). Reflecting on DSEI 2015, CAAT highlight the fact that, out of sixty-one countries who were invited to send delegations, fourteen have authoritarian regimes and four (Colombia, Iraq, Pakistan and Saudi Arabia) 'are identified by the UK government as having wide-ranging human rights concerns' (CAAT 2015b).

These lists are powerful. They quickly establish a moral equation, and can therefore be highly effective in fast-paced situations where there is a need to win an argument, or in contexts where brevity takes precedence over nuance. Such situations include handing out leaflets in public, conversations with potential arms trade employees at counter-recruitment events, selecting text for banners or websites, and providing soundbites for the media. Central to the success of the list is the *self-evidently* problematic quality of the recipient state; if that premise is accepted, then the arms sales themselves must be similarly questionable.

While lists may be used to discredit certain companies or arms fairs, more individual campaigns focus on specific controversial exporting relationships. In the 1990s British movements focused on the UK's arms sales to Indonesia, responding to the use of British weaponry in Indonesia's occupation of East Timor. In more recent years campaigns have opposed arms exports to Bahrain, Egypt and Turkey, and challenged the two-way arms trade with Israel. However, the most prominent focus has long been on arms sales to Saudi Arabia. This is perhaps unsurprising. In 1985 the UK government signed the first al-Yamamah deal with the Saudi government. This was the largest single defence contract in British history, and with it the UK replaced the US as the key supplier to the Royal Saudi Air Force (Nonneman 2001: 649–50). Since that time Saudi Arabia has been the primary customer for British arms exports.

Activists have challenged the UK–Saudi relationship throughout this time but have done so with particular intensity since 2015, when the Saudi-led coalition intervened in the Yemeni Civil War. The intervention has been marked by the repeated targeting of civilian infrastructure and killing of civilians, precipitating what one UN staffer called a 'humanitarian catastrophe' (O'Brien 2015). In the UK, attention has focused on the diplomatic cover provided by the British government for Saudi Arabia, the use of British-sold jets and bombs in the intervention, and the fact that the British government has licensed over £4.5 billion in new arms sales since the bombing began.[3] In response, CAAT has run a major campaign under the heading 'Stop Arming Saudi'. Stunts and actions associated with the campaign have been discussed in earlier chapters, including disruptions at the BAE Systems AGM, the Seeds of Hope 2 direct action, and the NPIW protest. On more unconventional territory, CAAT have attempted to pursue the campaign through legal processes, seeking a judicial review in an attempt to get arms exports to Saudi Arabia declared unlawful. This case and campaign is discussed in more detail below.

The focus on controversial exports and controversial states at work in the repressive regimes discourse is contoured by a series of relative silences. Implicit in every list of 'bad' regimes are those clients and customers who are not included, whose status is considered sufficiently non-controversial that they fail to develop the point. It is, frankly, a less arresting argument to oppose an arms fair because it includes delegations from Norway, France, Australia and Canada. Especially conspicuous in its absence is the US. After Saudi Arabia, the US is the main customer for UK arms exports (which totalled somewhere between £4.9 billion and £9.2 billion from 2008 to 2018), and British arms companies have major production operations in the US (Perlo-Freeman 2010: 259–60); however, the lists rarely include the US, nor indeed any NATO members except Turkey. These arms trading relationships are normalised in the process of calling attention to particular excesses.

Stavrianakis critiques the repressive regimes discourse for its role in reproducing the hierarchical structure of the international system. She argues that

> [a]rguing for an end to controversial exports – which are usually exports to the South – without a wider argument about the structure of military

power in international relations leaves the military dominance of Northern states intact and does nothing to challenge hierarchical North–South relations. (Stavrianakis 2010: 59)

This leads to a 'depoliticisation of militarism within the European world' (2010: 111) and the 'production of the South as a site of intervention and its resultant disciplining' (2010: 114).[4] While Stavrianakis identifies these issues in the context of mainstream NGO discourse, similar dynamics can be found in more direct action-oriented sections of the movement (and in some academic accounts (Gibbon and Sylvester 2017)).

In introducing this critique, I am not arguing that the anti-arms trade groups under discussion operate on straightforwardly depoliticised terms. Stavrianakis recognises that CAAT does go further than most NGOs insofar as it locates the problem in 'the relationship between arms capital and the state within the UK', where others such as Oxfam locate it more firmly in the South (2010: 59). CAAT have been careful to situate Britain's arms trading relationships with states like Saudi Arabia and Bahrain in their historical and colonial context (Hirst and CAAT 2000; Wearing 2016). It would also be misplaced to argue that there is *no* problematisation of the arms trade with respect to European or Northern militarism. CAAT is a prominent member of the European Network Against Arms Trade, through which it campaigns against the militarisation of the EU. At the time of the invasion and occupation of Iraq, it also highlighted arms sales to the US (which 'appears to be running amok') as a specific problem (CAAT 2003: 25).

However, when these various concerns have translated into campaign material, the overwhelming focus has remained on arms exports to the South. In conversation activists acknowledge the potential pitfalls here, but contend that focusing on particular problematic exports makes sense as a campaign strategy. As one CAAT staff member explained,

> when you're starting with a brief as big as 'stop the arms trade', the first thing you do as a campaign strategist is you break it down into transitional demands: what are some smaller, achievable objectives within this? How do we understand this campaign and make it real? And I can see that

looking at some of the worst instances of where UK weapons have been directly implicated in well-documented human rights abuses is a really sensible way to do that. (Interview N)

Another activist suggested that, when attempting to enlist public support for campaigns, starting off with deep-rooted or apparently uncontroversial practices (such as arms transfers to the US) is unlikely to build much momentum; it is more productive to begin by establishing a basic moral or ethical equation and then work from there (Interview B). As Charli Carpenter argues, negotiations like these are a common task for social movement actors, who seek to frame issues in a manner which resonates with the 'moral language familiar to international donors, belligerents, and the media' (2005: 297). Compromises and strategic essentialisms are commonplace, because attempts to mobilise or reshape norms are 'mediated by the strategic environment in which they operate' (2005: 311; see also Joachim 2003; Payne 2001).

The question of whether and how to make transitional demands has been heavily contested in radical political theory. It is useful here to distinguish between the sceptical position held by Day, and Slavoj Žižek's more strategic approach. As discussed in Chapter 1, Day argues that radical politics should avoid the 'politics of demand' in favour of a 'politics of the act'. His concern is that making demands on a political system tends to do more to legitimise and solidify that system than is ever conceded. It is on those terms that Day calls for a radical politics grounded in a prefigurative ontology (2005, 2011). Žižek recognises the double-edged nature of demands, but nevertheless argues that the art of politics consists in making demands that seem reasonable, but which 'strike at the core of hegemonic ideology and imply much more radical change' (2014: 111). He cites the call for universal healthcare in the US as an example of such a demand.

The Stop Arming Saudi campaign is an excellent example of a demand in Žižek's model. It is realistic, but cannot be met without a substantial revisioning of how British militarist geopolitics operate. In making this demand, campaigners thus highlight the substantial disjuncture between what most people would consider to be a reasonable demand and what the political system will permit. At its best, Stop Arming Saudi is a demand that is simultaneously moderate and radical, both demonstrating the absurdity of claims made by the British government to respect and uphold human rights *and* pointing towards the drastic upheavals necessary to redress the situation. However, Day's approach pushes us to think about the frameworks of intelligibility we situate ourselves within, and to consider the kinds of politics that we reproduce, when we issue a particular demand in a particular way. If Žižek's attention rests on the potential for demands to exploit fractures, Day challenges us to consider their role in remaking systems. There are two ways we can see the Stop Arming Saudi campaign (and the wider repressive regimes discourse) operating like this.

Liberal Militarism

The repressive regimes discourse works to cultivate general opposition to the arms trade by placing focus on its *excesses*, that is, on particularly problematic arms sales and arms trading relationships. It trades on the implication that the practice of selling arms to such clearly unacceptable regimes demonstrates the unscrupulous, hypocritical, unethical, or straightforwardly violent nature of the industry. In the context of making transitional or moderate demands while pursuing an abolitionist agenda, the idea is that such a framing introduces a basic critical perspective towards the arms trade that might then translate into more substantive critique (of both the 'non-excessive' arms trade and militarism more broadly). This is a more developed position than that of the NGOs, insofar as it refuses to stop with excesses and instead views them within a wider political framework that should be subject to challenge. However, this more substantive underlying critique does not necessarily insulate more radical positions from the charge that the performative effects of a focus on excesses can have relatively conservative implications.

One of the effects of placing overwhelming attention on excesses is the normalisation of that which is not considered excessive, that being the acceptable or unremarkable conduct from which certain practices or policies have departed. The repressive regimes discourse, with its use of lists and focus on particular problematic relationships, turns a critical gaze away from a significant portion of Britain's arms transfers. Whether these are viewed as politically unproblematic or as unfeasible campaign topics is clearly important when considering the political constitution of anti-arms trade activism, but perhaps less so when considering the performative effects of the discourse. That the vast majority of anti-arms trade public discourse focuses exclusively on states contained within the repressive regimes discourse, and very rarely mentions the UK's lucrative trading relationships with the US, France, South Korea and Italy, is not a passive gesture. It actively reproduces such relationships as unproblematic. Beyond the focus on particular bilateral trades (which itself will tend to maintain focus on excesses), we might consider the particular networks of militarism which are normalised through the discourse. It is particularly notable that transfers amongst NATO states are rarely challenged (with the exception of Turkey), their status too unremarkable to serve as grounds for a campaign.

By focusing on particular arms trading relationships, and so making the problem of the arms trade a problem of excesses, the repressive regimes discourse overlooks how liberal militarism functions, violently, normally. One of the major political moves of liberal militarism has been to render its violence unremarkable, banal, even administrative, with only occasional (and always humanitarian) spectacles (Dillon and Reid 2001; Evans 2013; Jabri 2012: 126–30). Its coercive apparatuses, including military bases, private security operators, and even drone strikes, are largely absent from (Western) public attention.[5] When incidents of 'excessive' violence carried out by agents of Western states do reach the eyes and ears of domestic populations, these are generally excused as regrettable accidents or isolated events tied to culpable individuals – never as a manifestation and inevitable consequence of liberal militarism itself (Owens 2003; Razack 2004). It is this normalised element that permits claims about the pacific role played by liberal states, and obfuscations of the charge of international aggression. In short, the ability to represent its violence as *non*-excessive has been a discursive strategy that sits at the heart of Western and liberal militarism.

This problem of normalisation is compounded insofar as the

repressive regimes discourse reproduces a distinction between legitimate and illegitimate arms transfers that is itself a productive narrative for liberal militarism. Liberal militarism depends on a series of hierarchical distinctions between legitimate and illegitimate forms of violence, warfare and arms transfer. The humanitarian, pacific and civilising status of liberal violence is constituted through identifications of illiberal or barbaric forms, which beg suppression, pacification and policing. This is a core epistemological premise which links classical to contemporary forms of imperialism. It is for precisely these reasons that the arms industry and Western governments are only too happy to identify and criticise illicit arms transfers (which invariably signals transfers amongst non-Western actors). CAAT and other abolitionist groups recognise that these gestures serve to give a humanitarian veneer to the arms transfers of the UK and other states – such is the foundation of their critique of the ATT.[6] However, the repressive regimes discourse leads us onto very similar territory.

In positioning the problem of the arms trade as one of excesses, the repressive regimes discourse tacitly accepts the terrain of distinction (between legitimate and illegitimate arms transfers), and so enters into debate about where the line should be drawn. In doing so, it implicitly recognises the existence of a legitimate arms trade, unuttered, behind that line. Of course, the specific lines being drawn by arms trade advocates and anti-arms trade activists are *very* different. Nonetheless, that difference betrays a similarity with respect to both the reproduction of a legitimate/illegitimate distinction, and the rarely questioned positioning of Western states on the right side of that divide. In this sense, the discourse operates within the contours of a narrative that has been central to liberal militarism and on which the legitimacy of organisations like NATO depends. In so doing, it obscures the space for a critique of Western and liberal militarism within anti-arms trade politics.

We can see how this focus on excesses performs certain normalising functions in CAAT's Stop Arming Saudi campaign, and especially in the 2017 judicial review. CAAT began legal proceedings when the government responded to the Saudi-led coalition's bombing of Yemen not by suspending arms sales, but by increasing them. CAAT argued that the government was in breach of its own arms export licensing laws, which prohibit the sale of weapons when there is a 'substantial risk' that they will be used to commit serious violations of human rights. The case was highly effective in both mobilising supporters and generating high levels of media coverage. Features covering the case, the conflict in Yemen, and Britain's role in arming Saudi Arabia appeared in every major British newspaper, and it received widespread television and radio coverage (Fisher 2017; Reuters 2017; Ross 2017). As well as being a powerful outreach tool, the case effectively raised tensions within the British government, itself divided on the question of selling arms to Saudi Arabia (Stavrianakis 2016b; Stone 2016b). A positive verdict would almost certainly cause chaos, forcing the government to either damage relations with a key ally or, more probably, tie itself in knots refusing to comply with the ruling. The case therefore makes very good campaigning sense.

However, we might also consider the performative work the case does in centring discourse around excesses. The nature of the case means that a framework which distinguishes between legal and illegal arms sales cannot but play a major role. Such a discourse distinguishes between particular arms transfers which do not fit within accepted legal bounds (and which should therefore be suspended), and the rest which do (and so should not). There are compelling reasons to think that granting export licences for arms sales to Saudi Arabia is clearly unlawful, and my argument here is not for a moment supposed to suggest that a halt in arms exports to Saudi Arabia is of anything other than urgent necessity. Nevertheless, the case also serves to reproduce the legal/illegal distinction, and to present arms sales to Saudi Arabia as an unusual excess. This framing obscures the co-implication of law and war, the ways in which both domestic and international law are, 'despite noble rhetoric to the contrary . . . formulated deliberately to privilege military necessity at the cost of humanitarian values' (Jochnick and Normand 1994: 50; see also Anghie 2005; Owens 2007: 72–90). There is something of a double bind. If arms sales to Saudi Arabia are ruled unlawful then the idea that law serves a pacific or restraining purpose is stabilised, as is the lawful practice of non-excessive liberal militarism. If, as seems more likely, arms sales to Saudi Arabia are ruled lawful, then the function of law as a legitimating device is more apparent than ever. In centring the legal/illegal distinction, CAAT therefore risk feeding into the normalising and legitimating terms of liberal militarism. This is not to argue that the case is not worthwhile, nor that it *only* or *necessarily* plays such a role; rather to point out that there are certain conservative implications even in the context of substantial critique.

Racialisation

The repressive regimes discourse also reproduces racialised framings of international politics which are themselves bound up in militarised imaginaries. This is the second way in which we might think critically about the role played by transitional demands. The discourse functions by relying on the *self-evidently* problematic nature of customer states. It is because Colombia, Saudi Arabia and Zimbabwe instinctively and reliably sound bad that the moral and political terms can be so swiftly established. This self-evidence taps into a sense of the kinds of people who should and should not be allowed weapons, and to the kinds of violence implicitly associated with different subjects – understandings which rely on the hierarchical and racialised frameworks of the international usually associated with standard of civilisation narratives.

The racialised character of the discourse is sometimes made explicit in the kinds of language activists use to talk about particular actors. Whilst CAAT, STAF and other groups are generally scrupulous in their public communications, one can often hear activists refer to Saudi Arabia and other Gulf states as 'barbaric', 'savage', or even 'medieval', and in the specific case of Saudi Arabia to make continual reference to beheadings as a specific marker of cruelty.[7] Those orientalising framings mark the violence of these states as fundamentally Other, as external to modernity, rather than as intimately and historically interwoven with Western practices of warfare.[8] They also function to reproduce an enlightened, civilised, modern 'us' who stands apart from and above such violence (Brown 2008: 149–205). These knowledge strategies were integral to both colonial and Cold War rationalities, and have been central to the War on Terror, providing 'the mantle of civilization, progress, and peace as cover for imperial militaristic adventures', sanctioning 'illiberal aggression toward what is marked as intolerable without tarring the "civilized" status of the aggressor' (Brown 2008: 179; see also Boletsi 2013: 39–45).[9] As such, their reproduction within anti-militarist discourse clearly invites critique.[10] However, perhaps more important than these explicit framings are the ways these racial codes are implicit in the repressive regimes discourse. We can see this when we examine the relationship between the discourse and public opinion.

The discourse is useful because it is a highly effective means of gaining public support. While activists may themselves have an abolitionist agenda, framings around particular problematic arms transfers allow them to find common ground with those who are politically moderate but who still oppose the sale of arms in certain circumstances. In this role, the discourse works extremely well, allowing for quick and convincing interventions in comment pieces (Smith 2018), press interviews (Dennis 2017; Doward 2017b), when designing campaign material, and when talking to members of the public. These are all situations where there is a certain imperative to frame debates in a manner which resonates swiftly with as many people as possible. In such contexts, the repressive regimes discourse is the obvious and most effective way of communicating. Principally, this is because the discourse does indeed reflect public opinion.

CAAT are keen to emphasise that the weight of public opinion supports the demands made within the context of the repressive regimes discourse. Polls commissioned by CAAT show that 62 per cent of UK adults consider the sale of arms to Saudi Arabia unacceptable (against 11 per cent who consider it acceptable). Other states regularly included within the discourse fare similarly, with Libya at 73 per cent to 4 per cent, China 63 per cent to 10 per cent, Pakistan 68 per cent to 7 per cent, and Iran 72 per cent to 4 per cent. On more general terms, 71 per cent agree that the UK government 'should not promote the sale of British military equipment to foreign governments with a poor record on human rights' (against 6 per cent who disagree), and 60 per cent agree that the government should not promote sales 'to foreign countries that aren't democracies' (against 9 per cent). These numbers put CAAT in a position to state that 'the UK public is rightly appalled by arms exports to abusive dictatorships like the one in Saudi Arabia' (CAAT 2017a; Doward 2017a). With respect to arms trading relationships largely sidelined by the discourse, 46 per cent consider the sale of arms to the US acceptable (with 28 per cent considering this unacceptable), with support for sales to France at 49 per cent and Germany at 45 per cent (against 25 per cent and 28 per cent respectively) (CAAT, personal communication).[11]

These healthy polling figures allow activists to frame the repressive regimes discourse and its associated demands as a common-sense position, with the weight of public opinion evidence of the moral force of their argument. Again, this resonates with Žižek's model; the demand to Stop Arming Saudi might not be fulfilled by the political establishment, but this only serves to show the fundamental disconnect between the state and the people. However, and notwithstanding the efficacy of this approach, it is notable that the shape of public opinion (alongside that of media interest) consequently has a significant effect on the particular way in which the arms trade is being problematised. While campaign discourses tend to frame favourable public opinion as a legitimating device, it is important to pay attention to the ways in which public opinion is not a neutral space of judgement, but is instead constituted through manifold overlapping framings, socialisations and prejudices. Or, more frankly, public opinion is itself a space of political contestation and reproduction. It is therefore important to interrogate how and why certain propositions attain the status of common-sense claims (Gramsci 2007: 323–51, 419–25), to consider what political processes determine the particular shape of public opinion, and which make some statements and demands seem reasonable and others not. Doing so takes us to dynamics integral to the reproduction of contemporary militarism.

The capacity for states to make and legitimise warfare depends on a series of category assumptions about the forms of sympathy and horror that attach themselves to different (racialised) subjects. These categorisations depend, at least in part, on the relationships between subjectivity and violence which direct blame, fear, empathy and grief in uneven ways. At its most basic, such unevenness positions 'our' violence as humane, pacific, unavoidable, and regrettable but necessary, while positioning 'theirs' as monstrous, barbaric, optional, and yet also essential (Razack 2004; Thobani 2014). These framings sit within a wider discursive field through which certain subjects are positioned as uncivilised, external to modernity, and operating under fundamentally different modes of rationality – a differentiation that has underpinned colonial forms of international relations from the classical era through to liberal militarism and the war on terror (Barkawi and Stanski 2012; Razack 2008; Silverblatt 2004). These framings are also straightforwardly racist, categorising black and brown bodies as particularly queer, dangerous, unpredictable, as always already violent, and therefore as necessitating various forms of militarised governance and elimination (Razack 2014). Islamophobia has been a particularly prominent form of this discourse in the UK over the past twenty years, with both media representation and public opinion surveys demonstrating an attitude which views Muslims as enemies within, fanatical, opposed to British values and essentially violent, and as therefore requiring militarised and/or securitising responses.[12]

The use of a discourse which trades on the *self-evidence* of the pariah status of Saudi Arabia (and others) risks reproducing narratives of the dangerous Other which are integral to militarist rationalities. Simultaneously, the silences the discourse enacts are themselves complicit in the racialised distribution of judgement and horror at work in liberal militarism, which views 'our' violence as *a priori* more legitimate and less terrible than 'theirs'. Sherene Razack argues that, far from transcending racial categorisation, humanitarian practices and discourses are productive of a contemporary colour line, 'with civilized white nations standing on one side and uncivilized Third World nations standing on the other' (2004: 10). The repressive regimes discourse clearly traces (and so carves) such a line, marking self and Other, innocence and danger, legitimacy and illegitimacy, even under the guise of calling the practices of the British government into question.

The public opinion and common-sense understandings that guide and legitimise anti-arms trade campaigns might therefore be precisely what anti-militarist politics needs to call into question, if it is to contest the processes by which 'ordinary citizens enter into ... fantasies of racial superiority in small, quotidian ways' (Razack 2004: 156). This poses a difficult problem for activists. While most would agree that these framings are problematic, and might claim that the discourse is not supposed to operate in this manner, narratives always function beyond their intentions. This is not to argue that the repressive regimes discourse *only* feeds into those racialised (or indeed exceptionalising) logics; its meaning is not singular. Nevertheless, it is to suggest that the discourse cannot be detached from them, and so that it cannot avoid a certain complicity. We can see this at work in an example.

In 2014 Prince Charles travelled to Saudi Arabia at the request of the UK government's Foreign and Commonwealth Office. Officially, the trip was unrelated to the arms trade; however, on the day after the Prince's visit, BAE Systems announced that it had finally come to an agreement over the sale of seventy-two Eurofighter Typhoon jets to the Saudi regime in a deal worth at least £4 billion (Norton-Taylor 2014). CAAT argued that this was one of a number of examples of the British government enlisting the UK royal family to promote arms sales. As part of the royal visit, the prince took part in the Janadriyah cultural festival in Riyadh, donning Saudi ceremonial dress and participating in a sword dance. Images of Prince Charles wearing a thobe, keffiyeh and wielding a sword were made public, and CAAT shared them on social media. It became one of their most widely shared social media posts to date, providing a dramatic opportunity to demonstrate collusion between arms capital and the state (CAAT 2014).

The photo was shared as an invitation to mockery, and it is in the nature of this mockery that we can read the ambiguities of the repressive regimes discourse. There are at least two ways of laughing at the image. The first, closer to CAAT's professed politics, focuses on the farcical lengths to which the UK government is going in order to sell weapons. Ridiculing Prince Charles's role as a glorified salesman, it is a laugh that mocks Britain's declining position in the world and the status anxiety that accompanies this post-imperial malaise. But there is also clearly a more straightforwardly othering and racialised laugh, which turns on the absurd debasement of the royal family, reduced to barbarity in desperate pursuit of arms sales. Here, the strangeness of Saudi dress and ritual signify Saudi Otherness, and so the corrupted nature of the arms trade. The comments left beneath the picture on Facebook (though heavily moderated) suggest that, for at least some people, the picture slotted neatly into that second story, one wondering 'if that's the sword they used to behead women for witchcraft!!'

Recovering Radicalism

The arguments in this chapter have significant implications for thinking about the relationship between militarism and resistance. That anti-militarist discourse can remain perfectly compatible with central features of contemporary militarism highlights both the ambiguous nature of anti-militarism and the depths, subtleties and common-sense positions through which public discourse is implicated in militarised rationalities. This poses a number of challenges. The first concerns the limits of making demands. Žižek makes bold claims about the potential for deconstructive demands to unsettle political systems by revealing their contradictions. The arguments here suggest that doing so can leave intact precisely that which might need to be called into question. In issuing demands, you are always circumscribed by what is articulable within a particular context. That is perhaps less a critique than a diagnosis, but it is troubling. It invites more detailed consideration of how apparently radical politics become bounded by dominant discourses which shape the terms of common sense. Trying to speak within that field of intelligibility is not just a neutral campaign strategy, but an active reproduction of certain political frameworks.

There is a broader point about the nature of radical politics and radical political subjects to be made here. I opened this chapter with a brief account of the role I have played in the Stop Arming Saudi campaign. Part of the reason for doing so was to acknowledge my own participation in the repressive regimes discourse. Even as I became increasingly uncomfortable with this particular mode of critique, I struggled to stop myself from deploying its slogans and lists and basic assumptions. At least in the context of making public-facing statements, it has a certain seductive force. It is notable that many of the activists with whom I work hold far more radical politics than the discourse implies, and even agree with this critique, but nonetheless find themselves reproducing it. If you want to make sense, and especially if you want to be taken seriously, there is little option other than this frankly quite conservative framing. From a prefigurative perspective, this asks demanding questions about how the work to generate alternative forms of subjectivity and social relation is limited, shaped and undermined by the wider discursive field.

However, the prominence of the discourse does not mean that it is the only way to problematise the arms trade. There are alternatives. These operate less to be intelligible or speak to a dominant common sense, than to shift the terms of intelligibility and expand from the common sense of the margins. One obvious alternative is to maintain a focus on arms transfers amongst Western states. Even when the problematic nature of those transfers is less easily accepted, anti-militarists might refuse to insulate these from critique, and to stress the violence with which they are entangled. An important example of such action is the Sisters Against the Arms Trade blockade discussed in Chapter 3. These campaigns and discourses are likely to be less galvanising, less media-friendly, less 'strategic'. They would need to involve alternative forms of communication and media strategy than the soundbite-friendly action associated with the repressive regimes discourse. But they may help to shift that discourse.

A second alternative, perhaps the wider context of the first, is to centre the critique of liberal militarism more firmly in anti-arms trade activism. This means demonstrating how Britain's arms sales, both to other 'Western' states and to those featured in the repressive regimes discourse, are implicated in a particular formation of violence that is both normal and excessive, legal and illegal. This does not mean ignoring arms sales to Saudi Arabia, Bahrain, or Turkey, but instead situating these within a wider framework which incorporates the normalised military dominance and violence of Western states, rather than as isolated and discrete evils. Arms sales to Saudi Arabia are no aberration; they are integral to the nature of British (liberal) militarism and its need to externalise its violence (Wearing 2018: 154–86). These relationships, their colonial foundations, and their neo-colonial presents are clearly legible through a critical focus on liberal militarism and the arms trade.

Third, there is an urgent need to contend with the racialised politics at the heart of both liberal militarism and the arms trade, and to recognise how this ties the arms trade into other forms of political violence. This involves being attentive to how colonial and racist narratives are very easily reproduced within anti-militarist discourse. While potentially challenging, such a shift would open up important avenues for radical coalitions. When drawing in a focus on liberal militarism and racialised violence, anti-arms trade campaigning finds substantial common ground with movements against police violence, migrant solidarity movements, even anti-gentrification campaigns. These connections are underexplored, although there is movement in this direction. A focus on such coalitions is less concerned with engaging with the hegemonic common sense, instead developing a more marginal common sense that may work to shift the wider discursive field. This is where the discussion at the end of Chapter 7 gives us both the problem and the route through. The whiteness of anti-militarism, and the lack of a substantive account of how militarism is racialised, makes the reproduction of the repressive regimes discourse far more likely. A more developed engagement with anti-racist politics in anti-militarism may lead to both a stronger movement and a more radical politics of critique.

Notes

1. For activist-facing critiques, see Feinstein (2012); Gilby (2014); Holden (2017).
2. In this chapter much of the empirical material is drawn from CAAT's reports and statements. This is primarily because CAAT is the major (abolitionist) user of the discourse, but also because CAAT's influential position within the wider movement means that it tends to set the terms for how the arms trade is framed.
3. Data on UK arms export licences is provided in an easily accessible format on CAAT's website, available at https://www.caat.org.uk/resources/export-licences.
4. A similar issue is identified by Pinar Bilgin and Adam David Morton, who point out how the 'failed states' discourse (upon which the list approach clearly relies) sustains 'inherently unequal structural relationships' between 'Western' 'zones of peace' and non-'Western' 'zones of conflict'. Indeed, they suggest, this is a discourse crucial to the legitimacy of the arms industry (Bilgin and Morton 2002: 69).
5. It should be noted that arms sales to clients are an important component of that normalised or non-spectacular liberal violence (Mabee 2016: 251–3). As such, it would be an overreach to say that no part of that system is challenged by the repressive regimes discourse. In the conclusion to this chapter I suggest that this relationship between the arms trade and liberal militarism offers important starting points for a more radical critique.

6. In responding to a story about illegal weaponry being sold at DSEI, a CAAT spokeswoman insisted, 'The really shocking thing about DSEi is not that arms companies sell "banned" or "illegal" equipment; it is that almost everything on display, however dangerous and destructive is "legal"' (Atwal 2013).
7. Other anti-war groups are less cautious about using these framings in their public material, as Stop the War Coalition's article '10 Years and 1000 Lashes for Blogger as Saudi Barbarism Rewarded with More UK Arms Sales' makes clear (Stop the War Coalition undated). While CAAT rarely publicly use this language, partly for the reasons outlined here, there are occasional lapses or exceptions (CAAT 2006, 2017b).
8. On the orientalising/Othering functions of these discourses, see Boletsi (2013: 41); Doty (1996); Said (1994, 2003). On the intertwined and co-constitutive histories of Western and Gulf militarisms, see Nonneman (2001); Wearing (2018: 11–46). On civilisational discourse in arms control politics, see Mathur (2014).
9. When confronted with this critique, activists often respond by insisting that they would just as readily use the term 'barbaric' (or similar) to refer to the practices of Western governments, in a manner akin to Gilbert Achcar's approach in his *Clash of Barbarisms* (2002). While there is some merit to this response, I am sympathetic to Boletsi's response that such a strategy fails to substantively trouble the civilisation/barbarism hierarchy or to shift the semantics of barbarism (and to her more substantive deconstructive strategy, which cannot be adequately engaged here) (2013: 51). On more straightforward terms it is notable that, despite claims that they would happily use this language for Western states, this rarely happens.
10. More subtle versions of these framings can also be found, such as in CAAT's concern that the Saudi regime's 'judicial and penal practices are inconsistent with Western principles' (Hirst and CAAT 2000: 27–8).
11. It is notable that only 24 per cent disagree with the statement that 'British companies that produce military equipment should not be allowed to sell it to foreign governments' (against a surprising 40 per cent who agree), but that over 45 per cent consider sales to France, Germany and the US to be acceptable (CAAT, personal communication). The contingency of foreignness is potentially revealed by such an apparent contradiction.
12. See Ciftci (2012); Croft (2012); Field (2007); Hussain and Bagguley (2012); Kapoor (2018); Qureshi and Zeitlyn (2013).

Conclusion

I finish writing this book in May 2018. As with the closing stages of any large project, it has taken over the last year of my life, leaving precious little time for anything else. I have hardly set foot in an activist meeting or attended a demo since DSEI last September. Nevertheless, the fantasy that we can ensconce ourselves away from the violent realities of the world in pursuit of that elusive intellectual headspace never holds for long. In April I convened a workshop at the LSE on the relationships between militarism, racism and colonialism, during which our plans for a quiet two days of discussion were aptly but unnervingly disrupted. First, by a group of Ghanaian activists, who held a protest outside the building where our workshop was taking place. The Ghanaian president, Nana Akufo-Addo, was scheduled to speak in the building, and the protestors were opposing a new Status of Forces Agreement between the US and Ghana, recently signed by Akufo-Addo and regarded by them as a neo-colonial imposition. And second, by security guards controlling access to the building in light of the presidential address, who paid little attention to our white workshop participants while subjecting those of Middle Eastern and South Asian descent to aggressive and physical interrogation. Not wishing to remain in the building under such conditions, and in solidarity with the activists outside, we suspended our workshop and joined the protest.

That universities are financially and intellectually interwoven with militarism, and that access to university spaces and resources is highly racialised, is hardly new information. Moreover, as one of our participants pointed out, that this harassment was particularly visible even to those of us coded as white should not occlude the fact that it is a routine experience for people of colour. And yet, the coincidence of our workshop with such stark manifestations of militarised and racialised power served as a blunt reminder that the privileged space of academic reflection is always already constituted by and intimately related to the systems of power we ostensibly wish to overturn. Just a few weeks before this event, BAE Systems agreed a provisional sale of a further forty-eight Typhoon jets to Saudi Arabia; one week after it, and just a few buildings away from the LSE in the Royal Courts of Justice, the Court of Appeal granted CAAT permission to appeal against the High Court judgment that allowed arms exports to Saudi Arabia to continue. These three events intervene in my writing process, their various urgencies and immediacies asking daunting questions. Does any of this – our activism, this ethnography – matter? What should we do? Who is this 'we'?

These are fair questions, crucial ones even, and I have no wish to sidestep them. However, as I stated in the Introduction, my intention is not to develop a grand account of the movement's capabilities, nor to outline strategic opportunities. The standard imperative in radical political theory at this stage is to articulate the discourses, assemblages and compositions which might aid in the construction of a counter-hegemony. These articulations are occasionally accompanied by declarations of frustration with political interventions which shy away from hegemonising gestures, which concern themselves with micropolitics, localism, direct action. Alex Williams and Nick Srnicek dismiss these formations as 'folk politics', arguing that they lack the potential to bring about meaningful and long-lasting change (2017; see also Dean 2018). In the face of political hegemonies so saturated with violence, the desire to construct counter-hegemonies is understandable, as is the frustration with resistant practices which do not (or will not) feed into such projects. There are important questions about how to build the kinds of practices and analyses I've engaged with throughout this book into sustainable, effective, even scalable movements, and I confess that on that front I have few answers. However, that impulse to hegemony also risks closures on how resistance can be thought and practised, potentially in a manner that leads to the reproduction of militarism within the politics of resistance. It is with those risks, and some potential routes through, that I want to engage here.

In Chapter 1 I argued that we can interpret direct action through the lens of Day's frustration with the hegemony of hegemony in radical politics – that is, with the assumption that effective social change can only be achieved simultaneously and *en masse*, either by making demands on the state or by replacing it with some new totality. The hegemony of hegemony ensures the perpetuation of political domination, the legitimacy of universalising and hierarchical political formations, and the subordination of that which does not fit the (alternative) order. For these reasons, Day argues that we should look to displace the logic of hegemony. Throughout the book I have sought to identify the anti-hegemonic politics of anti-militarism; those gestures and practices which do not straightforwardly build into a (counter-)hegemonic project. This does not mean that I have overlooked those aspects of anti-militarism which more obviously build hegemony, nor that it is simply bad when they do.[1] But it is important to be alive to the anti-hegemonic qualities of movements. They open new pathways, and hold spaces to disrupt the closures that hegemony can tend to demand.

Militarism is a seductive enemy. Anti-militarism brings you into contact with some deeply unpleasant characters, many of whom do an outstanding job of playing the villain. My yearly trip to BAE Systems' AGM in Farnborough is a regular opportunity to have my preconceptions reinforced; it is hard not to listen to the chairman, Roger Carr, calmly rationalise his company's many violences, and feel that you have found your foe. This animosity has its place, and can be highly effective at motivating and mobilising resistance. However, it also has a reactive dimension, stabilising the self-conception of the righteous anti-militarist subject, virtuous insofar as they are not that. 'You are evil, therefore I am good' (Deleuze 2006: 111). I have argued throughout the book that anti-militarist subjects are not innocent, that they participate in and reproduce militarism even as they resist it. Secure ontological differentiations between them and us, between militarists and anti-militarists, serve to frustrate engagement with this non-innocence, 'moraliz[ing] the self by disavowing commonality with the judged' (Butler 2005: 46).

Social movements and coalitions are always at risk of erecting sovereign boundaries, whereby firm distinctions are established between those on the inside and those on the outside. Decisions regarding with whom solidarity should be shared, what positions will be taken on various issues, and what tactics will be supported all serve to establish certain limits. While these closures are, to some extent, unavoidable, they are also always problematic. They codify space in ways which solidify exclusion, establish and enforce the boundaries of contestation, and demarcate the limits by which the subject of-and-in the collective is defined. In representing the inside as a space of pure opposition to the outside, such boundaries are likely to obscure how social power relations operate within movements. This is one way of understanding how patriarchal and racialised dynamics operate within anti-militarism, in a manner that is largely invisible to many of those involved.

The negotiation of politics within uniform or complete frameworks of coalition has been a serious problem for progressive political praxis. Day argues that this can be seen across much of liberal and postmarxist pluralism, pointing towards Hardt and Negri's popular conception of the multitude, which 'gloss[es] over too many real differences and struggles that are encountered by those trying to come together against neoliberalism, while inhabiting disparate regions, positions in political-economic structures and racial/cultural/sexual identifications' (2005: 178). In these situations, a commonality is presumed which obscures the varied and intersectional ways people experience oppression (usually at the expense of those whose marginalisation is the most acute); it is on such terms that socialist feminists 'were forced kicking and screaming to notice . . . the non-innocence of the category woman' (Haraway 1991: 157; see also hooks 2001; Moraga and Anzaldúa 1983). It cannot be sufficient to dismiss this experience as an uncomfortable legacy; it represents the violences (both theoretical and physical) which tend to result from any attempts towards large-scale consensus. As Lewis Call argues, 'a healthy polity requires not consensus but rather the endless interplay of radically dissenting voices' (2002: 39–40).

The declaration of political opposition often presupposes a subject whose existence may be premature, or should at least be considered more a question than an assumption. This is the 'we', us who are not that, who oppose that, who are collected and co-implicated by our opposition to that. As with all political movements, the pronoun is powerful within anti-militarism, and practised ears can interpret any particular articulation – and the tone, hand gestures, and general context within which it is spoken – with reference to its intended scale: we on the left / we who are anti-militarist / we within that we who are better anti-militarists, and so on. Judith Butler cites Adriana Cavarero's reflections on the subject:

> many revolutionary movements . . . seem to share a curious linguistic code based on the intrinsic morality of pronouns. The *we* is always positive, the *plural you* is a possible ally, the *they* has the face of an antagonist, the *I* is unseemly, and the *you* is, of course, superfluous. (Cavarero 2000: 90–1, cited in Butler 2005: 32; original emphasis)

There is a certain self-validating momentum to the 'we' which performs its unity and coherence, asserts its membership, and papers over its exclusions and hierarchies, eliding the ways these are always a work in progress.

Foucault, responding to Richard Rorty's charge that he does not appeal to a 'we' which might 'constitute the framework for a thought and define the conditions in which it can be validated', suggests that

> the problem is, precisely, to decide if it is actually suitable to place oneself within a 'we' in order to assert the principles one recognizes and the values one accepts; or if it is not, rather, necessary to make the future formation of a 'we' possible, by elaborating the question. Because it seems to me that the 'we' must not be previous to the question; it can only be the result – and the necessarily temporary result – of the question as it is posed in the new terms in which one formulates it. (Foucault 1984: 385)

As Call argues, 'the Foucaultian's emphasis on diversity does not preclude the possibility that [a subject] might place herself within a "we" – but she must be careful to do so only in a tactical and provisional way' (2002: 63). This we might read as a call for an anti-hegemonic conception of the 'we' that asserts collectivity without straightforwardly placing this into a hierarchy or imbuing it with sovereign claims.

Diversity of tactics generates something of this spirit, a fraught but productive attempt to ride the line between difference and unity, in which neither is quite allowed to dominate the other. Another attempt to theorise along these lines comes from Butler's account of the 'open coalition', a form of feminist organising that neither presumes nor tends towards unity:

> Perhaps a coalition needs to acknowledge its contradictions and take action with those contradictions intact. Perhaps also part of what dialogic understanding entails is the acceptance of divergence, breakage, splinter, and fragmentation as part of the often tortuous process of democratization ... Without the compulsory expectation that feminist actions must be instituted from some stable, unified, and agreed-upon identity, those actions might well get a quicker start and seem more congenial to a number of 'women' for whom the meaning of the category is permanently moot ... Coalitional politics requires neither an expanded category of 'women' nor an internally multiplicitous self that offers its complexity at once ... An open coalition, then, will affirm identities that are alternately instituted and relinquished according to the purposes at hand; it will be an open assemblage that permits of multiple convergences and divergences without obedience to a normative telos of definitional closure. (Butler 2006: 20–2)

This 'antifoundationalist approach to coalitional politics' (Butler 2006: 21) renders the coalition permanently incomplete, predicated precisely on a refusal to establish particular standards of subjectivity, on the celebration of its own opacity. Importantly this does not abandon the possibility for collective action; on the contrary, it expands the possibilities dramatically insofar as it refuses to impose totalising standards upon action and solidarity and celebrates a multiplicity of affinities and identities (which 'can come into being and dissolve depending on the concrete practices that constitute them' (Butler 2006: 21)).

In the moves to establish a diversity of tactics, we can see attempts by anti-militarists to produce contingent coalitions which facilitate political action without foreclosing the dissonances and divergences that constitute such spaces. The aim of STAF is not convergence, an eventual final position or consensus; it is to provide mutual facilitation and support, a forum in which affinities can be sought, and in which the space for differences is asserted. Of course, the coalition (and others like it) also hegemonises, also contains its own logics of exclusion. My intention is not to romanticise, but to point towards some practices that might trouble these closures.

Care is needed when taking the open coalition outside of its specifically feminist articulation in Butler, and the mobilisation here is not intended to suggest that a similar (or even remotely comparable) contestation over various and conflicting identities is experienced amongst anti-militarists. Nonetheless, this friction may be precisely where using the open coalition in this context is most provocative; it demands that 'we' situate questions and diversities concerning strategic choices, tactical limitations, organisational forms – those decisions and differences which tend most explicitly to divide anti-militarists – as questions of subjectivity. This does two things. The first is to highlight how an anti-militarist open coalition refuses central logics of militarism by refusing totalising conceptions of unity, narrow and subordinating conceptions of strategy (i.e. strategy as confrontation), and the impulse towards discipline in the name of 'The Cause'. The second is to mark again the ways in which questions of resistance are always simultaneously questions about who we are, and who we might otherwise be(come). This moves us onto the subject of prefiguration.

A prefigurative approach to anti-militarism is predicated on the understanding that militarism is not only a set of ideas, policies or institutions that can be critiqued or smashed – it is a series of social relations that are intimately entangled with and constitutive of our identities, value systems, everyday practices, and modes of interaction. In making space to explore alternative forms of social relation, prefiguration works to sap energy from prevailing configurations of power while seeking to uncover fresh lines of imbrication. It is not easy, nor sufficient in any straightforward sense, but it gestures towards a politics which refuses strategic rationalities which bracket (and so stabilise) the subject, which recognises the pervasive and micropolitical nature of militarism, and which remains committed to the 'language of example and beginning' (Landauer 2010: 310–11). It is a vital component of any resistance which is not destined to replicate that which it opposes. If militarism is a social relationship, then we destroy it by creating new social relationships.

I have conceptualised prefiguration as a dynamic interplay where speculative and creative interventions in the direction of anti-militarist 'ends' are explored and deconstructed in the process of (direct) action. It is not the attempt to live utopias, nor the abandonment of contestations; it indicates efforts to imagine and enact ways of being and relating otherwise, to cultivate counter-subjectivities, and to explore these various figurations. Whilst these transformations and explorations are viewed within their particular context, they are not necessarily contained there; as Shukaitis argues, '[m]oments of minor mutation, while often occupying a seemingly insignificant role within the larger social fabric, act as a fulcrum on which larger transformations in collective imagination are initiated' (2009: 14). Commitment to prefigurative politics involves an ongoing interrogation of how our subjectivity is implicated in systems of power, and the continual search for those authorities, hierarchies and militarised complicities which emerge in the practice of resistance. As such, and by definition, prefigurative politics does not aim towards finality. It is a process by which we come to know ourselves, and to become otherwise. I have argued that a prefigurative lens is valuable for reading the politics of anti-militarism both because it allows us to recognise these processes at work within the movement, and because it provides the tools to think critically about their limits.

That injunction to learn and explore within the context of prefiguration is not straightforward – it is difficult, context-specific, and demands careful labour. My hope is that this book feeds into such processes, while demonstrating how the tension between militarism and resistance can generate new readings of both. In seeing how militarism is reproduced even within spaces of resistance, we learn something about the depths by which political violence is produced within society. That should both inform and incite further resistance. But as a process, it is always unfinished. Butler reminds us that the inevitable failure of self-knowledge, the inescapable opacity which results when the subject turns inwards, is a crucial and productive failure, which establishes our subjectivity as relational, responsible, and perpetually incomplete (2005: 42; see also Rossdale 2015a). This is where the anti-militarist has to guard against the strategic pragmatism of abstraction and ontological differentiation. We do not know, and we have to hold that incompleteness and sense of complicity carefully, and make it useful, productive, political.

The account of militarism I have used in this book is broad, and challengingly so. I have been keen to push against accounts that view militarism as fixed, universal, or as restricted to particular political domains. Instead, I privileged an account which centres the generalised conscription of everyday life, and recognises that the social relations which underpin political violence are context specific, intelligible insofar as they are situated within particular racialised, gendered, political-economic, cultural and historical contexts. This is an approach which permits a nuanced account of the politics of militarism, but it also expands it beyond its traditional domains, spaces and practices. The concern here might be that such an expansion stretches the concept of militarism too far, rendering it either analytically unproductive or politically exhausting. That is certainly possible. However, it also situates anti-militarism as a politics of resistance to political violence, and one that can and should connect up with, draw in, and learn from other struggles. That is manifestly not to argue that all resistance should become anti-militarism, nor that anti-militarism should attempt to become everything. Instead, it is to suggest that a certain unfaithfulness and exploration might be worthwhile.

Does all of this get rid of militarism? Demilitarise? Produce a post-militarist future? Not really. Not quite. At various points in the book I have criticised the idea that anything can be straightforwardly demilitarised, and argued that we should guard against the sense of good conscience such accounts risk. And that should not necessarily be the goal. If militarism is a way of thinking about how violence is produced and organised within a particular social context, then it is perhaps unhelpful to think about a world beyond militarism. Militarism is not a stable politics from which we can extract ourselves, and so anti-militarism is not a journey to the outside. Instead, it might be thought as a particular politics which seeks to reveal, disrupt and subvert the social processes through which violence is made possible. It is an ethic of resistance, which recognises that its task is never complete, and that it must adapt to new forms and sites of militarism just as militarism adapts to new constellations of resistance. It is in that tension between militarism and resistance that we might find space for a prefigurative politics which refuses to become an alibi for innocence, which gives no secure guidelines or guarantees, and which demands both antagonistic contestation and a ceaseless openness to deconstruct that contestation.

Note

1. As Day argues, simply castigating all hegemonic gestures is its own hegemonising move (2005: 215).

LIST OF INTERVIEWS

Interview A: Interview with an activist, London, April 2011.
Interview B: Interview with an activist, London, May 2011.
Interview C: Interview with a group of activists 1, London, June 2011.
Interview D: Interview with a group of activists 2, London, June 2011.
Interview E: Interview with an activist, Bristol, July 2011.
Interview F: Interview with an activist, London, October 2011.
Interview G: Interview with an activist, London, February 2012.
Interview H: Interview with an activist, Leicester, March 2012.
Interview I: Interview with an activist, Hastings, July 2012.
Interview J: Interview with an activist, via e-mail, September 2012.
Interview K: Interview with an activist 1, London, November 2016.
Interview L: Interview with an activist 2, London, November 2016.
Interview M: Interview with an activist 1, London, December 2016.
Interview N: Interview with an activist 2, London, December 2016.
Interview O: Interview with an activist, London, January 2017.
Interview P: Interview with an activist, London, May 2017.

REFERENCES

Abraham, Amelia. 2017. 'Is Pride Still Doing What It Set Out to Do?' *I-D.* 7 July. https://i-d.vice.com/en_uk/article/9kbwmv/is-pride-still-doing-what-it-set-out-to-do.

Abrahamsen, Rita. 2018. 'Return of the Generals? Global Militarism in Africa from the Cold War to the Present.' *Security Dialogue* 49 (1–2): 19–31.

Achcar, Gilbert. 2002. *The Clash of Barbarisms: September 11 and the Making of the New World Disorder.* New York: Monthly Review Press.

Agamben, Giorgio. 2014. 'What Is a Destituent Power?' *Environment and Planning D: Society and Space* 32 (1): 65–74.

Agathangelou, Anna M. 2013. 'Neoliberal Geopolitical Order and Value.' *International Feminist Journal of Politics* 15 (4): 453–76.

Agathangelou, Anna M., M. Daniel Bassichis, and Tamara L. Spira. 2008. 'Intimate Investments: Homonormativity, Global Lockdown, and the Seductions of Empire.' *Radical History Review* 2008 (100): 120–43.

Åhäll, Linda. 2016. 'The Dance of Militarisation: A Feminist Security Studies Take on "the Political".' *Critical Studies on Security* 4 (2): 154–68.

Ahmed, Sara. 2004. 'Declarations of Whiteness: The Non-Performativity of Anti-Racism.' *Borderlands* 3 (2).

Akkerman, Mark. 2018. 'Militarization of European Border Security.' In *The Emergence of EU Defense Research Policy: From Innovation to Militarization,* edited by Nikolaos Karampekios,

Iraklis Oikonomou, and Elias G. Carayannis, 337–55. Cham: Springer International Publishing.

Alexander, Ronni. 2010. 'Confronting Militarization: Intersections of Gender(ed) Violence, Militarization, and Resistance in the Pacific.' In *Gender, War, and Militarism: Feminist Perspectives*, edited by Laura Sjoberg and Sandra Via, 69–79. Santa Barbara, CA: Praeger Security International.

Amar, Paul. 2013. *The Security Archipelago; Human-Security States, Sexuality Politics, and the End of Neoliberalism*. Durham, NC: Duke University Press.

Amnesty International. 2017. 'Yemen: Multibillion-dollar arms sales by USA and UK reveal shameful contradiction with aid efforts.' Amnesty.org. https://www.amnesty.org/en/latest/news/2017/03/yemen-multibillion-dollar-arms-sales-by-usa-and-uk-reveal-shameful-contradiction-with-aid-efforts/.

Amnesty UK. 2015. 'The London Arms Fair 2015: The Ad Campaign the Government Never Wanted.' Amnesty UK. https://www.amnesty.org.uk/london-arms-fair-2015-ad-campaign-dsei-torture-equipment.

Anghie, Antony. 2005. *Imperialism, Sovereignty, and the Making of International Law*. Cambridge; New York: Cambridge University Press.

Anti-Militarist Network. 2008. 'About.' Anti-Militarist Network. https://web.archive.org/web/20091217133749/http://www.antimilitaristnetwork.org.uk:80/about/.

Arendt, Hannah. 1970. 'Civil Disobedience.' *The New Yorker*. 12 September.

Ashley, Richard K. 1988. 'Untying the Sovereign State: A Double Reading of the Anarchy Problematique.' *Millennium* 17 (2): 227–62.

Atwal, Kay. 2013. 'Two Firms Thrown Out of ExCeL Arms Fair for Promoting Illegal Weapons.' *Newham Recorder*. 12 September. http://www.newhamrecorder.co.uk/news/two-firms-thrown-out-of-excel-arms-fair-for-promoting-illegal-weapons-1-2409647.

Bakunin, Mikhail. 1990. *Statism and Anarchy*. Cambridge; New York: Cambridge University Press.

Barkawi, Tarak, and Mark Laffey. 2006. 'The Postcolonial Moment in Security Studies.' *Review of International Studies* 32 (2): 329–52.

Barkawi, Tarak, and Keith Stanski, eds. 2012. *Orientalism and War*. London: Hurst.
Basham, Victoria M. 2013. *War, Identity and the Liberal State: Everyday Experiences of the Geopolitical in the Armed Forces*. London; New York: Routledge.
—. 2016a. 'Gender, Race, Militarism and Remembrance: The Everyday Geopolitics of the Poppy.' *Gender, Place & Culture* 23 (6): 883–96.
—. 2016b. 'Raising an Army: The Geopolitics of Militarizing the Lives of Working-Class Boys in an Age of Austerity.' *International Political Sociology* 10 (3): 258–74.
—. 2018. 'Liberal Militarism as Insecurity, Desire and Ambivalence: Gender, Race and the Everyday Geopolitics of War.' *Security Dialogue* 49 (1–2): 32–43.
Belkin, Aaron. 2012. *Bring Me Men: Military Masculinity and the Benign Facade of American Empire, 1898–2001*. London: Hurst.
Berghahn, Volker R. 1984. *Militarism: The History of an International Debate, 1861–1979*. Cambridge; New York: Cambridge University Press.
Bernazzoli, Richelle M., and Colin Flint. 2009. 'Power, Place, and Militarism: Toward a Comparative Geographic Analysis of Militarization.' *Geography Compass* 3 (1): 393–411.
Berrigan, Philip. 1970. *Prison Journals of a Priest Revolutionary*. New York; Chicago; San Francisco: Holt, Rinehart and Winston.
Bigo, Didier. 2002. 'Security and Immigration: Toward a Critique of the Governmentality of Unease.' *Alternatives* 27 (1_suppl): 63–92.
Bilgin, Pinar, and Adam David Morton. 2002. 'Historicising Representations of "Failed States": Beyond the Cold-War Annexation of the Social Sciences?' *Third World Quarterly* 23 (1): 55–80.
Bleiker, Roland. 2000. *Popular Dissent, Human Agency, and Global Politics*. Cambridge; New York: Cambridge University Press.
Boletsi, Maria. 2013. *Barbarism and Its Discontents*. Stanford, CA: Stanford University Press.
Bondurant, Joan V. 1988. *Conquest of Violence: The Gandhian Philosophy of Conflict*. Princeton, NJ: Princeton University Press.

Booth, Ken. 1991. 'Security and Emancipation.' *Review of International Studies* 17 (4): 313–26.
—, ed. 2005. *Critical Security Studies and World Politics*. Boulder, CO: Lynne Rienner.
—. 2007. *Theory of World Security*. Cambridge; New York: Cambridge University Press.
Bourke, Joanna. 2014. *Wounding the World: How Military Violence and War-Play Invade Our Lives*. London: Virago.
Bradshaw, Ross, Dennis Gould, and Chris Jones, eds. 1981. *From Protest to Resistance: The Direct Action Movement Against Nuclear Weapons*. Nottingham: Mushroom.
Braidotti, Rosi. 1994. *Nomadic Subjects: Embodiment and Sexual Difference in Contemporary Feminist Theory*. New York: Columbia University Press.
Brassett, James. 2009. 'British Irony, Global Justice: A Pragmatic Reading of Chris Brown, Banksy and Ricky Gervais.' *Review of International Studies* 35 (1): 219–45.
—. 2016. 'British Comedy, Global Resistance: Russell Brand, Charlie Brooker and Stewart Lee.' *European Journal of International Relations* 22 (1): 168–91.
Brigg, Morgan, and Roland Bleiker. 2010. 'Autoethnographic International Relations: Exploring the Self as a Source of Knowledge.' *Review of International Studies* 36 (3): 779–98.
Brown, Gavin, Anna Feigenbaum, Fabian Frenzel, and Patrick McCurdy, eds. 2017. *Protest Camps in International Context: Spaces, Infrastructures and Media of Resistance*. Bristol; Chicago: Policy Press.
Brown, Wendy. 2008. *Regulating Aversion: Tolerance in the Age of Identity and Empire*. Princeton, NJ: Princeton University Press.
Brown, Wilmette. 1990. *Black Women and the Peace Movement*. Bristol: Falling Wall Press.
Browning, Christopher S., and Matt McDonald. 2013. 'The Future of Critical Security Studies: Ethics and the Politics of Security.' *European Journal of International Relations* 19 (2): 235–55.
Bulmer, Sarah. 2013. 'Patriarchal Confusion?' *International Feminist Journal of Politics* 15 (2): 137–56.
Burke, Anthony. 2007. *Beyond Security, Ethics and Violence: War Against the Other*. London; New York: Routledge.

—. 2013. 'Security Cosmopolitanism.' *Critical Studies on Security* 1 (1): 13–28.
Butler, Judith. 2005. *Giving an Account of Oneself*. New York: Fordham University Press.
—. 2006. *Gender Trouble: Feminism and the Subversion of Identity*. London; New York: Routledge.
—. 2016a. *Frames of War: When Is Life Grievable?* London; New York: Verso.
—. 2016b. 'Rethinking Vulnerability and Resistance.' In *Vulnerability in Resistance*, edited by Judith Butler, Zeynep Gambetti, and Leticia Sabsay, 12–27. Durham, NC: Duke University Press.
Butler, Judith, Zeynep Gambetti, and Leticia Sabsay. 2016. 'Introduction.' In *Vulnerability in Resistance*, edited by Judith Butler, Zeynep Gambetti, and Leticia Sabsay, 1–11. Durham, NC: Duke University Press.
CAAT. 2003. *DSEi 2003 International Arms Market*. London: Campaign Against Arms Trade.
—. 2006. 'Written Evidence to Quadripartite Committee on Strategic Export Controls.' Parliament.UK. February. https://publications.parliament.uk/pa/cm200506/cmselect/cmquad/873/873we22.htm.
—. 2011a. 'This Is Not OK.' *CAAT News*. March.
—. 2011b. 'One Show Reports on UK Arms Companies.' *CAATblog*. 22 March. https://blog.caat.org.uk/2011/03/22/one-show-reports-on-uk-arms-companies/.
—. 2012. 'Arab Spring Repression No Barrier to UK Arms Exports in 2011.' Campaign Against Arms Trade. 1 May. https://www.caat.org.uk/media/press-releases/2012-05-01.
—. 2013. 'Arms Trade Treaty.' Campaign Against Arms Trade. 7 January. https://www.caat.org.uk/issues/att.
—. 2014. 'Prince Charles' Dance of Shame.' *CAATblog*. 20 February. https://blog.caat.org.uk/2014/02/20/prince-charles-dance-of-shame/.
—. 2015a. 'Company Map.' Campaign Against Arms Trade. https://www.caat.org.uk/resources/mapping/about-this-map.
—. 2015b. 'Buyers at DSEI 2015.' Campaign Against Arms Trade. 23 October. https://www.caat.org.uk/issues/arms-fairs/dsei/delegations.

—. 2015c. 'After the Paris Attacks: Militarisation and the Suppression of Protest.' *CAATblog*. 30 November. https://blog.caat.org.uk/2015/11/30/from-paris-to-london-militarisation-and-state-repression/.

—. 2016a. 'Resisting Police Militarisation in the US.' *CAATblog*. 18 January. https://blog.caat.org.uk/2016/01/18/resisting-police-militarisation-in-the-us/.

—. 2016b. 'Resisting Police Militarisation: Shut Down "Security and Policing".' *CAATblog*. 10 March. https://blog.caat.org.uk/2016/03/10/resisting-police-militarisation/.

—. 2016c. 'Security.' Campaign Against Arms Trade. September. https://www.caat.org.uk/issues/security.

—. 2017a. 'Almost Two Thirds of UK Oppose Arms Exports to Saudi Arabia – with Only 11% Supporting Them.' Campaign Against Arms Trade. https://www.caat.org.uk/media/press-releases/2017-02-05.

—. 2017b. 'Bianca Jagger to Lead Saudi Petition Hand-in to PM.' Campaign Against Arms Trade. 15 March. https://www.caat.org.uk/media/press-releases/2017-03-15.

—. 2017c. 'Campaigns – This Is Not OK.' Campaign Against Arms Trade. 3 April. https://www.caat.org.uk/campaigns/this-is-not-ok.

Calhoun, Craig. 1993. '"New Social Movements" of the Early Nineteenth Century.' *Social Science History* 17 (3): 385–427.

Call, Lewis. 2002. *Postmodern Anarchism*. Lanham, MD: Lexington Books.

Campbell, David. 1998. *Writing Security: United States Foreign Policy and the Politics of Identity*. Minneapolis: University of Minnesota Press.

Carpenter, R. Charli. 2005. '"Women, Children and Other Vulnerable Groups": Gender, Strategic Frames and the Protection of Civilians as a Transnational Issue.' *International Studies Quarterly* 49 (2): 295–334.

Carter, April. 1970. *Direct Action*. London: Peace News.

—. 1992. *Peace Movements: International Protest and World Politics Since 1945*. London; New York: Longman.

—. 2005. *Direct Action and Democracy Today*. Cambridge: Polity Press.

Cavarero, Adriana. 2000. *Relating Narratives: Storytelling and Selfhood*. London; New York: Routledge.
Ceadel, Martin. 1980. 'The First British Referendum: The Peace Ballot, 1934–5.' *The English Historical Review* 95 (377): 810–39.
Chabot, Sean, and Majid Sharifi. 2013. 'The Violence of Nonviolence: Problematizing Nonviolent Resistance in Iran and Egypt.' *Societies Without Borders* 8 (2): 205–32.
Chenoweth, Erica, and Maria J. Stephan. 2011. *Why Civil Resistance Works: The Strategic Logic of Nonviolent Conflict*. New York: Columbia University Press.
Chin, Christine B. N., and James H. Mittelman. 1997. 'Conceptualising Resistance to Globalisation.' *New Political Economy* 2 (1): 25–37.
Christoyannopoulos, Alexandre. 2011. *Christian Anarchism: A Political Commentary on the Gospel*. Exeter: Imprint Academic.
Ciftci, Sabri. 2012. 'Islamophobia and Threat Perceptions: Explaining Anti-Muslim Sentiment in the West.' *Journal of Muslim Minority Affairs* 32 (3): 293–309.
CIRCA. Undated. 'About.' CIRCA. http://web.archive.org/web/20120106084027/http://www.clownarmy.org:80/about/about.html.
Cockburn, Cynthia. 2012. *Antimilitarism: Political and Gender Dynamics of Peace Movements*. Basingstoke: Palgrave Macmillan.
Cockburn, Cynthia, and Cynthia Enloe. 2012. 'Militarism, Patriarchy and Peace Movements.' *International Feminist Journal of Politics* 14 (4): 550–7.
Cohn, Carol. 1987. 'Sex and Death in the Rational World of Defense Intellectuals.' *Signs: Journal of Women in Culture and Society* 12 (4): 687–718.
Cole, Chris. 2017. '"I Never, Ever, Listen to Radio 4".' *Peace News*. https://peacenews.info/node/8818/%E2%80%98i-never-ever-listen-radio-4%E2%80%99.
Cole, Chris, Mary Dobbing, and Amy Hailwood. 2010. *Convenient Killing: Armed Drones and the 'Playstation' Mentality*. London: Fellowship of Reconciliation.
Coleman, Lara Montesinos. 2015. 'Ethnography, Commitment, and Critique: Departing from Activist Scholarship.' *International Political Sociology* 9 (3): 263–80.

Control Arms. 2013. 'States Vote Overwhelmingly for Ground-Breaking Arms Trade Treaty.' Control Arms. http://controlarms.org/en/news/states-vote-overwhelmingly-for-ground-breaking-arms-trade-treaty/.

Conway, Adam. 2008. 'We Fought the Law . . . and the Law Ran and Hid.' In *Faslane 365: A Year of Anti-Nuclear Blockades*, edited by Angie Zelter, 125–44. Edinburgh: Luath.

Conway, Daniel. 2012. *Masculinities, Militarisation and the End Conscription Campaign: War Resistance in Apartheid South Africa*. Manchester; New York: Manchester University Press.

Conway, Janet. 2003. 'Civil Resistance and the Diversity of Tactics in the Anti-Globalization Movement: Problems of Violence, Silence, and Solidarity in Activist Politics.' *Osgoode Hall Law Journal* 41 (2): 505–30.

Cortright, David. 2008. *Peace: A History of Movements and Ideas*. Cambridge; New York: Cambridge University Press.

Coward, Martin. 2009. 'Network-Centric Violence, Critical Infrastructure and the Urbanization of Security.' *Security Dialogue* 40 (4–5): 399–418.

—. 2017. 'Against Network Thinking: A Critique of Pathological Sovereignty.' *European Journal of International Relations* 24 (2): 440–63.

Coy, Patrick G. 2013. 'Whither Nonviolent Studies?' *Peace Review* 25 (2): 257–65.

Crane-Seeber, Jesse Paul. 2016. 'Sexy Warriors: The Politics and Pleasures of Submission to the State.' *Critical Military Studies* 2 (1–2): 41–55.

CrimethInc Ex-Workers Collective. 2012. 'The Illegitimacy of Violence, the Violence of Legitimacy.' CrimethInc. https://crimethinc.com/2012/03/27/the-illegitimacy-of-violence-the-violence-of-legitimacy.

Critchley, Simon. 2008. *Infinitely Demanding: Ethics of Commitment, Politics of Resistance*. London; New York: Verso.

Croft, Stuart. 2012. 'Constructing Ontological Insecurity: The Insecuritization of Britain's Muslims.' *Contemporary Security Policy* 33 (2): 219–35.

Dauphinee, Elizabeth. 2010. 'The Ethics of Autoethnography.' *Review of International Studies* 36 (3): 799–818.

Day, Richard J. F. 2005. *Gramsci Is Dead: Anarchist Currents in the Newest Social Movements*. London; Ann Arbor, MI: Pluto Press.

—. 2011. 'Hegemony, Affinity and the Newest Social Movements: At the End of the 00s.' In *Post-Anarchism: A Reader*, edited by Duane Rousselle and Süreyya Evren, 95–116. London: Pluto Press.

de Cleyre, Voltairine. 2005. *Exquisite Rebel: The Essays of Voltairine de Cleyre – Feminist, Anarchist, Genius*. Edited by Sharon Presley and Crispin Sartwell. Albany: State University of New York Press.

de Goede, Marieke. 2005. 'Carnival of Money: Politics of Dissent in an Era of Globalizing Finance.' In *The Global Resistance Reader*, edited by Louise Amoore, 379–91. London; New York: Routledge.

Dean, Jodi. 2018. *Crowds and Party*. London; New York: Verso.

Deleuze, Gilles. 2006. *Nietzsche and Philosophy*. London; New York: Continuum.

Deleuze, Gilles, and Claire Parnet. 1987. *Dialogues*. Translated by Hugh Tomlinson and Barbara Habberjam. New York: Columbia University Press.

Dennis, Martine. 2017. 'What Matters More in the Arms Trade – Money or Morals?' *Inside Story*. Al Jazeera. https://www.aljazeera.com/programmes/insidestory/2017/08/matters-arms-trade-money-morals-170808200834677.html.

Der Derian, James. 1995. 'The Value of Security: Hobbes, Marx, Nietzsche, and Baudrillard.' In *On Security*, edited by Ronnie D. Lipschutz, 24–45. New York: Columbia University Press.

—. 2009. *Virtuous War: Mapping the Military-Industrial-Media-Entertainment Network*. New York: Routledge.

Derrida, Jacques. 1982. *Margins of Philosophy*. Chicago: University of Chicago Press.

—. 1993. *Aporias*. Stanford, CA: Stanford University Press.

Dillon, Michael. 1996. *Politics of Security: Towards a Political Philosophy of Continental Thought*. London; New York: Routledge.

Dillon, Michael, and Julian Reid. 2001. 'Global Liberal Governance: Biopolitics, Security and War.' *Millennium Journal of International Studies* 30 (1): 41–66.

Disarm DSEI. 2015. 'What Is DSEI?' *Disarm DSEI*. Blog. https://dsei.org/what-is-dsei/.

Dixon, Paul. 2012. 'Bringing It All Back Home: The Militarisation of Britain and the Iraq and Afghanistan Wars.' In *The British Approach to Counterinsurgency: From Malaya and Northern Ireland to Iraq and Afghanistan*, edited by Paul Dixon, 112–46. New York: Palgrave Macmillan.

Doherty, Brian, Alexandra Plows, and Derek Wall. 2003. '"The Preferred Way of Doing Things": The British Direct Action Movement.' *Parliamentary Affairs* 56 (4): 669–86.

Doty, Roxanne Lynn. 1996. *Imperial Encounters: The Politics of Representation in North–South Relations*. Minneapolis: University of Minnesota Press.

—. 2010. 'Autoethnography – Making Human Connections.' *Review of International Studies* 36 (4): 1047–50.

Douglass, Jim. 2013. 'Civil Disobedience as Prayer.' *Red Letter Christians*. Blog. https://www.redletterchristians.org/civil-disobedience-as-prayer/.

Doward, Jamie. 2017a. 'Most Britons Believe Selling Arms to Saudis Is "Unacceptable".' *The Guardian*. 5 February. https://www.theguardian.com/world/2017/feb/05/most-britons-believe-selling-arms-to-saudis-is-unacceptable.

—. 2017b. 'British Arms Sales to Repressive Regimes Soar to £5bn Since Election.' *The Guardian*. 9 September. http://www.theguardian.com/world/2017/sep/09/arms-sales-repressive-regimes-saudi-arabia.

Driver, Christopher. 1964. *The Disarmers: A Study in Protest*. London: Hodder and Stoughton.

DuBois, W. E. B. 1915. 'The African Roots of War.' *Atlantic Monthly* 115: 707–14.

Duffy, Carol Ann. 2009. 'Last Post.' *BBC News*. 6 August. http://news.bbc.co.uk/today/hi/today/newsid_8175000/8175790.stm.

Dunne, Tim, and Nicholas J. Wheeler. 2004. '"We the Peoples": Contending Discourses of Security in Human Rights Theory and Practice.' *International Relations* 18 (1): 9–23.

Eastwood, James. 2018. 'Rethinking Militarism as Ideology: The Critique of Violence after Security.' *Security Dialogue* 49 (1–2): 44–56.

Edgerton, David. 1991. 'Liberal Militarism and the British State.' *New Left Review* 1 (185): 138–69.

Edkins, Jenny. 2003. 'Security, Cosmology, Copenhagen.' *Contemporary Politics* 9 (4): 361-70.

Edkins, Jenny, and Véronique Pin-Fat. 2005. 'Through the Wire: Relations of Power and Relations of Violence.' *Millennium Journal of International Studies* 34 (1): 1-24.

Edkins, Jenny, and Maja Zehfuss. 2005. 'Generalising the International.' *Review of International Studies* 31 (3): 451-72.

EDO Decommissioners. 2009. *If I Had A Hammer ... Decommissioning the War Machine*. Leaflet.

Ellis, Carolyn. 2007. 'Telling Secrets, Revealing Lives: Relational Ethics in Research with Intimate Others.' *Qualitative Inquiry* 13 (1): 3-29.

Elshtain, Jean Bethke. 1995. *Women and War*. Chicago: University of Chicago Press.

Enloe, Cynthia. 1989. *Bananas, Beaches & Bases: Making Feminist Sense of International Politics*. London: Pandora.

—. 1996. 'Margins, Silences and Bottom Rungs: How to Overcome the Underestimation of Power in the Study of International Relations.' In *International Theory: Positivism and Beyond*, edited by Steve Smith, Ken Booth, and Marysia Zalewski, 186-202. Cambridge; New York: Cambridge University Press.

—. 2000. *Maneuvers: The International Politics of Militarizing Women's Lives*. Berkeley, CA: University of California Press.

—. 2004. *The Curious Feminist: Searching for Women in a New Age of Empire*. Berkeley, CA: University of California Press.

Eschle, Catherine. 2013. 'Gender and the Subject of (Anti)Nuclear Politics: Revisiting Women's Campaigning Against the Bomb.' *International Studies Quarterly* 57 (4): 713-24.

—. 2017. 'Beyond Greenham Women? Gender Identities and Anti-Nuclear Activism in Peace Camps.' *International Feminist Journal of Politics* 19 (4): 471-90.

Evans, Brad. 2013. *Liberal Terror*. Cambridge; Malden, MA: Polity Press.

Evans, Rob. 2007. 'Export Department Closure Leaves Defence Firms Out in the Cold.' *The Guardian*. 26 July. https://www.theguardian.com/business/2007/jul/26/1.

Fanon, Frantz. 2004. *The Wretched of the Earth*. Translated by Richard Philcox. New York: Grove Press.

Farmer, Paul. 1996. 'On Suffering and Structural Violence: A View from Below.' *Daedalus* 125 (1): 261–83.

Feigenbaum, Anna. 2017. *Tear Gas: From the Battlefields of World War I to the Streets of Today*. London; Brooklyn, NY: Verso.

Feigenbaum, Anna, Fabian Frenzel, and Patrick McCurdy. 2013. *Protest Camps*. London; New York: Zed Books.

Feinstein, Andrew. 2012. *The Shadow World: Inside the Global Arms Trade*. London: Penguin.

Fekete, Liz. 2013. 'Total Policing: Reflections from the Frontline:' *Race & Class* 54 (3): 65–76.

Feminism and Nonviolence Study Group. 1983. *Piecing It Together: Feminism and Nonviolence*. Buckleigh: Feminism and Nonviolence Study Group.

Field, Clive D. 2007. 'Islamophobia in Contemporary Britain: The Evidence of the Opinion Polls, 1988–2006.' *Islam and Christian–Muslim Relations* 18 (4): 447–77.

Finchett-Maddock, Lucy. 2013. 'The Case of the Naughty in Relation to Law.' In *Disobedience: Concept and Practice*, edited by Elena Loizidou, 83–97. Abingdon: Routledge.

Fisher, Lucy. 2017. 'Javid Ignored Advice on Saudi Arms Deal, Court Told.' *The Times*. 8 February. https://www.thetimes.co.uk/article/javid-ignored-advice-on-saudi-arms-deal-court-told-p9x2jc3jx.

Foucault, Michel. 1982. 'The Subject and Power.' *Critical Inquiry* 8 (4): 777–95.

—. 1984. 'Polemics, Politics, and Problematizations: An Interview with Michel Foucault.' In *The Foucault Reader*, edited by Paul Rabinow, 381–90. New York: Pantheon Books.

—. 1997. 'On the Genealogy of Ethics: An Overview of Work in Progress.' In *Ethics: Subjectivity and Truth, The Essential Works of Michel Foucault 1954–1984, Vol. 1*, edited by Paul Rabinow, 253–80. London: Allen Lane.

—. 2002. 'Useless to Revolt?' In *Power: The Essential Works of Michel Foucault 1954–1984, Vol. 3*, edited by J. D. Faubion. London: Penguin.

—. 2007a. *Security, Territory, Population: Lectures at the Collège de France, 1977–1978*. Edited by Michel Senellart. Translated by Graham Burchell. New York: Picador.

—. 2007b. *The Politics of Truth*. Edited by Sylvère Lotringer. Los Angeles: Semiotext(e).

Franks, Benjamin. 2003. 'The Direct Action Ethic.' *Anarchist Studies* 11 (1): 13–41.

Frazer, Elizabeth, and Kimberly Hutchings. 2014a. 'Revisiting Ruddick: Feminism, Pacifism and Non-Violence.' *Journal of International Political Theory* 10 (1): 109–24.

—. 2014b. 'Feminism and the Critique of Violence: Negotiating Feminist Political Agency.' *Journal of Political Ideologies* 19 (2): 143–63.

Frowd, Philippe M., and Adam J. Sandor. 2018. 'Militarism and Its Limits: Sociological Insights on Security Assemblages in the Sahel.' *Security Dialogue* 49 (1–2): 70–82.

Ǧahānbiglū, Rāmīn. 2014. *Introduction to Nonviolence*. New York: Palgrave Macmillan.

Galtung, Johan. 1969. 'Violence, Peace, and Peace Research.' *Journal of Peace Research* 6 (3): 167–91.

Gardner, Morgan. 2005. *Linking Activism: Ecology, Social Justice, and Education for Social Change*. New York: Routledge.

Gee, David. 2014. *Spectacle, Reality, Resistance: Confronting a Culture of Militarism*. London: ForcesWatch.

Gee, David, and Anna Goodman. 2013. *Young Age at Army Enlistment Is Associated with Greater War Zone Risks*. London: ForcesWatch and Child Soldiers International.

Gelderloos, Peter. 2007. *How Nonviolence Protects the State*. Cambridge, MA: South End Press.

Gibbon, Jill, and Christine Sylvester. 2017. 'Thinking Like an Artist-Researcher about War.' *Millennium Journal of International Studies* 45 (2): 249–57.

Gilby, Nicholas. 2014. *Deception in High Places: A History of Bribery in Britain's Arms Trade*. London: Pluto Press.

Gillan, Kevin, Jenny Pickerill, and Frank Webster. 2008. *Anti-War Activism: New Media and Protest in the Information Age*. Basingstoke: Palgrave Macmillan.

Gilman-Opalsky, Richard. 2011. *Spectacular Capitalism: Guy Debord and the Practice of Radical Philosophy*. London; New York: Minor Compositions.

Gilmore, Jonathan. 2015. *The Cosmopolitan Military: Armed Forces and Human Security in the 21st Century.* Basingstoke: Palgrave Macmillan.

Goldman, Emma. 1969. *Anarchism and Other Essays.* New York: Dover Publications.

—. 1996. *Red Emma Speaks.* London: Wildwood House.

Gordon, Uri. 2007. *Anarchy Alive!: Anti-Authoritarian Politics from Practice to Theory.* London; Ann Arbor, MI: Pluto Press.

—. 2018. 'Prefigurative Politics Between Ethical Practice and Absent Promise.' *Political Studies* 66 (2): 521–37.

Graeber, David. 2007. *Possibilities: Essays on Hierarchy, Rebellion, and Desire.* Oakland, CA: AK Press.

—. 2009. *Direct Action: An Ethnography.* Edinburgh: AK Press.

—. 2011. 'Occupy Wall Street's Anarchist Roots.' *Al Jazeera.* 30 November. https://www.aljazeera.com/indepth/opinion/2011/11/2011112872835904508.html.

Gramsci, Antonio. 1971. *The Prison Notebooks.* New York: International Publishers.

—. 2007. *Selections from the Prison Notebooks of Antonio Gramsci.* Edited by Quintin Hoare and Geoffrey Nowell-Smith. London: Lawrence and Wishart.

Grayson, Kyle. 2008. 'Human Security as Power/Knowledge: The Biopolitics of a Definitional Debate.' *Cambridge Review of International Affairs* 21 (3): 383–401.

Greenawalt, Kent. 1987. *Conflicts of Law and Morality.* Clarendon Law Series. New York: Oxford University Press.

Greer, Stephen. 2012. *Contemporary British Queer Performance.* Performance Interventions. Basingstoke; New York: Palgrave Macmillan.

Griffin, Ben. 2013. 'Veterans for Peace UK Demonstrate at the Cenotaph.' *Peace News.* https://www.peacenews.info/node/7474/veterans-peace-uk-demonstrate-cenotaph.

Grünewald, Guido, and Peter van den Dungen, eds. 1995. *Twentieth-Century Peace Movements: Successes and Failures.* Lewiston, NY: Edwin Mellen Press.

Hagen, Jamie J. 2016. 'Queering Women, Peace and Security.' *International Affairs* 92 (2): 313–32.

Halberstam, Jack. 2011. *The Queer Art of Failure.* Durham, NC: Duke University Press.

Halkon, Ruth. 2015. 'Banksy and Friends Take on London Arms Fair with Chilling Poster Campaign.' *Daily Mirror.* 16 September. http://www.mirror.co.uk/news/uk-news/banksy-friends-leave-chilling-poster-6452956.

Hallward, Maia Carter, and Julie M. Norman. 2015. 'Understanding Nonviolence.' In *Understanding Nonviolence: Contours and Contexts,* edited by Maia Carter Hallward and Julie M. Norman, 14–35. Malden, MA: Polity Press.

Hambling, David. 2015. 'The U.K. Fights ISIS with a Missile the U.S. Lacks.' *Popular Mechanics.* 4 December. http://www.popularmechanics.com/military/weapons/a18410/brimstone-missile-uk-david-cameron-isis/.

Haraway, Donna Jeanne. 1991. 'A Cyborg Manifesto: Science, Technology, and Socialist Feminism in the Late Twentieth Century.' In *Simians, Cyborgs, and Women: The Reinvention of Nature,* 149–82. New York: Routledge.

Harcourt, Bernard E. 2012. 'Political Disobedience.' *Critical Inquiry* 39 (1): 33–55.

Hardt, Michael, and Antonio Negri. 2003. *Empire.* Cambridge, MA: Harvard University Press.

—. 2004. *Multitude: War and Democracy in the Age of Empire.* New York: Penguin.

Heckert, Jamie. 2011. 'Sexuality as State Form.' In *Post-Anarchism: A Reader,* edited by Duane Rousselle and Süreyya Evren, 195–207. London: Pluto Press.

Hetherington, William. 2015. *Swimming Against the Tide: The Peace Pledge Union Story, 1934–2014.* London: Peace Pledge Union.

Higate, Paul, ed. 2003. *Military Masculinities: Identity and the State.* Westport, CT: Praeger.

—. 2012. 'Drinking Vodka from the "Butt-Crack".' *International Feminist Journal of Politics* 14 (4): 450–69.

Hill, Jason D. 2013. *Civil Disobedience and the Politics of Identity: When We Should Not Get Along.* New York: Palgrave Macmillan.

Hirsch, Marianne. 2016. 'Vulnerable Times.' In *Vulnerability in Resistance,* edited by Judith Butler, Zeynep Gambetti, and Leticia Sabsay, 76–96. Durham, NC: Duke University Press.

Hirst, Chrissie, and CAAT. 2000. *The Arabian Connection: The UK*

Arms Trade to Saudi Arabia. London: Campaign Against Arms Trade.

Holden, Paul, ed. 2017. *Indefensible: Seven Myths That Sustain the Global Arms Trade.* London: Zed Books.

hooks, bell. 1995. 'Feminism and Militarism: A Comment.' *Women's Studies Quarterly* 23 (3/4): 58–64.

—. 2001. *Ain't I a Woman: Black Women and Feminism.* Pluto Classics. London: Pluto Press.

Horn, Denise M. 2010. 'Boots and Bedsheets: Constructing the Military Support System in a Time of War.' In *Gender, War, and Militarism: Feminist Perspectives*, edited by Laura Sjoberg and Sandra Via, 57–68. Santa Barbara, CA: Praeger Security International.

Horrox, James. 2010. 'Reinventing Resistance: Constructive Anarchism in Gustav Landauer's Social Philosophy.' In *New Perspectives on Anarchism*, edited by Nathan Jun and Shane Wahl, 189–208. Plymouth: Lexington Books.

Howard, Neil, and Keira Pratt-Boyden. 2013. 'Occupy London as Pre-figurative Political Action.' *Development in Practice* 23 (5–06): 729–41.

Howell, Alison. 2018. 'Forget "Militarization": Race, Disability and the "Martial Politics" of the Police and of the University.' *International Feminist Journal of Politics* 20 (2): 117–36.

Hudson, Kate. 2005. *CND – Now More than Ever the Story of a Peace Movement.* London: Vision Paperbacks.

Hussain, Yasmin, and Paul Bagguley. 2012. 'Securitized Citizens: Islamophobia, Racism and the 7/7 London Bombings.' *The Sociological Review* 60 (4): 715–34.

Hutchings, Kimberly. 2008. 'Making Sense of Masculinity and War.' *Men and Masculinities* 10 (4): 389–404.

—. 2018. 'Pacifism Is Dirty: Towards an Ethico-Political Defence.' *Critical Studies on Security* 6 (2): 176–92.

Hwang, Ihntaek. 2018. 'Militarising National Security Through Criminalisation of Conscientious Objectors to Conscription in South Korea.' *Critical Studies on Security* 6 (3): 296–311.

Inayatullah, Naeem. 2011. 'Introduction.' In *Autobiographical International Relations: I, IR*, edited by Naeem Inayatullah, 1–12. Abingdon; New York: Routledge.

Indymedia UK. 2010a. 'EDO Blockaded Again.' 2010. Indymedia UK. 14 December. https://www.indymedia.org.uk/en/2010/12/470666.html.

Indymedia UK. 2010b. 'Update from EDO Blockade.' 2010. Indymedia UK. 14 December. https://www.indymedia.org.uk/en/2010/12/470680.html?c=on#c261178.

Inwood, Joshua, and Anne Bonds. 2016. 'Confronting White Supremacy and a Militaristic Pedagogy in the U.S. Settler Colonial State.' *Annals of the American Association of Geographers* 106 (3): 521–9.

Jabri, Vivienne. 2012. *The Postcolonial Subject: Claiming Politics/ Governing Others in Late Modernity*. London; New York: Routledge.

Jackson, Kirk. 2013. 'The Arms Trade Treaty: A Historic and Momentous Failure.' *Ceasefire Magazine*. 29 April. https://ceasefiremagazine.co.uk/failure-arms-trade-treaty/.

Jasiewicz, Ewa. 2009. 'A Perspective on the Decommissioning as Viewed from Gaza.' In EDO Decommissioners, *If I Had A Hammer . . . Decommissioning the War Machine*. Leaflet, 9–16.

Jauhola, Marjaana. 2010. 'Building Back Better? – Negotiating Normative Boundaries of Gender Mainstreaming and Post-Tsunami Reconstruction in Nanggroe Aceh Darussalam, Indonesia.' *Review of International Studies* 36 (1): 29–50.

Jeffords, Susan. 1989. *The Remasculinization of America: Gender and the Vietnam War*. Bloomington: Indiana University Press.

Joachim, Jutta. 2003. 'Framing Issues and Seizing Opportunities: The UN, NGOs, and Women's Rights.' *International Studies Quarterly* 47 (2): 247–74.

Jochnick, Chris af, and Roger Normand. 1994. 'The Legitimation of Violence: A Critical History of the Laws of War.' *Harvard International Law Journal* 35 (1): 49–95.

Jun, Nathan. 2011. 'Reconsidering Post-Structuralism and Anarchism.' In *Post-Anarchism: A Reader*, edited by Duane Rousselle and Süreyya Evren, 231–49. London: Pluto Press.

Juris, Jeffrey S. 2008. *Networking Futures: The Movements Against Corporate Globalization*. Durham, NC: Duke University Press.

Kaldor, Mary. 2003. *Global Civil Society: An Answer to War*. Cambridge; Malden, MA: Polity Press.

Kapoor, Ilan. 2004. 'Hyper-Self-Reflexive Development? Spivak on

Representing the Third World "Other".' *Third World Quarterly* 25 (4): 627–47.

Kapoor, Nisha. 2018. *Deport, Deprive, Extradite: 21st Century State Extremism*. New York: Verso.

Kelly, John. 2013. 'Popular Culture, Sport and the "Hero"-fication of British Militarism.' *Sociology* 47 (4): 722–38.

Khalid, Maryam. 2011. 'Gender, Orientalism and Representations of the "Other" in the War on Terror.' *Global Change, Peace & Security* 23 (1): 15–29.

—. 2015. 'Feminist Perspectives on Militarism and War.' In *The Oxford Handbook of Transnational Feminist Movements*, edited by Rawwida Baksh-Soodeen and Wendy Harcourt, 632–50. New York: Oxford University Press.

Klein, Naomi, and Yotam Marom. 2012. 'Why Now? What's Next? Naomi Klein and Yotam Marom in Conversation About Occupy Wall Street.' *The Nation*. 9 January. https://www.thenation.com/article/why-now-whats-next-naomi-klein-and-yotam-marom-conversation-about-occupy-wall-street/.

Kumar, Deepa. 2004. 'War Propaganda and the (AB)Uses of Women.' *Feminist Media Studies* 4 (3): 297–313.

Laclau, Ernesto, and Chantal Mouffe. 2001. *Hegemony and Socialist Strategy: Towards a Radical Democratic Politics*. London; New York: Verso.

Laffin, Arthur J. 2003. *The Plowshares Disarmament Chronology, 1980–2003*. Marion, SD: Rose Hill Books.

Landauer, Gustav. 2010. *Revolution and Other Writings: A Political Reader*. Translated by Gabriel Kuhn. Oakland, CA: PM Press.

Landstreicher, Wolfi. 2009. *Willful Disobedience*. N.p.: Ardent Press.

Laudani, Raffaele. 2013. *Disobedience in Western Political Thought: A Genealogy*. Cambridge; New York: Cambridge University Press.

Laware, Margaret L. 2004. 'Circling the Missiles and Staining Them Red: Feminist Rhetorical Invention and Strategies of Resistance at the Women's Peace Camp at Greenham Common.' *NWSA Journal* 16 (3): 18–41.

Lewis, Paul, and Rob Evans. 2013. *Undercover: The True Story of Britain's Secret Police*. London: Faber and Faber.

Liddington, Jill. 1989. *Long Road to Greenham: Feminism and Anti-Militarism in Britain Since 1820*. London: Virago.

Löfflmann, Georg. 2013. 'Hollywood, the Pentagon, and the Cinematic Production of National Security.' *Critical Studies on Security* 1 (3): 280–94.

Loizidou, Elena. 2013. 'Disobedience Subjectively Speaking.' In *Disobedience: Concept and Practice*, edited by Elena Loizidou, 108–24. Abingdon; New York: Routledge.

Lorde, Audre. 2007. *Sister Outsider: Essays and Speeches*. Berkeley, CA: Crossing Press.

Losurdo, Domenico. 2010. 'Moral Dilemmas and Broken Promises: A Historical-Philosophical Overview of the Nonviolent Movement.' *Historical Materialism* 18 (4): 85–134.

Luther King, Jr., Martin. 1991. 'Letter from Birmingham City Jail.' In *Civil Disobedience in Focus*, edited by Hugo Adam Bedau, 68–84. London; New York: Routledge.

Mabee, Bryan. 2016. 'From "Liberal War" to "Liberal Militarism": United States Security Policy as the Promotion of Military Modernity.' *Critical Military Studies* 2 (3): 242–61.

Mabee, Bryan, and Srdjan Vucetic. 2018. 'Varieties of Militarism: Towards a Typology.' *Security Dialogue* 49 (1–2): 96–108.

McCann, Eamonn. Undated. *The Raytheon 9*. Derry: Derry Anti-War Coalition.

—. 2007. 'Qana, Derry: The Dead Lie in Familiar Shapes.' *Cúisle Mo Croí*. Blog. 4 September. https://katemc.wordpress.com/2007/09/04/qana-derry-the-dead-lie-in-familiar-shapes/.

McCulloch, Jude, and Vicki Sentas. 2006. 'The Killing of Jean Charles de Menezes: Hyper-Militarism in the Neoliberal Economic Free-Fire Zone.' *Social Justice* 33 (4 (106)): 92–106.

McDonald, Matt. 2005. 'Be Alarmed? Australia's Anti-Terrorism Kit and the Politics of Security.' *Global Change, Peace & Security* 17 (2): 171–89.

—. 2012. *Security, the Environment and Emancipation: Contestation Over Environmental Change*. New York: Routledge.

—. 2013. 'Discourses of Climate Security.' *Political Geography* 33 (March): 42–51.

McDonald, Matt, and Lee Wilson. 2017. 'Trouble in Paradise: Contesting Security in Bali.' *Security Dialogue* 48 (3), 241–58.

MacKenzie, Megan. 2015. *Beyond the Band of Brothers: The US Military and the Myth That Women Can't Fight*. Cambridge: Cambridge University Press.

McSorley, Kevin. 2016. 'Doing Military Fitness: Physical Culture, Civilian Leisure, and Militarism.' *Critical Military Studies* 2 (1–2): 103–19.

McSorley, Kevin, and Joseph Burridge. 2013. 'Too Fat to Fight? Obesity, Bio-Politics and the Militarisation of Children's Bodies.' In *War and the Body: Militarisation, Practice and Experience*, edited by Kevin McSorley, 62–77. New York: Routledge.

McSweeney, Bill. 1999. *Security, Identity, and Interests: A Sociology of International Relations*. Cambridge; New York: Cambridge University Press.

Maeckelbergh, Marianne. 2009. *The Will of the Many: How the Alterglobalisation Movement Is Changing the Face of Democracy*. London; New York: Pluto Press.

—. 2011. 'Doing Is Believing: Prefiguration as Strategic Practice in the Alterglobalization Movement.' *Social Movement Studies* 10 (1): 1–20.

Mahrouse, Gada. 2014. *Conflicted Commitments: Race, Privilege, and Power in Transnational Solidarity Activism*. Montreal: McGill-Queen's University Press.

Manchanda, Nivi. 2015. 'Queering the Pashtun: Afghan Sexuality in the Homo-Nationalist Imaginary.' *Third World Quarterly* 36 (1): 130–46.

Mangan, J. A., ed. 2003. *Militarism, Sport, Europe: War without Weapons*. London; Portland, OR: Frank Cass.

Mann, Michael. 1987. 'The Roots and Contradictions of Modern Militarism.' *New Left Review* 1 (162): 35–50.

Mantello, Peter. 2012. 'Playing Discreet War in the US: Negotiating Subjecthood and Sovereignty Through Special Forces Video Games.' *Media, War & Conflict* 5 (3): 269–83.

Mason, Kelvin. 2014. 'Becoming Citizen Green: Prefigurative Politics, Autonomous Geographies, and Hoping Against Hope.' *Environmental Politics* 23 (1): 140–58.

Masters, Cristina. 2014. *Militarism, Gender and (In)Security: Biopolitical Technologies of Security and the War on Terror*. London: Routledge.

Mathur, Ritu. 2014. '"The West and the Rest": A Civilizational

Mantra in Arms Control and Disarmament.' *Contemporary Security Policy* 35 (3): 332–55.

Mattausch, John. 1989. *A Commitment to Campaign: A Sociological Study of CND*. Manchester; New York: Manchester University Press.

May, Todd. 1994. *The Political Philosophy of Poststructuralist Anarchism*. University Park, PA: Pennsylvania State University Press.

Meaden, Bernadette. 1999. *Protest for Peace*. Glasgow: Wild Goose Publications.

Miah, Shamim. 2013. '"Prevent"ing Education: Anti-Muslim Racism and the War on Terror in Schools.' In *The State of Race*, edited by Nisha Kapoor, Virinder S. Kalra, and James Rhodes, 146–62. Houndmills: Palgrave Macmillan.

Millar, Katharine M. 2016. '"They Need Our Help": Non-Governmental Organizations and the Subjectifying Dynamics of the Military as Social Cause.' *Media, War & Conflict* 9 (1): 9–26.

Milmo, Cahal. 2014. '"Torture Gear" Brochures at World's Largest Weaponry Fair.' *The Independent*. 21 March. http://www.independent.co.uk/news/uk/home-news/torture-gear-brochures-at-world-s-largest-weaponry-fair-backfire-9208852.html.

Mohan, Giles, and Kristian Stokke. 2000. 'Participatory Development and Empowerment: The Dangers of Localism.' *Third World Quarterly* 21 (2): 247–68.

Mohanty, Chandra Talpade. 1984. 'Under Western Eyes: Feminist Scholarship and Colonial Discourses.' *Boundary 2* 12/13: 333–58.

—. 2003. *Feminism without Borders: Decolonizing Theory, Practicing Solidarity*. Durham, NC; London: Duke University Press.

Montgomery, Anne. 2010. 'Divine Obedience.' In *Swords into Plowshares: Nonviolent Direct Action for Disarmament*, edited by Anne Montgomery and Arthur J. Laffin, 1–7. Eugene, OR: WIPF & Stock.

Moraga, Cherríe, and Gloria Anzaldúa, eds. 1983. *This Bridge Called My Back: Writings by Radical Women of Color*. New York: Kitchen Table.

Muppidi, Himadeep. 2012. *The Colonial Signs of International Relations*. London: Hurst.

Nagel, Joane. 1998. 'Masculinity and Nationalism: Gender and Sexuality in the Making of Nations.' *Ethnic and Racial Studies* 21 (2): 242–69.

Nayak, Meghana. 2006. 'Orientalism and "Saving" US State Identity after 9/11.' *International Feminist Journal of Politics* 8 (1): 42–61.

Needham, Andrea. 2016. *The Hammer Blow: How 10 Women Disarmed a War Plane*. London: Peace News.

Neocleous, Mark. 2008. *Critique of Security*. Edinburgh: Edinburgh University Press.

Nepstad, Sharon Erickson. 2008. *Religion and War Resistance in the Plowshares Movement*. New York: Cambridge University Press.

Neufeld, Mark. 2004. 'Pitfalls of Emancipation and Discourses of Security: Reflections on Canada's "Security with a Human Face".' *International Relations* 18 (1): 109–23.

New Keywords Collective. 2016. 'Europe/Crisis: New Keywords of "the Crisis" in and of "Europe".' *Near Futures Online*. http://nearfuturesonline.org/europecrisis-new-keywords-of-crisis-in-and-of-europe.

Newman, Saul. 2010a. *The Politics of Postanarchism*. Edinburgh: Edinburgh University Press.

—. 2010b. 'Voluntary Servitude Reconsidered: Radical Politics and the Problem of Self-Domination.' *Anarchist Developments in Cultural Studies* 1: 31–49.

Nonneman, Gerd. 2001. 'Saudi–European Relations 1902–2001: A Pragmatic Quest for Relative Autonomy.' *International Affairs (Royal Institute of International Affairs 1944–)* 77 (3): 631–61.

Norton-Taylor, Richard. 2014. 'The Future British King, Saudi Princes, and a Secret Arms Deal.' *The Guardian*. 24 February. https://www.theguardian.com/uk-news/defence-and-security-blog/2014/feb/24/arms-gulf-prince-charles.

Nuciari, Marina. 2006. 'Models and Explanations for Military Organization: An Updated Reconsideration.' In *Handbook of the Sociology of the Military*, edited by Giuseppe Caforio, 61–86. New York: Springer Science & Business Media.

Nunes, João. 2012. 'Reclaiming the Political: Emancipation and Critique in Security Studies.' *Security Dialogue* 43 (4): 345–61.

O'Brien, Stephen. 2015. 'Statement to the Security Council on

Yemen.' ReliefWeb. 28 July. https://reliefweb.int/report/yemen/under-secretary-general-humanitarian-affairs-and-emergency-relief-coordinator-stephen-0.

—. 2016. 'Statement to the Security Council on Yemen.' ReliefWeb. 31 October. https://reliefweb.int/report/yemen/under-secretary-general-humanitarian-affairs-and-emergency-relief-coordinator-10.

Odysseos, Louiza. 2001. 'Laughing Matters: Peace, Democracy and the Challenge of the Comic Narrative.' *Millennium: Journal of International Studies* 30 (3): 709–32.

—. 2012. 'Governing Dissent in the Central Kalahari Game Reserve: "Development", Governmentality, and Subjectification Among Botswana's Bushmen.' In *Situating Global Resistance: Between Discipline and Dissent*, 45–62. Abingdon: Routledge.

On the Verge. 2008. Documentary. SchMOVIES.

Onlywomen Press Collective. 1983. *Breaching the Peace*. London: Onlywomen Press.

Ormrod, David. 1987. 'The Churches and the Nuclear Arms Race, 1945–85.' In *Campaigns for Peace: British Peace Movements in the Twentieth Century*, edited by Nigel Young and Richard Taylor, 189–220. Manchester: Manchester University Press.

Owens, Patricia. 2003. 'Accidents Don't Just Happen: The Liberal Politics of High-Technology "Humanitarian" War.' *Millennium: Journal of International Studies* 32 (3): 595–616.

—. 2007. *Between War and Politics: International Relations and the Thought of Hannah Arendt*. Oxford; New York: Oxford University Press.

Pallister-Wilkins, Polly. 2009. 'Radical Ground: Israeli and Palestinian Activists and Joint Protest Against the Wall.' *Social Movement Studies* 8 (4): 393–407.

Parashar, Swati. 2018. 'Discursive (In)Securities and Postcolonial Anxiety: Enabling Excessive Militarism in India.' *Security Dialogue* 49 (1–2): 123–35.

Parkin, Frank. 1968. *Middle Class Radicalism: The Social Bases of the British Campaign for Nuclear Disarmament*. Manchester: Manchester University Press.

Payne, Rodger A. 2001. 'Persuasion, Frames and Norm Construction.' *European Journal of International Relations* 7 (1): 37–61.

Peace Pledge Union. Undated. 'White Poppies for Peace.' Peace Pledge Union. http://www.ppu.org.uk/whitepoppy/.

Peoples, Columba, and Nick Vaughan-Williams. 2010. *Critical Security Studies: An Introduction*. London; New York: Routledge.

Perlo-Freeman, Sam. 2010. 'The United Kingdom Arms Industry in a Globalized World.' In *The Global Arms Trade: A Handbook*, edited by Andrew T. H. Tan, 250–65. London; New York: Routledge.

Pickerill, Jenny, and Paul Chatterton. 2006. 'Notes Towards Autonomous Geographies: Creation, Resistance and Self-Management as Survival Tactics.' *Progress in Human Geography* 30 (6): 730–46.

Pratt, Nicola. 2007. 'The Queen Boat Case in Egypt: Sexuality, National Security and State Sovereignty.' *Review of International Studies* 33 (1): 129–44.

Press TV. 2010. 'The Big Story: The Decommissioners.' 4 August.

Prividera, Laura C., and John W. Howard III. 2006. 'Masculinity, Whiteness and the Warrior Hero: Nationalism and the Marginalization of Women.' *Women & Language* 29 (2): 29–37.

Prozorov, Sergei. 2007. *Foucault, Freedom and Sovereignty*. Aldershot; Burlington, VT: Ashgate.

Puar, Jasbir K. 2007. *Terrorist Assemblages: Homonationalism in Queer Times*. Durham, NC: Duke University Press.

—. 2017. *The Right to Maim: Debility, Capacity, Disability*. Durham, NC: Duke University Press.

Puar, Jasbir K., and Maya Mikdashi. 2012a. 'Interpenetration and Its Discontents.' *Jadaliyya*. 8 September. http://www.jadaliyya.com/Details/26818/Pinkwatching-And-Pinkwashing-Interpenetration-and-its-Discontents.

—. 2012b. 'On Positionality and Not Naming Names: A Rejoinder to the Response by Maikey and Schotten.' *Jadaliyya*. 10 October. http://www.jadaliyya.com/Details/27195/On-Positionality-and-Not-Naming-Names-A-Rejoinder-to-the-Response-by-Maikey-and-Schotten.

Puar, Jasbir K., and Amit Rai. 2002. 'Monster, Terrorist, Fag: The War on Terrorism and the Production of Docile Patriots.' *Social Text* 20 (3): 117–48.

Qureshi, Kaveri, and Benjamin Zeitlyn. 2013. 'British Muslims,

British Soldiers: Cultural Citizenship in the New Imperialism.' *Ethnicities* 13 (1): 110–26.

Rahman, Momin. 2014. 'Queer Rights and the Triangulation of Western Exceptionalism.' *Journal of Human Rights* 13 (3): 274–89.

Rai, Milan. 2013a. 'Taking a Lead from the Global South.' *Peace News.* May. https://www.peacenews.info/node/7234/taking-lead-global-south.

—. 2013b. 'PN Summer Camp 2013: Who, What, Where, Why and When.' *Peace News.* August. https://www.peacenews.info/node/7284/pn-summer-camp-2013-who-what-where-why-and-when.

Randle, Michael. 1987. 'Non-Violent Direct Action in the 1950s and 1960s.' In *Campaigns for Peace: British Peace Movements in the Twentieth Century,* edited by Nigel Young and Richard Taylor, 131–61. Manchester: Manchester University Press.

Rasmussen, Tom. 2016. 'Keep Pride as a Protest.' *I-D.* 23 June. https://i-d.vice.com/en_uk/article/bjnw7q/keep-pride-as-a-protest.

Rawls, John. 1971. *A Theory of Justice.* Cambridge, MA: Belknap Press of Harvard University Press.

Razack, Sherene. 2004. *Dark Threats and White Knights: The Somalia Affair, Peacekeeping, and the New Imperialism.* Toronto: University of Toronto Press.

—. 2007. 'Stealing the Pain of Others: Reflections on Canadian Humanitarian Responses.' *Review of Education, Pedagogy, and Cultural Studies* 29 (4): 375–94.

—. 2008. *Casting Out: The Eviction of Muslims from Western Law and Politics.* Toronto: University of Toronto Press.

—. 2014. 'The Manufacture of Torture as Public Truth: The Case of Omar Khadr.' In *At the Limits of Justice: Women of Colour on Terror,* edited by Suvendrini Perera and Sherene Razack, 57–85. Toronto: University of Toronto Press.

ReelNews. 2016. *Veterans For Peace Mark Remembrance Sunday 2016.* https://www.youtube.com/watch?v=Rsr15SZfVUw.

Reuters, Thomson. 2017. *Campaigners Start UK Court Case to Stop Saudi Arms Sales.* https://www.reuters.com/video/2017/02/07/campaigners-start-uk-court-case-to-stop?videoId=371076125&videoChannel=14073.

Richter-Montpetit, Melanie. 2014. 'Beyond the Erotics of Orientalism: Homeland Security, Liberal War and the Pacification of the Global Frontier.' Toronto: York University.

Richter-Montpetit, Melanie, and Cynthia Weber. 2017. 'Queer International Relations.' *Oxford Research Encyclopedia of Politics.* http://oxfordre.com/politics/view/10.1093/acrefore/97801902 28637.001.0001/acrefore-9780190228637-e-265.

Rigby, Andrew. 1999. 'The Peace Pledge Union: From Peace to War, 1936-1945.' In *Challenge to Mars: Essays on Pacifism from 1918 to 1945*, edited by Peter Brock and Thomas Paul Socknat, 169-85. Toronto: University of Toronto Press.

Robinson, Christine M. 2008. 'Order in Chaos: Security Culture as Anarchist Resistance to the Terrorist Label.' *Deviant Behavior* 29 (3): 225-52.

Robinson, Nick. 2016. 'Militarism and Opposition in the Living Room: The Case of Military Videogames.' *Critical Studies on Security* 4 (3): 255-75.

Rooum, Donald. 2003. *Wildcat: Anarchists Against Bombs*. London: Freedom Press.

Roseneil, Sasha. 1995. *Disarming Patriarchy: Feminism and Political Action at Greenham*. Buckingham; Philadelphia: Open University Press.

Ross, Alice. 2017. 'Judicial Review Aiming to Stop UK Arms Sales to Saudi Arabia to Begin.' *The Guardian*. 7 February. http://www.theguardian.com/world/2017/feb/07/review-halt-uks--campaign-against-arms-trade-saudi-arabia-begin-yemen.

Rossdale, Chris. 2010. 'Anarchy Is What Anarchists Make of It: Reclaiming the Concept of Agency in IR and Security Studies.' *Millennium Journal of International Studies* 39 (2): 483-501.

—. 2015a. 'Enclosing Critique: The Limits of Ontological Security.' *International Political Sociology* 9 (4): 369-86.

—. 2015b. 'Dancing Ourselves to Death: The Subject of Emma Goldman's Nietzschean Anarchism.' *Globalizations* 12 (1): 116-33.

—. 2016. 'Activism, Resistance and Security.' In *Ethical Security Studies: A New Research Agenda*, edited by Jonna Nyman and Anthony Burke, 201-15. Abingdon; New York: Routledge.

Rossdale, Chris, and Maurice Stierl. 2016. 'Everything Is Dangerous:

Conduct and Counter-Conduct in the Occupy Movement.' *Global Society* 30 (2): 157–78.

Routledge, Paul. 2003. 'Convergence Space: Process Geographies of Grassroots Globalization Networks.' *Transactions of the Institute of British Geographers* 28 (3): 333–49.

Rundberg, Anna-Linnea. 2008. 'What the Hell Do You Need Training For?' In *Faslane 365: A Year of Anti-Nuclear Blockades*, edited by Angie Zelter, 110–17. Edinburgh: Luath.

Said, Edward W. 1994. *Culture and Imperialism*. London: Vintage.

—. 2003. *Orientalism*. London: Penguin.

Sancho, Guiomar Rovira. 2014. 'Networks, Insurgencies, and Prefigurative Politics: A Cycle of Global Indignation.' *Convergence* 20 (4): 387–401.

Satia, Priya. 2018. *Empire of Guns: The Violent Making of the Industrial Revolution*. New York: Penguin.

Schell, Jonathan. 2004. *The Unconquerable World: Power, Nonviolence, and the Will of the People*. London: Allen Lane.

SchNEWS. Undated. 'Arms Trade Spoofs.' SchNEWS. http://web.archive.org/web/20151206134912/http://www.schnews.org.uk/satire/index-arms-trade.html.

Schotten, Heike, and Haneen Maikey. 2012. 'Queers Resisting Zionism: On Authority and Accountability Beyond Homonationalism.' *Jadaliyya*. 10 October. http://www.jadaliyya.com/Details/27175/Queers-Resisting-Zionism-On-Authority-and-Accountability-Beyond-Homonationalism.

Schrader, Benjamin. 2017. 'The Affect of Veteran Activism.' *Critical Military Studies* DOI: 10.1080/23337486.2017.1334300, forthcoming in print.

Schwichtenberg, Cathy. 1987. 'Articulating the People's Politics: Manhood and Right-Wing Populism in The A-Team.' *Communication* 9 (3–4): 379–98.

Scott, James C. 2000. *Weapons of the Weak: Everyday Forms of Peasant Resistance*. New Haven, CT: Yale University Press.

—. 2012. *Two Cheers for Anarchism: Six Easy Pieces on Autonomy, Dignity, and Meaningful Work and Play*. Princeton, NJ; Oxford: Princeton University Press.

Shaheen, Jack G. 2015. *Reel Bad Arabs: How Hollywood Vilifies a People*. Northampton, MA: Olive Branch Press.

Shapiro, Michael J. 1992. *Reading the Postmodern Polity: Political Theory as Textual Practice*. Minneapolis; Oxford: University of Minnesota Press.

Sharp, Gene. 1959. 'A Time for Action.' *Peace News*. 30 January.

—. 2005. *Waging Nonviolent Struggle: 20th Century Practice and 21st Century Potential*. Boston: Extending Horizons Books.

Shaw, Martin. 1991. *Post-Military Society: Militarism, Demilitarization, and War at the End of the Twentieth Century*. Philadelphia: Temple University Press.

Shiva, Vandana. 1988. *Staying Alive: Women, Ecology, and Survival in India*. New Delhi: Kali for Women.

Shukaitis, Stevphen. 2009. *Imaginal Machines: Autonomy & Self-Organization in the Revolutions of Everyday Life*. London: Minor Compositions.

Silverblatt, Irene. 2004. *Modern Inquisitions: Peru and the Colonial Origins of the Civilized World*. Durham, NC: Duke University Press.

Singer, Peter. 1973. *Democracy and Disobedience*. Oxford: Clarendon Press.

Šisler, Vít. 2008. 'Digital Arabs: Representation in Video Games.' *European Journal of Cultural Studies* 11 (2): 203–20.

Sitze, Adam. 2013. 'Foreword.' In *Disobedience in Western Political Thought: A Genealogy*, by Raffaele Laudani, vii–xxvi. Cambridge; New York: Cambridge University Press.

Skjelsbæk, Inger. 2001. 'Sexual Violence and War: Mapping Out a Complex Relationship.' *European Journal of International Relations* 7 (2): 211–37.

Sklar, Deidre. 1994. 'Can Bodylore Be Brought to Its Senses?' *The Journal of American Folklore* 107 (423): 9–22.

Smith, Andrew. 2018. 'London Is About to Host a Roll Call of the World's Most Vile Regimes. We Must Protest.' *TalkRADIO*. 30 August. http://talkradio.co.uk/opinion/london-about-host-roll-call-worlds-most-vile-regimes-we-must-protest-17083017958.

Smith, William. 2013. *Civil Disobedience and Deliberative Democracy*. London; New York: Routledge.

Snow, John. 2006. 'Why I Don't Wear a Poppy on Air.' *Channel 4 News*. 8 November. https://www.channel4.com/news/by/jon-snow/blogs/wear-poppy-air.

Space Hijackers. Undated. 'Arms Dealers & The Baby Show.' Space Hijackers. http://www.spacehijackers.org/html/projects/dseibabies/thebabyshow.html.

—. 2005. 'Arms Dealers Sex Toy Party.' Space Hijackers. https://spacehijackers.org/html/projects/dsei05/index.html.

—. 2007. 'Tuesday September 11th – Tank Day.' Space Hijackers. http://spacehijackers.org/html/projects/dsei07/tuesday.html.

—. 2011a. 'Life Neutral Solutions.' Life Neutral Solutions. https://web.archive.org/web/20120229030601/http://www.lifeneutralsolutions.com/.

—. 2011b. 'Life Neutral Solutions – Industry.' Life Neutral Solutions. https://web.archive.org/web/20111124131447/http://lifeneutralsolutions.com:80/industry.html.

Sparkles Not Shrapnel. 2011. 'Why We Are (Part of) Sparkles Not Shrapnel.' Sparkles Not Shrapnel. http://www.sparklesnotshrapnel.org.uk/why.

Spike Peterson, V. 2010. 'Gendered Identities, Ideologies, and Practices in the Context of War and Militarism.' In *Gender, War, and Militarism: Feminist Perspectives*, edited by Laura Sjoberg and Sandra Via, 17–29. Santa Barbara, CA: Praeger Security International.

Spivak, Gayatri. 1988. 'Can the Subaltern Speak?' In *Marxism and the Interpretation of Culture*, edited by Cary Nelson and Lawrence Grossberg, 271–313. Basingstoke: Macmillan Education.

Stavrianakis, Anna. 2006. 'Call to Arms: The University as a Site of Militarised Capitalism and a Site of Struggle.' *Millennium Journal of International Studies* 35 (1): 139–54.

—. 2010. *Taking Aim at the Arms Trade: NGOs, Global Civil Society and the World Military Order*. London; New York: Zed Books.

—. 2016a. 'Legitimising Liberal Militarism: Politics, Law and War in the Arms Trade Treaty.' *Third World Quarterly* 37 (5): 840–65.

—. 2016b. 'Arming the Saudi War in Yemen: The Cracks in the Mirror of British Internationalism.' OpenDemocracyUK. 20 September. https://www.opendemocracy.net/anna-stavrianakis/arming-saudi-war-in-yemen-cracks-in-mirror-of-british-internationalism.

Stavrianakis, Anna, and Jan Selby. 2012. 'Militarism and International Relations in the Twenty-First Century.' In *Militarism* and *International Relations: Political Economy, Security, Theory*, edited by Anna Stavrianakis and Jan Selby, 3–18. New York: Routledge.

Stiehm, Judith Hicks. 1982. 'The Protected, the Protector, the Defender.' *Women's Studies International Forum*, Special Issue Women and Men's Wars 5 (3): 367–76.

Stierl, Maurice. 2012. '"No One Is Illegal!" Resistance and the Politics of Discomfort.' *Globalizations* 9 (3): 425–38.

Stoler, Ann Laura. 2010. *Carnal Knowledge and Imperial Power: Race and the Intimate in Colonial Rule: With a New Preface*. Berkeley, CA: University of California Press.

Stone, Jon. 2016a. 'Protesters Who Blockaded London Arms Trade Fair Acquitted after Judge Sees Evidence of Illegal Weapons on Sale.' *The Independent*. 15 April. http://www.independent.co.uk/news/uk/politics/dsei-protesters-acquitted-london-arms-fair-illegal-weapons-sales-a6985766.html.

—. 2016b. 'Britain's Arms Control Committee Can't Agree What to Do About Selling Bombs to Saudi Arabia.' *The Independent*. 15 September. http://www.independent.co.uk/news/uk/politics/saudi-arabian-arms-sales-uk-row-ban-vote-committee-arms-export-control-senate-a7309291.html.

Stop the Arms Fair. 2013. 'About.' Stop the Arms Fair. https://www.stopthearmsfair.org.uk/about/.

Stop the War Coalition. Undated. '10 Years and 1000 Lashes for Blogger as Saudi Barbarism Rewarded with More UK Arms Sales.' Stopwar.org. http://www.stopwar.org.uk/index.php/usa-war-on-terror/903-everyone-knows-the-american-president-cant-commit-qmurderq).

Street, Tim, and Martha Beale. 2007. *Study War No More: Military Involvement in UK Universities*. London: Campaign Against Arms Trade. https://www.studywarnomore.org.uk/documents/studywarnomore.pdf.

Summers, Anne. 1976. 'Militarism in Britain before the Great War.' *History Workshop Journal* 2 (1): 104–23.

Sylvester, Christine. 1992. 'Feminists and Realists View Autonomy and Obligation in International Relations.' In *Gendered States: Feminist (Re)Visions of International Relations Theory*, edited by V. Spike Peterson. Boulder, CO; London: Lynne Rienner.

—. 2002. *Feminist International Relations: An Unfinished Journey.* Cambridge; New York: Cambridge University Press.
Target Brimar. Undated. 'Target Brimar.' Campaign flier.
Tatchell, Peter. 1995. *We Don't Want to March Straight: Masculinity, Queers, and the Military.* London; New York: Cassell.
Taylor, Faith. 2016. *No Pride In War Action Against BAE Systems.* https://www.youtube.com/watch?v=iI5JqMsKTC0.
Taylor, Richard. 1988. *Against the Bomb: The British Peace Movement, 1958–1965.* Oxford: Oxford University Press.
Teather, David. 2009. 'Ministry of Defence Hopes New Toy Action Figures Will Help Image.' *The Guardian.* 6 May. http://www.theguardian.com/lifeandstyle/2009/may/07/british-armed-forces-action-man.
The Ammerdown Group. 2016. *Rethinking Security: A Discussion Paper.* https://rethinkingsecurityorguk.files.wordpress.com/2016/10/rethinking-security-executive-summary.pdf.
Thobani, Sunera. 2014. 'Fighting Terror: Race, Sex, and the Monstrosity of Islam.' In *At the Limits of Justice: Women of Colour on Terror,* edited by Suvendrini Perera and Sherene Razack, 57–85. Toronto: University of Toronto Press.
Thomas, Mark. 2007a. *As Used on the Famous Nelson Mandela: Underground Adventures in the Arms and Torture Trade.* London: Ebury.
—. 2007b. 'Martin and Me.' *The Guardian.* 4 December. http://www.theguardian.com/world/2007/dec/04/bae.armstrade.
—. 2009. 'Doth I Protest Too Much?' *The Guardian.* 25 October. http://www.theguardian.com/commentisfree/libertycentral/2009/oct/25/doth-i-protest-too-much.
Thoreau, Henry David. 1993. *Civil Disobedience, and Other Essays.* New York: Dover Publications.
Tidy, Joanna. 2015a. 'Gender, Dissenting Subjectivity and the Contemporary Military Peace Movement in *Body of War.*' *International Feminist Journal of Politics* 17 (3): 454–72.
—. 2015b. 'Forces Sauces and Eggs for Soldiers: Food, Nostalgia, and the Rehabilitation of the British Military.' *Critical Military Studies* 1 (3): 220–32.
Tilly, Charles. 2010. 'War Making and State Making as Organized

Crime.' In *Bringing the State Back In*, edited by Peter B. Evans and Dietrich Rüschemeyer, 169–91. Cambridge: Cambridge University Press.

Tobey, Kristen. 2017. *Plowshares: Protest, Performance, and Religious Identity in the Nuclear Age*. University Park, PA: Pennsylvania State University Press.

UN. 2013. 'Arms Trade Treaty.' United Nations Office For Disarmament Affairs. https://www.un.org/disarmament/convarms/arms-trade-treaty-2/.

Vagts, Alfred. 1959. *A History of Militarism*. New York: Free Press.

Veterans for Peace. 2015. *Action Man: Battlefield Casualties*. http://battlefieldcasualties.co.uk.

—. 2016. *Veterans for Peace Handbook*. Veterans for Peace. http://vfpuk.org/wp-content/uploads/2016/11/Handbook-2016-AGM.pdf.

Viesnik, Dan. 2009. 'Clarion Call from "The Spirit of Christmas".' *CAATblog*. 12 November. https://blog.caat.org.uk/2009/11/12/clarion-call-from-the-spirit-of-christmas/.

Vinthagen, Stellan. 2015. *A Theory of Nonviolent Action: How Civil Resistance Works*. London: Zed Books.

Vipont, Elfrida. 1960. *The Story of Quakerism*. London: Bannisdale Press.

Vrasti, Wanda. 2008. 'The Strange Case of Ethnography and International Relations.' *Millennium* 37 (2): 279–301.

Wæver, Ole. 1995. 'Securitization and Desecuritization.' In *On Security*, edited by Ronnie D. Lipschutz, 46–87. New York: Columbia University Press.

Walker, R. B. J. 1987. *One World, Many Worlds: Struggles for a Just World Peace*. London: Zed Books.

—. 1992. *Inside/Outside: International Relations as Political Theory*. Cambridge: Cambridge University Press.

—. 1997. 'The Subject of Security.' In *Critical Security Studies: Concepts and Cases*, edited by Keith Krause and Michael C. Williams, 61–82. London: Routledge.

Wall, Derek. 1999. *Earth First! And the Anti-Roads Movement: Radical Environmentalism and Comparative Social Movements*. London; New York: Routledge.

Walter, Nicolas. 2011. *Damned Fools in Utopia: And Other Writings on Anarchism and War Resistance*. Edited by David Goodway. Oakland, CA; London: PM Press.

Walton, Sam. 2017. 'The judge deciding we are not guilty doesn't make trying to disarm #Saudi jets bound for #Yemen any more right. But it is quite handy.' Tweet. *@SamWalton*. Blog. 2 October. https://twitter.com/SamWalton/status/925373630032302082.

Ward, Colin. 1982. *Anarchy in Action*. London: Freedom Press.

Ware, Vron. 2013. 'Can You Have Muslim Soldiers? Diversity as a Martial Value.' In *The State of Race*, edited by Nisha Kapoor, Virinder S. Kalra, and James Rhodes, 121–45. Houndmills: Palgrave Macmillan.

Wearing, David. 2016. *A Shameful Relationship: UK Complicity in Saudi State Violence*. London: Campaign Against Arms Trade. https://www.caat.org.uk/campaigns/stop-arming-saudi/a-shameful-relationship.pdf.

—. 2018. *AngloArabia: Why Gulf Wealth Matters to Britain*. Cambridge: Polity Press.

Weber, Cynthia. 2016. *Queer International Relations: Sovereignty, Sexuality and the Will to Knowledge*. New York: Oxford University Press.

Weldes, Jutta. 2003. 'Popular Culture, Science Fiction, and World Politics: Exploring Intertextual Relations.' In *To Seek Out New Worlds: Science Fiction and World Politics*, edited by Jutta Weldes, 1–27. New York: Palgrave Macmillan.

Wetta, Frank Joseph, and Martin A. Novelli. 2003. '"Now a Major Motion Picture": War Films and Hollywood's New Patriotism.' *The Journal of Military History* 67 (3): 861–82.

Wibben, Annick T. R. 2016. 'The Promise and Dangers of Human Security.' In *Ethical Security Studies: A New Research Agenda*, edited by Jonna Nyman and Anthony Burke, 102–15. Abingdon; New York: Routledge.

—. 2018. 'Why We Need to Study (US) Militarism: A Critical Feminist Lens.' *Security Dialogue* 49 (1–2): 136–48.

Wieck, David. 1996. 'The Habit of Direct Action.' In *Reinventing Anarchy, Again*, edited by H. J. Ehrlich, 375–6. Edinburgh; San Francisco: AK Press.

Wilkinson, Eleanor. 2009. 'The Emotions Least Relevant to Politics?

Queering Autonomous Activism.' *Emotion, Space and Society* 2 (1): 36–43.

Williams, Alex, and Nick Srnicek. 2017. *#Accelerate Manifesto: For an Accelerationist Politics*. Mexico City: Gato Negro Ediciones.

Wood, Lesley J. 2014. *Crisis and Control: The Militarization of Protest Policing*. London: Pluto Press.

Woodhead, Thomas. 2009. 'Why I Smashed EDO and Why I Waited to Be Held Accountable for My Actions.' In EDO Decommissioners, *If I Had A Hammer . . . Decommissioning the War Machine*. Leaflet, 17–18.

Wyatt, Daisy. 2015. 'Alternative "Adverts" for a Major Arms Fair Are Appearing Around London.' *The Independent*. 15 September. http://www.independent.co.uk/arts-entertainment/art/news/posters-from-banksys-dismaland-protesting-major-arms-fair-appear-across-london-10502053.html.

Wyn Jones, Richard. 1999. *Security, Strategy, and Critical Theory*. Boulder, CO: Lynne Rienner.

Yates, Luke. 2015. 'Rethinking Prefiguration: Alternatives, Micropolitics and Goals in Social Movements.' *Social Movement Studies* 14 (1): 1–21.

Yearly Meeting of the Religious Society of Friends (Quakers) in Britain. 2009. *Quaker Faith & Practice*. London: Quaker Peace & Service.

Young, Alison. 1990. *Femininity in Dissent*. Sociology of Law and Crime. London; New York: Routledge.

Young, Nigel. 1987a. 'Tradition and Innovation in the British Peace Movement: Towards an Analytical Framework.' In *Campaigns for Peace: British Peace Movements in the Twentieth Century*, edited by Nigel Young and Richard Taylor, 5–22. Manchester: Manchester University Press.

—. 1987b. 'War Resistance and the British Peace Movement Since 1914.' In *Campaigns for Peace: British Peace Movements in the Twentieth Century*, edited by Nigel Young and Richard Taylor, 23–48. Manchester: Manchester University Press.

Zalewski, Marysia. 1996. '"All These Theories Yet the Bodies Keep Piling Up": Theory, Theorists, Theorising.' In *International Theory: Positivism and Beyond*, edited by Steve Smith, Ken Booth, and

Marysia Zalewski, 340–53. Cambridge; New York: Cambridge University Press.

Zalewski, Marysia, and Anne Sisson Runyan. 2013. 'Taking Feminist Violence Seriously in Feminist International Relations.' *International Feminist Journal of Politics* 15 (3): 293–313.

Zelter, Angie. 2004. 'Civil Society and Global Responsibility: The Arms Trade and East Timor.' *International Relations* 18 (1): 125–40.

—. 2009. 'Trident Ploughshares Support for Decommissioners.' In EDO Decommissioners, *If I Had A Hammer . . . Decommissioning the War Machine*. Leaflet, 20–1.

Zinn, Howard. 2002. *Disobedience and Democracy: Nine Fallacies of Law and Order*. Cambridge, MA: South End Press.

Žižek, Slavoj. 2014. *Trouble in Paradise: From the End of History to the End of Capitalism*. London: Allen Lane.

INDEX

accountability, 209, 220–7, 230, 235
Achcar, Gilbert, 260n
act, politics of, 29–31, 90, 134, 247
activist training, 101, 131, 143–4, 212, 230–1
affinity groups, 91, 93, 231
agency
  direct action and, 40, 151, 215, 223, 230, 235
  security and, 84–5, 87–9, 92–7
  solidarity and, 197
Akufo-Addo, Nana, 262
All Africa Women's Group, 202–3
anarchism, 39, 125–6, 128, 135, 160, 234
  direct action, 21–2, 32
  diversity of tactics, 175–6, 205n
  influence on anti-militarism, 22–5
  prefiguration, 34–5
Anarchists Against the Wall, 21
anti-hegemony, 13, 30–1, 85, 89, 94, 106, 111, 113, 135, 152, 162–3, 203, 208, 210, 263, 266
  see also counter-hegemony; hegemony
anti-militarism
  definitions, 5, 269–70
  history of, 22–7, 43n
  radical nature of, 257–9, 269–70

Anti-Militarist Network, 178, 186, 191–2
anti-nonviolence, 174–5, 178, 186–91, 194–6
arm tubes, 73–4, 81n, 96, 98–101, 103, 164–5
arms trade, 47–9, 259n
Arms Trade Treaty, 239–42, 250
arrest, activist perspectives on, 18–19, 100–1, 129, 131, 150, 183, 209, 211, 216–24, 226–8, 231
Ashley, Richard K., 89

BAE Systems, 47, 240
  Annual General Meeting, 157, 171n, 263
  direct action against, 1–2, 16–17, 147–9
  Pride participation, 76–8
  Saudi Arabia, 1–2, 256, 262
  surveillance of CAAT, 47, 114, 121
Bahrain and Bahrainis, 157, 187, 198–9, 243–4, 246
Bakunin, Mikhail, 34
Banksy, 155–6
Basham, Victoria, 59
Berrigan, Philip, 92, 141, 222, 232
Berry, Matt, 157–8, 160
Bilgin, Pinar, 259n
Billig, Michael, 54

308 / Resisting Militarism

Black Bloc, 115–16, 132–3, 135–6, 138n, 176, 192
Black Lives Matter, 73n, 199
Bleiker, Roland, 10
Block the Factory, 97–103, 164–6, 228
Boletsi, Maria, 260n
Booth, Ken, 86
Bourke, Joanna, 53, 55
Braidotti, Rosi, 39–40
Brigg, Morgan, 10
Brimar Systems *see* Target Brimar
British Aerospace *see* BAE Systems
Brock, Hugh, 24
Brown, Wilmette, 188, 202
Burke, Anthony, 112
Burridge, Joseph, 54
Butler, Judith, 265–8

CAAT (Campaign Against Arms Trade), 11, 235
  Arms Trade Treaty critique, 239, 250
  BAE Systems opposition, 47
  DESO closure campaign, 48
  diversity of tactics, 178–9
  DSEI opposition, 49, 50–1, 63n
  humour as strategy, 155, 256–7
  influence in movement, 259n
  judicial review of arms sales to Saudi, 227, 250–2, 262
  local campaigning, 50–1, 63n
  nonviolence, 184, 194–5
  repressive regimes discourse, 237–8, 242–7, 252–4, 260n
  Royal Family, 48, 256–7
  security reframed by, 86–7
  STAF support, 178–9
  Stop Arming Saudi campaign, 1, 237, 244–5, 250–4, 256–7
  surveillance by BAE systems, 47, 114, 121
  whiteness, 196, 200–1
Calhoun, Craig, 32
Call, Lewis, 264
Campaign for Nuclear Disarmament, 24, 44n, 192
Campbell, David, 110
Carpenter, Charli, 247

Cavarero, Adriana, 265
Chatterton, Paul, 145
Christian Pacifism, 221–2
CIRCA (Clandestine Insurgent Rebel Clown Army), 116–17, 161–2, 167
civil disobedience, 23–5, 126, 208, 224–6, 234
  see also disobedience
Clarion Events, 49, 52
Cockburn, Cynthia, 185, 192
Committee of 100, 24–5, 32
common sense, 254–5, 257–9
counter-hegemony, 28–9, 113, 130, 132–3, 168, 262–3
  see also anti-hegemony; hegemony
Coward, Martin, 50
Crane-Seeber, Jesse, 167
CrimethInc, 189–90
Critchley, Simon, 141–2
critical mass bike rides, 166–7
Critical Security Studies, 84–9, 92, 94, 106–7n
Cullen, Darren, 171n

dabke dancing, 18, 213, 235
DAC (Direct Action Committee Against Nuclear War), 24–5
Day, Richard J. F., 28–30, 35, 90, 132, 247–8, 263–4, 270n
de Goede, Mareike, 156, 163–4
Deleuze, Gilles, 206–7
demands, politics of, 29–31, 44n, 90, 134, 246–8, 252–4, 257–8, 263
Derrida, Jacques, 112, 137n
die-in, 13, 71, 147–51, 197, 231,
direct action
  definitions, 5–7, 20–2
  agency, 40, 151, 215, 223, 230, 235
  anarchism, 21–2, 32
  disobedience, 211–13
  empowerment, 40–3
  history in anti-militarism 22–7
  prefiguration, 32–3, 43, 89–90, 227, 268
  relationship with strategy, 38–40

representative politics,
 alternative to, 27–33, 41, 43, 49, 92
 resistance and, 7
 security and, 90–5
 white privilege, 102–3, 175, 198–9, 204, 205n
Disarm DSEI
 local campaigning, 50–1
 non-cooperation with police, 117, 212–13
 participation in STAF, 178–9
 repressive regimes discourse, 242, 244
 scepticism of nonviolence, 186, 191
Disarm the Gallery, 49, 52–3, 72
disobedience, 13–14, 206–10
 cultivation of, 210–16, 234–6
 radical potential of, 207–9, 213, 216, 234–6
 relationship with obedience, 208, 225–7, 232–4
 see also civil disobedience
diversity of tactics, 13, 174–5
 active labour required, 181–3
 challenges, 177–8, 183–4, 194–5, 203
 history, 175–6
 prefigurative qualities, 176–7, 203, 266–7
 role in anti-militarism, 25, 178, 204–5n
 role in STAF, 178–82, 267
 violence and nonviolence, 184, 193–5
Dixon, Paul, 56
Doty, Roxanne Lynn, 10
Drone Wars, 169
DSEI (Defence and Security Equipment International), 11, 48–9, 229, 243–4
 DSEI 2005, 114, 162–3
 DSEI 2007, 123–6
 DSEI 2011, 49, 72, 144, 150, 152–4, 179–82
 DSEI 2013, 219–20
 DSEI 2015, 17–19, 120, 155–6, 201, 213, 222, 229
 DSEI 2017, 202–3
 local campaigning, 50–1, 63n
 security focus, 82–3
 see also Clarion Events
DSO (Defence & Security Organisation), 48, 243
DuBois, W. E. B., 196
Duffy, Carol Ann, 71

Earth First!, 26–7
East London Against Arms Fairs, 63n, 178
EDO Decommissioners, 90–4, 126, 205n, 222–3, 228, 230
EDO MBM *see* Smash EDO/EDO Decommissioners
Egypt, 198, 243, 244
Elbit Systems *see* Block the Factory
empowerment, 12, 20, 40–3
Enloe, Cynthia, 53, 56–7, 63n, 70, 81n, 146
ethnography, 7–10
ExCeL *see* DSEI

face masks, 109, 115–16, 126–9, 132
Fanon, Frantz, 187
Farnborough International Air Show, 49, 51, 52
Faslane 365, 38, 231
Faslane Peace Camp, 143
feminist anti-militarism, 26, 36, 65–71, 73–6, 80, 140–1, 191, 196
Finchett-Maddock, Lucy, 208, 234
Finmeccanica *see* Disarm the Gallery
FITwatching, 117
Foucault, Michel, 136, 170, 207, 234, 265
France, 245, 249, 254, 260n
Frazer, Elizabeth, 191, 205n

Gandhi, Mohandas, 24, 221
Gelderloos, Peter, 188
Germany, 254, 260n
Ghana, 261
Gilman-Opalsky, Richard, 135–6
Goldman, Emma, 21–2, 34, 207

Gordon, Uri, 27, 33, 36–7, 175–7
Graeber, David, 9, 116, 133, 176
Green and Black Cross, 117, 119, 131, 213
Greenham Common Women's Peace Camp, 13, 86
  diversity of tactics, 204–5n
  feminist politics, 26, 68–9
  influence on movement, 25–6, 143
  nonviolence, 205n
  prefigurative politics, 26, 132, 145–6
  sex worker solidarity, 202

Halberstam, Jack, 130
Haraway, Donna, 141, 264
Harcourt, Bernard, 208
Hardt, Michael, 51, 83, 177, 264
Hastings, Tom, 218
Heckert, Jamie, 135–6
Heckler & Koch *see* Shut Down Heckler & Koch
hegemony, 28–30, 61, 89, 94, 113, 123, 130, 203, 263
  see also anti-hegemony; counter-hegemony
heroism
  as feature of militarism, 58–9, 61, 66, 160, 166, 170
  as reproduced by anti-militarists, 7, 62, 183, 197, 199, 209, 214–16
Hogbin, Martin, 114
homonationalism, 78–9
hooks, bell, 196
Howell, Alison, 63n
humour, 13, 151–64
Hutchings, Kimberly, 191, 205n

Islamophobia, 255
Israel, 17–19, 21, 51, 90–2, 98, 155, 214, 231, 244
Italy, 249

Jackson, Kirk, 239–40
Jasiewicz, Ewa, 215
Jun, Nathan, J., 36
Juris, Jeffrey S., 8–9, 14–15n

Khalid, Maryam, 54, 67
King, Martin Luther, Jr., 224
Klein, Naomi, 30
Kronlid, Lotta, 16–17
Kurds, 198

Landauer, Gustav, 34–6, 38, 42, 268
Landstreicher, Wolfi, 56–7, 140–1, 268
Laudani, Raffaele, 208–9, 225, 234
liberal militarism, 57–8, 240–1, 249–50, 258–9
Lockheed Martin, 219
Loizidou, Elena, 211, 224, 234

Mabee, Bryan, 46, 83
McDonald, Matt, 86–7, 95, 107n
McSorley, Kevin, 54, 167
Marom, Yotam, 30–1
May, Todd, 206–7
Mikdashi, Maya, 79
militarism
  definitions, 3–5, 45–6, 55–7, 269–70
  arms trade, 47–9, 259n
  as local, 50–2
  as networked, 49–50, 53
  banal militarism, 54–5, 57, 58–9, 62, 83, 140, 249
  class, 57, 59
  desire for, 59–60, 167–70
  distinction from militarisation, 63n
  everyday militarism, 53–5, 58–9
  gender, 57, 59, 66–9, 74, 76
  homonationalism, 78–9
  institutions, 46–9
  law, 224, 241, 250–2
  liberal militarism, 57–8, 240–1, 249–50, 258–9
  masculinity, 59, 62, 66–70, 145, 162–3, 166, 168–70
  nationalism, 57
  pinkwashing, 77–8
  police, 83, 106n, 199–201
  popular culture, 58–9, 63n, 166, 168–9

race, 57, 59, 196, 199–203, 252–7, 258–9
  reproduced by anti-militarists, 57, 80, 141, 162–3, 189–91, 199–200, 248–57
  security, 82–4, 86–7, 106–7n, 111
  sexuality, 57, 67–8, 72–3
  subjectivity, 55, 60, 139–41, 257–8, 263–4, 267–8
  universities, 49, 59–60
  values, 55–8, 60
Millar, Katharine, 58
Ministry of Defence, 24, 48, 158–9
Montgomery, Sister Anne, 225
Morton, Adam David, 259n
Movement for Black Lives, 73

National Gallery, 49, 52–3, 71–2
National History Museum, 49, 52, 72
NATO, 245, 249–50
naughtiness, 208, 234–5
Needham, Andrea, 16–17, 31, 122, 220–1, 235
Negri, Antonio, 51, 83, 177, 264
Newman, Saul, 114–15, 136, 208, 234
Nichols, Bob, 90–1
No Conscription Fellowship, 22–3
No Pride in War, 76–80
nonviolence, 13, 23, 133, 221
  critiques of, 186–91
  distinction between nonviolence and pacifism, 205n
  diversity of tactics, 174–5, 184, 193–5
  prefigurative qualities, 184–6
  role in anti-militarism, 24, 184–6, 205n
  tensions in movement, 178, 191–5, 203–4

Occupy Movement, 30–1, 73, 143, 208
open coalition, 266–7

pacifism *see* nonviolence/Christian Pacifism

Palestine and Palestinians, 17–19, 21, 98–9, 102, 198, 213–4
Pallister-Wilkins, Polly, 20–1
Parashar, Swati, 83
Peace Ballot, 43–4n
peace camps, 91, 143–6, 212
  see also Greenham Common Women's Peace Camp
  see also Peace News: Peace News Gatherings
Peace News, 23–4
  nonviolence, 184
  Peace News Gatherings, 69–70, 81n, 103–5, 143–4, 148, 180
  unsettling whiteness, 198, 200–1
Peace Pledge Union, 60–2, 64n, 184
Pickerill, Jenny, 145
playfulness, 125–6, 167, 235
Plowshares/Ploughshares, 11–12, 44n
  attitudes to arrest and prosecution, 217–22
  Christian pacifism, 217, 221–2, 225
  legal strategies, 217–19, 236n
  nonviolence, 184
  symbolism, 92
  tactics, 19, 91–2, 217–18
  Trident Ploughshares, 178, 191–2
  whiteness, 196
  see also Seeds of Hope; Seeds of Hope 2
police
  activist strategies towards, 18, 95–103, 117–22, 125–6, 128–9, 211–13, 231
  militarism of, 83, 106n, 199–201
  surveillance of activists, 102, 114–15, 121
popular culture, militarism in, 58–9, 63n, 160, 166, 168–9
prefiguration
  definitions, 6–7, 33–4, 142, 173–4
  accountability, 221, 223, 230

prefiguration (*cont.*)
  anti-nonviolence, 174–5, 188, 190, 195–6
  as analytic, 6–7, 37–8, 142, 167–70, 200, 204, 258, 268
  direct action, 20, 32–3, 43, 89–90, 227, 268
  disobedience, 210, 213
  diversity of tactics, 174, 176–7, 181–2, 203
  experimentation, 36, 105, 142, 164, 168, 177, 203
  Greenham Common Women's Peace Camp, 26, 132, 145–6
  humour, 152, 160–2
  Landauer, Gustav, 34–6, 38, 268
  learning, 36, 70, 142, 167–70, 268–9
  nonviolence, 174–5, 184–6
  peace camps, 105, 143–6
  process, focus on, 36–7, 39, 142
  resistance and, 14, 169–70, 177, 267–70
  security, 90, 103, 134
  vulnerability, 147, 151
Prince Charles *see* Royal Family
prosecution for direct action, activist perspectives on, 209, 216–33
Puar, Jasbir, 78–9
public opinion, 253–5

Quakers, 23, 184, 221–2
queer anti-militarism, 67–8, 71–3, 76–80, 140, 202

racism, 175, 196–204, 252–7, 261
Randle, Michael, 24–5, 32
Raytheon 9, 51, 91, 228, 230
Razack, Sherene, 255
Red Arrows, 76–7
representative politics, radical critique of, 12, 20, 27–33, 41, 43, 49, 92
repressive regimes, 14
  discourse as racialised, 252–7, 259
  liberal militarism, 248–52

  use of discourse by activists, 201, 242–7, 257–8
resistance
  as method, 3, 7–8, 169–70
  constituted within militarism, 14, 36, 94, 139–41, 164–70, 257–8, 268–70
  direct action, 7
  humour and, 156
  micropolitics, 36, 54–5, 60, 140–2
  prefiguration, 14, 169–70, 177, 267–70
  to security, 84, 108–9, 111–14, 122–3, 125–6, 128–37
  vulnerability and, 147, 149–51, 185
Robinson, Christine M., 117–18
Roseneil, Sasha, 205n
Royal Family, 48, 256–7
Ruddick, Sara, 191
Rundberg, Anna-Linnea, 212
Russell, Bertrand, 24, 32

Saibene, Ornella, 90–1
Saudi Arabia
  arms sales, 1–2, 73, 256–7, 262
  homonationalism and, 78
  judicial review of arms sales, 237, 250–2, 262
  public opinion about arms sales, 253–4
  racialisation of, 252–3, 255–7
  relationship to BAE Systems, 157
  relationship to British state, 244, 258
  role in 'Arab Spring', 157, 198
  Stop Arming Saudi campaign, 1, 155, 237, 244–8, 250–7
  Yemeni Civil War, 1, 73, 237, 245
Science Museum, 49, 52, 171n
Scott, James C., 215, 234
Security and Policing Exhibition, 49, 51, 201
security, 13
  agency, 87–9, 92–7
  alternative practices, 103–6
  contestation, 95–7

deconstruction, 109–14, 126
direct action, 90–5
militarism, 82–4, 86–7, 111
resistance and, 84, 108–9, 111–14, 122–3, 125–6, 128–37
social movements, 84, 86
subversion of state practices, 97–103, 125–6, 146, 231
see also security culture; Critical Security Studies
security culture, 114–22, 165, 167
Seeds of Hope (1996), 16–17, 31, 47, 90–1, 122, 205n
accountability, 218, 220–1
acquittal, 228, 230
symbolism, 33
Seeds of Hope 2 (2017), 1–2, 47, 237
accountability, 221, 228–9
acquittal, 228–9
symbolism, 33
Selby, Jan, 3
Shapiro, Michael, 169
Sharp, Gene, 24
Shukaitis, Stevphen, 136–7, 268
Shut Down Heckler & Koch, 50, 148–9, 178
Sisters Against the Arms Trade, 73–6, 198, 216, 258
Smash EDO, 11, 230–1
citizen's weapons inspection, 96–7
diversity of tactics, 91, 178
Hammertime demonstration, 126–31
humour as strategy, 156
local campaigning, 50–1
non-cooperation with police, 117, 212–13
scepticism of nonviolence, 186
STAF participation, 179
Smith, Elijah, 90–1
solidarity, 13, 41, 80, 115, 119, 129, 133, 259, 216, 264
diversity of tactics, 175–8, 192–4, 203, 266
negotiating power relations, 74–6, 197–8, 201–2

nonviolence, 186–7, 190, 193–4
South Korea, 249
sovereignty
anti-sovereign organising, 85, 89, 92–4, 106, 134–5
sovereignty/anarchy, 89, 94, 103, 110, 113, 125, 132, 135
Space Hijackers, 12, 52, 137, 167
Life Neutral Solutions, 152–4
sex toy action, 162–3
tank auction, 123–6, 213, 235
Sparkles Not Shrapnel, 71–3, 235
Spies for Peace, 93–4, 118
spontaneity, 129, 131
Srnicek, Nick, 262
STAF (Stop the Arms Fair) Coalition, 11, 49, 216
diversity of tactics, 178–81, 192, 195, 267
founding, 179
marginalised voices, 198
repressive regimes discourse, 242–3, 252
scepticism of nonviolence, 186, 192, 195
Stop Arming Israel day of action, 17–19
Stavrianakis, Anna, 3, 57, 187, 240–2, 245–6
Stop the War Coalition, 260n
strategy, anti-militarist critique of, 12, 20, 38–40, 43, 57, 140, 176–7, 267
Summers, Anne, 43n
superglue, 98, 100, 128, 219
Sylvester, Christine, 132, 145–6
Syria and Syrians, 73–6, 198, 216

Tadman, Harvey, 90–1
Target Brimar, 49–51, 178, 229–30
Thatcher, Margaret, 61, 86
Thomas, Mark, 155
tripods, 98, 107n
Turkey, 244, 245, 249

United States, 245–7, 249, 254, 260n, 261

universities, militarism and, 49, 59–60

Vagts, Alfred, 55
Veggies, 131
VfP (Veterans for Peace)
  Battlefield Casualties campaign, 157–60
  medals discarded, 170
  No Pride in War participation, 76, 79–80
  remembrance ceremony, 61–2
Vinthagen, Stellan, 232
vulnerability
  as mode of resistance, 147, 149–51, 185
  infiltration and, 118–19, 121–2

Walker, R. B. J., 88
Walter, Nicolas, 44n, 107n, 118
Walton, Sam, 1–2, 16, 33, 221, 229
War Resisters' International, 185–6
Ward, Colin, 90, 93
Ware, Vron, 204

white poppies, 42, 60–1
whiteness, 13, 175
  attempts to unsettle, 197–8, 200–3
  in conceptions of militarism, 175, 199–200, 204
  of movement, 196–7, 204, 259
  white privilege in direct action, 102–3, 175, 198–9, 204, 205n
Wieck, David, 20
Wilkinson, Eleanor, 182
Williams, Alex, 262
Wilson, Joanna, 16–17
Wilson, Lee, 87
Women for Syria, 74–6, 198
Woodhead, Tom, 90–1, 222–3
'Woody' Woodhouse, Daniel, 1–2, 16, 33

Yates, Luke, 142
Yemen and Yemenis, 1, 73, 198, 229, 237, 245, 250–1
Young, Nigel, 22–3

Zelter, Angie, 17, 217–18
Žižek, Slavoj, 247–8, 254, 257

EU representative:
Easy Access System Europe
Mustamäe tee 50, 10621 Tallinn, Estonia
Gpsr.requests@easproject.com

www.ingramcontent.com/pod-product-compliance
Lightning Source LLC
Chambersburg PA
CBHW052057300426
44117CB00013B/2164